ARAB-MUSLIM VIEWS OF THE WEST
FROM THE NINTH CENTURY TO THE TWENTIETH

ARAB-MUSLIM VIEWS OF THE WEST
FROM THE NINTH CENTURY TO THE TWENTIETH
The Neglected Bridge Builders

Christopher Nouryeh

The Edwin Mellen Press
Lewiston•Queenston•Lampeter

Library of Congress Cataloging-in-Publication Data

Nouryeh, Christopher.
   Arab-Muslim views of the West from the ninth century to the twentieth : the neglected
bridge builders / Christopher Nouryeh.
      p. cm.
   [Includes bibliographical references and index.]
   ISBN 0-7734-5958-8
   1. East and West. 2. Civilization, Arab--Western influences. 3. Civilization,
Islamic--Western influences. I. Title.

   CB251.N67   2005
   303.48'25601820109--dc22

                                                      2005056234
hors série.

A CIP catalog record for this book is available from the British Library.

             The Edwin Mellen Press   The Edwin Mellen Press
                    Box 450   Box 67
               Lewiston, New York   Queenston, Ontario
               USA 14092-0450   CANADA L0S 1L0

                        The Edwin Mellen Press, Ltd.
                        Lampeter, Ceredigion, Wales
                        UNITED KINGDOM SA48 8LT

                   Printed in the United States of America

Dedicated to

My wife Andrea and daughter, Anita

Table of Contents

Preface

This work offers a broad historical view of Arab-Muslim views of the West from the ninth century to the second half of the twentieth. In what is a contemporary information culture loaded to overflow with the production and reproduction of words, images, facts, and opinions on a continuously changing daily basis, and in a world profoundly shaken and troubled by the seemingly intractable tensions and open wounds between East and West, one might be forgiven for supposing that there is little concerning this subject's historical dimension which remains uncovered and in serious need of being said. This book works simultaneously on two levels - historical and philosophical- to demonstrate that, sadly, rather the opposite is true. Not only are many of the major Islamic writers and thinkers, as well as the debates in which they figured and the ongoing legacies they engendered, either unknown or ignored in the mainstream of Western representation of Islamic thought and history, but the very philosophical framework which the best examples offer in terms of bridge-building ideas between East and West are routinely overlooked. In the present work this fascinating and important intellectual landscape is opened up in its diverse points of view before the English speaking reader for the first time in a well articulated discussion of people, ideas and history as well as the multiple possible meanings of these points of departure for our lives in a contemporary world facing a myriad of crossroads and too often an impasse built into place by the persistence of the unthought. This work therefore functions to stem the blind and dangerous advance of narrow political assumptions and practice linked to the unthought across the horizons of tomorrow, and to open up spaces for intercultural dialogue, critique and thought based on existing legacies of open-ness which have been sadly brushed aside to make way for the clamor of crude and simplisticly closed minded dogmas on both sides of the so-called East-West divide. This book, then, is an important resource of ideas, and hopefully inspiration, for the world of social issues and political circumstances surrounding us today.

The work opens up from two straightforward questions, one historical and the other concerning scholarly methodology. Firstly, how and in what ways, since the ninth century, has the West gained ever increasing space in the Arab-Muslim consciousness, leading ultimately to the development of spaces for intercultural critique in the second half of the twentieth century? Secondly, why is it that no thorough treatment of this theme, until now, has existed? Both questions throw open more questions in their turn and invite us to think rather than closing the door with the declaration of the immediate answers which reproduce old certainties. In a preliminary survey of the existing and authoritative range of material on what is roughly the same thing the author calls to our attention a tendency among these diverse works to sideline, blot from sight, and chop to incomplete fragments the Arab-Muslim's lookout and view of self in relation to the West. Upon closer scrutiny this shared tendency among a diversity of authors, though perhaps unthought, is unhappily no mere accident. The received structure of knowledge regarding Islamic thought and culture, which Said initially identified as Orientalism, contains a systemic assortment of inbuilt negative assumptions which freely reproduce themselves - often unconsciously - if not held carefully up to analytical scrutiny. It is therefore of the order of necessity for the author to retrace the often highly influential works of his venerable predecessors in the subject in order to lay bare why such systemic cover ups of crucial areas of historical and intellectual reality have produced the urgent need, today, of writing a book which redresses these dangerous and misleading imbalances.

From this initial point of departure the myriad of conceptions underlying the work's historical investigation come into play. In opposition to the legacy of

Orientalism which sustains a lack of distinction between the imaginary and the real, in large part to secure a 'modern' and 'Western' identity or 'Reason' against an imagined 'Orient', and thereby fosters a tendency to think in terms of essences - images, representations, binaries - the author invokes the Platonic concept of the other as an 'eye mirror'. At the core of this project is the ideal of self-understanding through the other in a triangle of selfhood, difference and coexistence. As where as the Orientalist paradigm would persist in sabotaging, for the general public, fruitful encounters between the East and West by way of fixating the Arab-Muslim world into an object and thereby arresting its continuous transformation, the author presents a vivid picture of an Arab-Muslim intellectual history rich with challenging thought and debate circuiting around the questions of Islamic identity and history, Western culture and achievement, and the deeply interwoven roots of both in the context of an emerging experience of global modernity in both its brighter and darker aspects. Above all, in contrast to the received Orientalist view, this story indicates a process of continuous and creative transformation. In fact, the Platonic conception of the 'eye mirror' is very alive and expressed in a diversity of ways in the works introduced and analyzed here. Simultaneously, this work is also an interrogation of the self for the author, an odyssey to arrive at the truth of one man's life who has lived the extended trajectory of a Middle Easterner who has made his home in the U.S.A. and who has thereby faced the West, walked through the West, and looked back. In so doing he confronts the question of how we are to look at the past: we must, he explains, "look to the past not for a homeopathic treatment or a quick fix, as the Islamists and autocrats do, but for a beacon of wisdom devoid of mythology and resentment baggage; in short, for a guide to a brighter Arab-Muslim culture". This too, then, is a work of both productive forgetting and forgiveness.

The result of the far reaching and surprising historical investigations in this work is to show that, for Western general publics, the "Arab-Muslim view of the West is a peculiar lookout which hasn't yet been seen for what it truly is". Highlighting the historical plurality of Islamic societies, the author's research exhibits a far ranging and creative flexibility in the history of Islamic thought which points to a general conceptual framework which is decidedly international in its dimensions. This unfortunately ignored tradition of thought towers in complexity and breadth of vision over the later so-called 'fundamentalism', and the former in its more open and democratic inclination, the author suggests, will very likely prove the rock against which the misconceived fundamentalist project will finally crash in the context of the inner dynamic of Islamic societies. Yet an important precondition for this possibility is a change of perceptions and attitudes in the West itself, through a dismantling of received Orientalist dogma and its accompanying political policies. At the core of this book, then, with its contents grounded in points of view multiply dispersed in historical time and geographic space, is the conviction that Islam and the West can't be thought apart from each other historically or in the contemporary conjuncture of modernity. Both Islam and the West, even assuming such generalized blocks of identity make the slightest sense, imperatively require each other in order to both achieve a proactive rather than reactive modernity combined with the necessary forgetfulness and forgiveness for the disturbing web of atrocities both past and present. The heart of soul of a more vital and humanistic modernity depends upon neither the conflation of modernity and Western particularism, nor the stunted and irrelevant denials of Islamist ideology, but rather a recognition of modernity's complex and multi-cultural genealogy as a democratic possibility based on bold and radical historical reevaluation for both 'Islam' and the 'West'. In its historical range, this book reconsiders the relations between European Enlightenment and Arab-Muslim philosophy, and re-conceives the origins of classical modernity as a scientific discourse in light of Islamic involvements and contributions. The very definition of the Renaissance, as defined by Husserl, is accordingly challenged on several fronts. Both the complex intellectual climate of the Ottoman Empire in relation to Enlightenment and the French Revolution, as well as the Egyptian intellectual aftermath in relation to Napoleon, are investigated and compared to show a diversity of views in subjects ranging from the principles and practice of revolutionary republicanism to the question of technology and its possible benefits. Rifa'a al-Tahtawi's reflections on the ideas and achievements of European science and technology inspire his hope that the Enlightenment can influence Islamic culture to reconnect with its own roots in philosophy and the rational sciences. He analyzes the ideals of justice and freedom in the French constitution and relates them to Islamic conceptions of equity, finding in the ground of *Ijtihad* the potential motor of transforming Egyptian society along its own path to Enlightened modernity. His contemporary, Ali Mubarak, conceived *Ijtihad* as the instrument for achieving the harmonizing bridge between Islam and Europe. He additionally ventures an analysis of European ascendency in which he highlights the role of imperialism and questions the initial possibility of European accomplishment in the absence of Arab-Muslim philosophy and science. Ultimately, both nineteenth century thinkers concur on the fundamental Islamic precept which exhorts the pursuit of science, economics, and administration. In Tunisia, Khayr al-Din al-Tunisi, in his call for European inspired reforms, warns Muslims against "denouncing an other's praiseworthy deportment that tallies with the *Shari'a* simply because everything pertaining to a non-Arab-Muslim's conduct and disposition must in their mind be discarded as worthless". He writes: "Freedom is the magnitude of a culture's domain of knowledge that European nations themselves have attained". For such thinkers, who extend both criticism and admiration to the West, the idea of any inherent contradiction between the modern world and an 'essential' Islam is surely an alien and implausible thought. Their ideas, rather, point to the creative and reflective dimension of the Islamic tradition which remains open to changing historical configurations. These thoughts, and many others, by such influential but little known Muslim thinkers and activists surely unveil an altogether different reality to that representation driven home for Western publics - by the likes of Bernard Lewis - of a closed and unthinking 'Islam' which is capable only of lashing out with reactive and irrational animosity grounded in the darkness of a remote pre-modern history.

There are also interesting reinterpretations offered of more well known figures such as the Persian philosopher Jamal al-Din al-Afghani, particularly through his relation to the Egyptian Muhammed Abduh. Their many layered debates about the proper relation of religion and reason, traditionalism and dogma, and the role of science in social history were to considerably influence the thinking of subsequent generations. Sheik al-Jisr, in his efforts to create a synthesis of the two thinkers' ideas, also advanced a complex critique of philosophical materialism while also promoting the embrace of scientific achievement·and reason. He therefore argued that Qur'anic interpretation, far from being threatened in its legitimacy by scientific progress, should be grounded in the continuously evolving discoveries of scientific method about the natural world, in order to reach a more perfect interpretation of a divine text which comports, by its own admission, with reason.

The multiple examples of such thinkers demonstrate the main contention of the project - that a new vision of self knowledge can and should be obtained through the other. In spite of examples of reactive modes of thought in Islam, which unfortunately seize and dominate the attention of the popular media while concurring deplorably with Orientalist prejudice, there are plentiful examples of such proactive thought in Islamic discourse based on the principle of the Platonic 'eye mirror' available for scholarly and public inquiry and reflection. This book, crucially, brings such evidence - albeit belatedly - to the table, while also offering an interesting philosophical perspective which presents sign posts for navigating a path beyond both the futile and destructive trappings of a fading but still dominant received Orientalist panoply, and its abysmal counterpart in frozen and self defeating Islamic discourses of authenticity, to a shared space of modernity as democratic possibility without privileged ontology.

Ali Mirsepassi
New York University

Ali Mirsepassi is Professor of Middle Eastern Studies at New York University, author of *Intellectual Discourses and Politics of Modernization* (Cambridge University Press, 2000). He has published extensively in journals such as Contemporary Sociology, Radical History, Social Text, and Nepata. He is currently completing a book titled *Social Hope and Philosophical Despair*. He is also coeditor of *Localizing Knowledge in a Globalizing World* (Syracuse University Press); also editor of *Beyond the Boundaries of the Old Geographies*: *Natives, Citizens, Exiles, and Cosmopolitans* (in Progress).

Acknowledgments

I would like to thank my friends and colleagues Michael Simpson, Peter Baley, John Barthelme, and Nadine Jennings, for sharing their thoughts and expertise in the subject of East-West relations and their friendship with me throughout this project. Financial support of this project included two grants from National Endowment for the Humanities Faculty development Program at SUNY-Potsdam College, New York. I would also like to thank my friends and colleagues as well as my students at SUNY-Canton College and University of Technology for the support and understanding the difficult task of preparing this manuscript. A special thanks to my Mentor and friend and colleague Ali Mirsepassi of New York University for his magnificent support and observation and guidance. Finally I thank my wife Andrea and daughter Anita for their emotionally generous support of this project. I would not have written this book without your love and support. Shukran!

1

Instead of an Introduction

Part One

1

'Instead of an Introduction' may sound unusual. That's because it introduces nothing new. Nor for that matter does the work as a whole. After all, the subject—East-West relations—is as old as the hills. If anything, I simply infuse it with some thoughtful vigor just to render its ambient world a bit easier to breathe in for a change.[1] And I hope this fresh air wafts through the entire work, keeping it clear of any rhetorical effects, improvisations, and, above all, biased judgments.

2

The theme, too, Arab-Muslim view of the West, is nothing uncommon either. I know of at least four works (discussed briefly below). Mine here would be the fifth. Though I think it differs. For instance, it presents an all-out history of the theme; it doesn't dismiss orientalism out of hand, or bracket occidentalism (a counter-orienalism of sorts), but rather deals with them in such a way as to explore bridge-building possibilities between East and West, a relatively neglected topic of the familiar theme or subject.[2] Put otherwise, it monitors with sensitive ears and eyes how, since the ninth century, the West gains more and more space in Arab-Muslim consciousness (historians, geographers, travelers). Also how, in the second half of twentieth century, that space morphs into an intercultural critique in the hands of a few philosophers who then probe what it takes to bring about harmony. This critique takes the stage in the last two chapters of my work.

---

[1] The fetid air of other books on the subject is just hard to breathe. See Edward Said, *From Oslo to Iraq* (New York: Pantheon Books, 2004), pp. 261-297.

[2] At least one study I know, which has additionally made a difference in my life (see Part Two of this text), deals with the theme historically, though in a different way than mine. See Thierry Hentsch, *Imagining the Middle* East, trans. Fred A. Reed (New York: Black Nose Books, 1992).

more space in Arab-Muslim consciousness (historians, geographers, travelers). Also how, in the second half of twentieth century, that space morphs into an intercultural critique in the hands of a few philosophers who then probe what it takes to bring about harmony. This critique takes the stage in the last two chapters of my work.

Part Two of this text broaches the topic of my personal relation to East-West relations. It starts as an encounter between the West and me—right from the first day of my arrival in the USA in 1967. Over the years, it assumes the dimensions of mission of the loftiest honor. The effect produced on me is, to use a strong word, revolutionary. I discover in myself, in my memories of pain and suffering, the ardent will commanding me, like a voice from a dream, to carry out that mission. I do. Which, to cut corners, is to transform my pain and suffering into an agonism, a creative war against them. A stroke of luck fulfills the words of that dream. In 2003, I have a second encounter: I read four magnificent works (discussed below as well) that supply me with the tools for shaping, ordering, and organizing my work for war (discussed below as well).

So you see, this work reflects a personal investment, a kind of odyssey, if you will, in which I tie myself to a worthy task until the sirens of pent-up resentment get out of hearing. Then I get on to searching the world for a sunny spot of humanity, if there's one.

3

There's, thank goodness. It's in today's and tomorrow's world leaders (or power-elites). For me, they embody that sunny spot. Romantic as I am, I think they can promote amity and good will in the world if they want to. I'll go even farther, they must promote them because the law of change demands it. The law, if I may say, that lays down the law. And that's the law of change in nature and nations alike. You see, Vico says exactly that: change marks both the world and the world of nations. But he's more concerned with the latter. Since humans have made the world of nations, he says, they can know it; and since they can know it, they can re-make it—for better, not for worse, naturally, especially "when circumstances are thus and so and not otherwise."[3] A historical, all-too historical truth no human on earth dares to deny.[4]

Today—and Vico looks on as if to say—circumstances are indeed thus and so and not otherwise. For instance, sick of carnage, people yearn for change—for re-building, for re-making things. For that, they look to their leaders. Like me, they're romantic, too. They think leaders are refined, well-bred, high-spirited types with natures that are the antithesis of the vicious and unbridled; their disciplined selves evince dislike for blind indulgence of an affect as well as will for recouping what loss in spirituality they incur. Are we too romantic about this? If yes, the world's surely for worse. Then our leaders are no leaders but spiders spinning mythologies to manipulate us, while they live in clover, taking their ease. And do so knowing nothing but the same thing: more mythologies and more manipulations. What a boring, empty, monotonous artifact of human ingenuity! What nihilism stifling human creativity! Correct me if I'm wrong.[5]

4

The foregoing paragraphs help, I hope, frame my work's theme and title: *Arab-Muslims view of the West: A Historical Revaluation*. As such, it brings up, at least for me, three questions to be pondered watched, and slept on: why is it that no thorough treatment of the theme exists? What, historically speaking, motivates my work to steal the thunder of all irredentism (political and

---

[3] See Erich Auerbach, *Literary Language and its Public in Late Latin Antiquity and In The Middle Ages*, trans. Ralph Manheim (New York: Bollingen Foundation, 1965). In the first half of his introduction to the book, Auerbach explicates lucidly Vico's theory of historical knowledge and change.

[4] See Friedrich Nietzsche, *Beyond Good and Evil*, trans. Walter Kaufmann (New York: Vintage Books, 1989), section 9, p. 15. For more study of how humans positively transform history, see Michel Foucault, "28 January 1976," *Society Must Be Defended*, trans. David Macey (New York: Picador, 2003), pp. 65-84.

[5] For this thought, I'm indebted to Nussbaum: "Acting and living well are things that depend on human effort, things that human beings can always control, no matter what happens around them in the world." See Martha Nussbaum, "Tragedy and Self-sufficiency: Plato and Aristotle on Fear and Pity," *Essays on Aristotle's Poetics*, ed. Amelie Oksenbery Rorty (Princeton: Princeton University Press, 1992), p. 263.

intellectual)?[6] And how does it thematically link up with modern Arab-Muslim cultural theory discussed in the last two chapters? As an initial line of inquiry, I consider briefly the works of the four writers (referred to earlier), each of which, in its peculiar way, tackles the theme. These writers are Bernard Lewis, Amin Maalouf, Kamal Abdel-Malek, and Carole Hillenbrand. Apropos of the works, however, permit me to describe two problems; they shed more light on my own work and the series of questions I've just set down.

First problem: each work is a partial handling of the subject. Lewis treats Turkish- and Persian-Muslims, and few Arab-Muslims, and so leaves much to be desired; Maalouf and Hillenbrand a two-hundred years' worth of Crusades history; while Abdel-Malek a hundred years' worth of travel history to the USA— 1895-1995. Now I fully support freedom of choice in writing, and respect it profoundly. After all, I myself choose to limit my study to Arab-Muslim view of the West. Yet the difference between us amounts to this: while they each, so to speak, shortchange the theme, chopping a long history in pieces, my study puts the pieces back together in a continuum; and again, while their method blots out of sight Arab-Muslims' lookout, their view of self in relation to their view of the West (for the latter reflects the former), my study restores that lookout, even considers, though briefly, Ottoman-Muslim relations to the West as a link in the long chain of Arab-Muslim complex view of the West and self. That's not all.

Their truncated histories tend, I think, to sanction (without intending it to be so, of course) demeaning images of Arab-Muslims today—for example, a masked man, scudding through the desert on horse- or camelback, brandishing his scimitar, heads for a landed Western bomber and hacks off its cockpit. Such imagery generates, in turn, thought-parasites that embed themselves in Western public's feelings or perceptions—exotic, fanatic, bigoted, savage. They, too, blot out all ethical-religious and cultural subtexts from sight, leading astray or prejudicing even the most intelligent and level-headed among the public. There's the rub, you see: stereotypes clinging to Arab-Muslim character like poison ivy,

---

[6] I extend the specific meaning of the word "irredentism" (applied in the case of Jerusalem) to the general field of politics and intellect. See Walīd Khālidi, *Islam, the West, and Jerusalem* (Washington, D.C., 1996), p. 20.

which the intellectuals of the Arab-Muslim world still find ever so difficult to shake off Western imagination. Truth to tell, the whole kit and caboodle is pure fiction, with no reality corresponding to it. To persist in thinking otherwise is nihilism of the worst order.[7] It's like positing that a circle drawn up on paper corresponds to one in reality, too.

5

Second problem: the choice each writer makes also tends to sideline significant work, little or not known in the West, performed during the second half of twentieth century. A few Arab-Muslim cultural theorists write out their vision on how to establish harmony and socio-political relations between East and West.[8] Here you can't miss their spiritual-intellectual excitement—the same that beats in the breast of their medieval counterparts. True, the latter's writings are more critical of the West than a cultural critique of East-West relations. Even so, the aim of understanding self through the other is an unmistakable epiphenomenon. The cultural theorists, on the other hand, target harmony like a hunting dog, with the aim of deliberately grasping the West and Self through knowledge of the West. You see, both medieval and modern writers share similar needs: to transcend their limitations, to understand and promote themselves in an autonomous way. What's more, they want to believe in themselves as creators while still obeying something divine and higher than themselves. All this, obviously, couldn't be subsumed into our four writers' purview of things.

Nor for that matter could the vision of Arab-Muslim cultural theorists. It's too complex, too extensive, and perhaps for that reason, unwieldy. At any rate, this vision has it that to produce harmony between them, to learn to coexist together, East and West each does well to re-view itself: to know itself and its

---

[7] Nietzsche on nihilism: the most extreme nihilism "places the value of things precisely in the lack of any reality corresponding to these values and in their being merely symptoms of strength on the part of the value positers, a simplification for the sake of life." *Will To Power*, trans. Walter Kaufmann (new York: Vintage Books, 1968), p. 14.

[8] This is an additional reason or idea for which I undertake my study here. Another, with which many Westerners and Easterners may be familiar, is the egregious misunderstanding by the West of Arab-Muslim ethos. Ethos which, like every ethos in the world, remains hidden from sight.

difference from the other. Is that enough to achieve all three—selfhood, difference, coexistence? No. For this knowledge can efficaciously occur when the one looks into the other's eye. Why the other's eye? Because knowledge of self may not be grasped simply by looking at oneself in a mirror. For that amalgam to strike roots, one has to look into the other's eye. The pupil serves as the mirror. Knowledge of self, then, these theorists argue, goes by way of the other; it's an ontological operation, not a psychological one. In a word, when each side contemplates itself in the other's soul, it'll then recognize its human (also divine) element. As Plato says.[9] That's why they juxtapose critiques of East and West in their work—as if to say, we Westerners and Easterners are brothers in war against our common enemy: ignorance. War is here understood as creativity, or, like the war I'm fighting, as agonism.[10] Put otherwise, these theorists transpose, as it were, Plato's ontology into a politics. The kind of politics, I hasten to add, designed to politicize difference as initial step toward cultural bridge-building between East and West.[11]

---

[9] See Plato, *Alcibiades, The Dialogues of Plato*, trans. B. Jowett, vol. II, 3rd ed. (London: University of Oxford Press, 1891), pp. 504-509.

[10] A good example of such brotherly war or creative agonism is Roshdi Rāshed's short book *Science in Islam and Classical Modernity*, 2002. He starts off by quoting an important statement of the philosopher Husserl's: "It is well known that during the Renaissance, European humanity underwent a revolutionary turnaround: against the prevailing Middle Ages modes of existence which is now no longer valued, preferring instead a new kind of freedom." Well, it's barely known, actually. That's why Rāshed goes on to show irrecusably that the philosopher—as a speaker of universals, as a strategist with a vantage point and firm position or conviction—may, for that very reason, have inferred inaccurately or incorrectly; after all, classical modernity harks back to the simultaneous or combined contributions of medieval Europe, Islam, and Greco-Roman antiquity. He then finishes by advancing what he thinks the historian-to-come should keep in mind when it comes to being a devotee of truth: "He or she should go in search of true paths, and leave aside the myths and legends which led such great minds as Husserl's astray." The upshot here is that Husserl goes against the grain and, solipsistically, insists on seeing all of himself in mirror of his own eye. I take up Rāshed's thought in more detail in my last chapter.

[11] This politicization of difference is most vital today. When you politicize difference, that is, when you negotiate your position vis-à-vis the other (and vice versa), you no longer make a bid for power by driving a wedge between you and the other (between one nation and another, one people and another, one religion and another, as power elites do today). Instead, your new power, call it cosmopolitics, leads you to the recognition of the values of difference in the formation of selfhood. You're you, or produce yourself, on the basis of the other, not in spite of it. As has been said, "self-knowledge goes by the way of the other." For further information on cosmopolitics, see J. Derrida, *Ethics, Institutions, and the Right to Philosophy*, trans. Peter Perecles Trifonas (New York: Rowman & Littlefield Publishers, Inc., 2002), pp. 1-17. On the

I'd like to sum up by advancing a two-fold working hypothesis. First, imagine the problems of historical fragmentation and ontological distance acknowledged, if not overcome, what then? Well, the chances Western ethos communicating with Arab-Muslim ethos, one ethnographic self with another would surely get greater; further, if such communication is concomitantly buttressed by honest interpretation of history and texts, those chances could get greater still. Secondly, suppose East and West apologize to each other for mutually inflicted atrocities (isn't it time they did so, though, now more than ever?); suppose also they probe history and texts in good conscience, what then? Well, the outcome would simply be breathtaking: all mental impasses between them, all loggerheaded, stupid behaviors and manipulations would vanish in half a jiffy. And this earth, think on it, would no more be the dark and dangerous abyss that was—but a beautiful kingdom once again.

All the same, more goodies still—too irresistible, I assure you, to pass up or keep silent about. Of all figures, East-West old distrust, too, would no longer be. I mean the jinnee disguised now as poltergeist, now as terrible siren would burst like a bubble. The former, named orientalism (the bug-a-boo of every Mid-Eastern country), making its home in the treacherous depths of Christianity, and moving things around actively, furtively, stirring up nefarious feelings in Western public, blinding it to Arab-Muslims, their character, their ethics, their merits and achievements; the latter, the siren, booming its lurid songs into the other hemisphere, rousing deadly hatred among Arab-Muslims at once toward each other and the West, its ethics, its character, its merits and its accomplishments. This changeling jinnee, again, would be no more. Nor indeed would it re-call Arab-Muslims to the fate that seemed to have put a curse upon them before their birth. "We hate, we must hate," as once upon a time runs the compelling force within them.

question of self-knowledge through the Other, see Theirry Hentsch, *Imagining the Middle East*, trans. Fred A. Reed (New York: Black Rose Books, 1992), p. 205.

In the ecstasy of that thought, East and West would once and for all shrink back from their fate with the whole force of the repression by which their mutual hatred and distrust have been held down within them. Then—and this may sound a bit weird or strange or both—they would take pride in their mutual hatred and anguish, and would say so to each other publicly. Then they would, as others have done, apologize to each other publicly, and perhaps even (who knows?) will themselves to engage in a serious commitment to radical ethico-cultural self-remaking. I think the golden opportunity is for such a thought, fictional as it may be, to blend with the reality of life as the thought of pragmatists and philosophers does with the reality of existence. Zarathustra's model and behavior comes to mind here: not only he hates his friends and loves his enemies; he discovers in that very same passion, and proudly so, a mnemonic aid to consciousness or self-knowledge: "The way to yourself," he says, "is the also the way of your affliction."[12] In this, he echoes Rousseau and a whole tradition of Western spiritual schooling behind him.[13]

This is the kind of spiritual schooling of which some (perhaps many) Arab-Muslims and I from the East partake. It's, to repeat, the quintessence of my mission, too: to carry out an all-out study of Arab-Muslim view of the West from the ninth century to the present.[14] And to do so with three purposes in mind: to show that Arab-Muslims' soul is capacious enough to think in international terms; that Arab-Muslim fundamentalism must crash on the rock of Arab-Muslim medieval and modern invention of "democratic thought"; and that an in-depth

---

[12] F. Nietzsche, *Zarathustra, The Portable Nietzsche*, trans. Walter Kaufmann, 3rd edition (New York: Penguin Books, 1982), p. 174.

[13] See Jean-Jacques Rousseau, *Julie: ou la nouvelle Heloise*: "Le chemin des passions me conduit a la philosophie veritable." The road of passions leads me to the true philosophy. I emphasize these ideas because, like Rousseau, like Nietzsche both of whom write and think in the tradition of the Stoic philosopher Epictetus, believe that, first, the highest good is to be found not in externals, but within the self, and, secondly, mankind is one vast brotherhood.

[14] I don't want to be understood as saying that this view is shared by every single Arab-Muslim individual. But it does mean that Arab-Muslim intellectuals, medieval or modern, have attempted to educate the public in and about the meaning of that view. There's scholarly indication (too extensive to record here) that the majority of Arab-Muslims today are quite conversant in this matter and wish that some bridging of differences can be achieved.

perception of Arab-Muslim ethos may go a long way to predispose the West to aid in the cultivation of human excellence in the Mid-East region. I deem these purposes an important step leading to self-mastery, itself a precondition for converting an impossible dream to a possible East-West rapprochement. Arab-Muslim cultural theorists believe it's possible to effect that conversion.

8

Allow me now to present to you a brief review of each of the four writers. The review, again, should help to situate my work in relation to his and hers, on the one hand, and, on the other, to bolster my proposal to close the historico-cultural gap, perhaps even also to shoo away all thought-parasites I mentioned before, all bugaboos and poltergeists, all ungrounded speculations from the minds of Western and Eastern publics.

Bernard Lewis, if I'm right, must be the most prolific of the four writers on East-West relations. He has also published two books on Muslim view of the West. In most of these works he attends more to Turkish- and Persian Muslim than to Arab-Muslim view of the West. Even so, he apparently and on the whole refuses to do without throwing some heavy punches, I mean without stereotyping and judging—for example, "Islam had no awareness of or interest in Western history or culture"; and again, "it remained closed off to new ideas," and so on and so forth.[15] Notice his ungracious, uncalled-for disparagements of Muslims, which he offers up to the West's palate paragraph in, paragraph out.[16] Does he ever alter his tune? Not really. In the end, you read through hundreds of pages and not find a single genuine encounter with a text; not even a tidbit of insight into why Muslims (Turkish, Persian, or Arab) evince no such interest, why they remain closed off to new ideas. Or, if this is really the case, how their peculiar

---

[15] Bernard Lewis, *The Muslim Discovery of Europe* (New York: W.W. Norton & Company, 2001); also *What Went Wrong? A Clash between Islam and Modernity in the Middle East* (New York: Oxford University Press, 2002). Lewis never deviates from those mantra-like statements.

[16] Not only that, he repeats almost verbatim the same arbitrary, formulaic judgment of Arab-Muslims in 1962 as he does in 1981, and, again, in 2002. Amazing! There seems to be no other drive, say, some understanding, some in-depth perception that participates in this writer's scholarship.

ethos—the residence, its home, its familiar place of dwelling inasmuch as the manner, attitude, values, and beliefs in which Arab-Muslims daily relate to themselves and to others—again, how such ethos might have barred the way, and for a good reason, to accommodating new ideas. You find nothing of the kind. Not a speck, not a trace of it at all.[17]

Amin Maalouf of Lebanon is another—how shall I put it?—enlightened writer. His book, primarily about war and battles, spans two centuries of the Crusades seen through Arab eyes; and, to say it without bias, it barely fares any better than Lewis's bass histories. To cut corners, the cursory, fragmentary procedure is almost identical. And like Lewis, he loves (what a word!) to prate against Arab-Muslims in his spirit. For example, he first cites Ibn Jubayr, a 12th century traveler, who, according to Maalouf, fears that imitating the 'Franj' (West) is mortal danger for Islam. Then from this supposition, and without wondering how, why, or wherefore, Maalouf dissects, scalpel in hand, as it were, what seems to him to be the "symptomatic malady from which his [Ibn Jubayr's] congeners suffered." Then, extrapolating from Jubayr, he tells you what he sees, gazing behind the symptoms: "throughout the Crusades, the Arabs refused to open their own society to ideas from the West. And this, in all likelihood, was the most disastrous effect of the aggression of which they were the victims."[18] If I read these words correctly, Maalouf not only derogates Arab-Muslims; he also makes them out to be their own worst enemies, as if lying in wait for themselves in desert caves and crags—. You never read or hear anything more barren, actually, not to say more boring from a bungling surgeon.

Certainly, Lewis and Maalouf insert some interesting anecdotes that may tickle your fancy now and then. For example, Maalouf presents an impressive account of the birth and development of medieval Assassins.[19] On a less serious note, Lewis reports how Ibn Jubayr observes a pretty Frankish bride: "she walked

---

[17] See *From Oslo to Iraq*. Saïd uses two words to sum up Lewis's latest book: "superficial and dismissive," p. 264.

[18] Amin Maalouf, *The Crusades Through Arab Eyes* (New York: Schoken Books, 1985).

[19] Ibid., pp. 98-112.

with grace and dignity, swaying her jewels and adornments, stepping like a dove or a passing cloud." Then he looks away, fearing a state of priapism: "and may God save me from evil thoughts provoked by such sights."[20]   Yet soon such charm and fascination fade out in the overarching languid effect of their discourse, sending you to sleep. It's often sent me to sleep, especially upon my hearing the same tedious judgment over and over again. For they judge as do their counterparts, the orientalists, judge, frequently gratuitously, to boot. And when they judge, lacking a sense of what's real and what's imaginary, you can be sure the fires go out, the grass wilts, the wind dies, and life all but stops.

9

The next two writers have an edge on Maalouf and Lewis. At least they don't judge. Kamal Abdel-Malek presents a catalogue of disparate images. But they're (according to their publication dates) detailed, lively, entertaining, and occasionally insightful images of Arab-Muslim travelers' experiences in North America. The author's own 1999 crackling, witty image of Sheikh Mustapha's experience—the "American-Arab Sabeel Company, Ltd" (Water Charity)—is beautifully scripted, as if for filming. Here are a few more images: a love tour, the jeans and the switchblade, the flying sphinx in America, the land of magic, America—you cheeky devil, America: paradise and hellfire, and so on. All in all, the entire book reflects, in part, a trend: Mid-Easterners' on-going exodus to the West in quest, sad to say, of a new way of life in which to make up for their being the children of their fatherlands and motherlands. In any case, the images and the individual stories behind them are narrowly conceived. They have nothing to do with either the new politico-cultural activities afoot in the Mid-East or with any historical unfolding that sustains a systematic of view of the West.[21]

The same, to certain extent, holds for Carole Hillenbrand's work. But first, I should recognize her project for what it does and doesn't do. To begin with, she utilizes Arabic sources to depict medieval Arab-Muslims' plight,

---

[20] Bernard Lewis, p. 98.

[21] Kamal Abdel-Malek, *America in an Arab Mirror: Images of America in Arabic Travel Literature: An Anthology*, 1895-1995 (New York: St. Martin's Press, 2000).

12

including moments of triumph, during the Crusades invasion of the Mid-East. Above all, she makes no judgments. This is doubly refreshing when you come to it from the dank atmosphere of Maalouf's and Lewis's works. And yet, given her work's trajectory, it discounts the evolution of Arab-Muslim view and self-view vis-á-vis the world and the West. It also discounts the awareness on the part of some Arab-Muslim thinkers that turning over a new leaf—despite sentimental, angry portrayal of the West, despite Mid-Eastern autocrats' local atrocities—is inevitable, now more than ever (my own work's most crucial motif).[22] And so her account replicates Maalouf's, even if it exceeds the latter by claiming that the Crusades experience has pretty much shaped Arab-Muslim present. (I take this opportunity to stress the practical importance of the West's taking note of these evolutions: at least of integrating their study into its academy's curricula by opening academe's doors to the best minds in Islam and Arab-Muslim culture.[23])

Hillenbrand's claim brings me to a pause. Whose present exactly, I ask? All Arab-Muslims? Local autocrats? Islamist groups? Hillenbrand singles out the last; she then extrapolates and generalizes. Incidentally, I wonder why she discounts the second. In any case, she links Islamist insurgence, as if symbiotically (or perhaps telepathically?) to medieval Arab-Muslim feeling of resentment against the Franks. Such reactive feelings, she maintains, go far enough to define today's fundamentalist mindset. She finishes by asserting that the Crusades not only continue today; they also exert internal social and political pressure as well. Hence the persistent demand, according to her, for a Muslim

---

[22] For more valuable information, see Fatema Mernissi, *Islam and Democracy*, trans. Mary Jo Lakeland (Cambridge: Perseus Publishing, 2002), pp. 22-41. In these pages Mernissi describes the efforts of many medieval Arab-Muslim savants to instruct the public in the glory of reason and intellectual freedom. I, of course, add to her description from a different perspective.

[23] See Mohammad Arkhoun, *Rethinking Islam*, trans. Robert D. Lee (Boulder: Westview Press, 1994), p. 8. Arkhoun is right to chastise the West for keeping Arab-Muslim culture at a respectful distance, that is, for marginalizing it, as if it fears losing its authority or hegemony if it doesn't. He intimates that the West, in sidetracking the culture of the Other (which is essential for its own self-understanding), betrays the fact that its very culture not only stands on shaky grounds, but also lacks solidarity.

state.[24] And this demand, again, draws fuel from the self-contained, original, and pure culture of medieval Arab-Muslims.

Even so, I ask: what about Arab-Muslim multi-faceted reactions to orientalism, to Western domination and occupation of land? Does that count for nothing? What of Muhammad himself as well? His companions? The four successive Caliphs? Surely, their spiritual-ethical purism is and has been misconstrued, if not distorted by today's Islamists as mush as by autocrats.[25] For example, all of them find in Muhammad's and the four caliphs' wars (though a completely different experience by a different people for a different reason) a solution for today's problems. But the solution, you see, is projected onto the diabolical West. That is, it forecasts onto its past the elaborate politics of today's West. In so doing, it unwittingly turns in on itself, then, suddenly, lashes out against Arab-Muslim cultural theorists who look to the past not for a homoeopathic treatment or a quick fix, as Islamists and autocrats do, but for a beacon of wisdom devoid of mythology and resentment baggage; in short, for a guide to a brighter Arab-Muslim culture.[26] All that and more Hillenbrand leaves out of count.[27] Once again, she does so, understandably, by dint of her choice and specific purpose.

10

Let there be no misunderstanding: I've found all four works quite enlightening, and for that reason used them extensively. By juxtaposing their conclusions I've come to see how to insert my own thought in the interstices of their statements. For instance, by placing Hillenbrand's next to Maalouf's and

---

[24] Recently, al-Zarqāwi of Iraq, for example, has called for a Muslim state, though his demand hardly tallies with Hillenbrand's symbiotic account. But he doesn't claim any connection to Medieval Arabs. Nor for that matter does Khomeini of Iran at the time of the revolution.

[25] It's a disturbing irony, to say the least, that yesterday's admirable Islamic creed—non-violence, community, social justice, championship of the poor—is today's doctrine of oil-rich autocrats and ideology-ridden mullahs and murderous bigots.

[26] I highly recommend Habib Boulares, *The Fear and the Hope*, trans. Lewis Ware (London: Zed Books Ltd, 1990). This is an intelligent, thoughtful study that yields untold rewards when juxtaposed with Hillenbrand's book.

[27] Carole Hillenbrand, *The Crusades: Islamic Perspectives* (New York: Routledge, 2000).

Lewis's, I've learned to suspend judgment, the better to observe her use of language; indeed, she writes in a language stripped of dialectics and oratorical effects, which for me tend to counter their superimposed, unconscionable derogations of Muslims and Arab-Muslims alike. On the other hand, I appreciate her and Abdel-Malek's ability to transcend that stage of carelessness or prejudice at which the real as distinct from the imaginary is still relatively lacking. However, Lewis's and Maalouf's works remain invaluable sources of wide-ranging historical information not available in the other two works. All in all, then, I intend to glean from these works all the knowledge that's fit to enhance and extend further every nook and corner of my work.

11

Apropos of that, the important question may now be raised: why so far has there been no revaluation of Arab-Muslim long-range view of the West? Or, what amounts to the same, why has it been ignored, shrugged off, or perhaps put out of public's mind altogether? After all, scores of scholars, Easterners and Westerners alike, have been writing on East-West relations, particularly on orientalism, the exotic East (Orient)—exoticism, incidentally, is an emergency figure of distantiation when bourgeois Christians can't assimilate the other.[28] Why, then, this lack of interest? Or, if there's interest at all, why is it so scattered, scanty, lukewarm, prejudiced, boring, and clever, to boot? These questions have something of an ironic ring about them. Ironic, but also tragic and tempestuous like a hurricane of the skies, which sweeps down on life, upsets everything, uproots the mind like a leaf, and carries away the heart as in an abyss. I have in mind orientalism.

The word's etymology may reveal what's in that abyss. It derives from 'oriental,' the latter from 'orient,' and 'orient' from the Latin 'oriri,' meaning 'to rise.' Does this etymology meet up with modern history? Or is it a forgone coincidence? Anyhow, I ask because this age-old mummy (a.k.a. poltergeist) is up again, confounding people, raised to it, no doubt, by the hurricane of media

---

[28] See Roland Barthes, "Myth Today," *A Barthes Reader*, ed. Susan Sontag (New York: The Noonday Press, 1982), pp. 141-2.

and academia, no less than by the high winds of 9/11, Afghanistan and Iraq wars. Then outbursts and lightnings sweep down on life: more and more debates, articles, and books get written by Western orientalists, including, believe it or not, Arab orientalists. Their heavy rains deluge the Orient, covering it with images after their own—an arbitrary, abstract generalization—thus fulfilling the old bourgeois-Christian concept of the Orient as a figura of exoticism.[29] Arab-Muslims and Islam suffer similar abysmal and defacing fate. For two centuries now they receive a goodly share of this strange brew of fabrications, so that their very identity drowns in its abyssal miasma.

12

For example, Irshad Manji's book appears in 2003. It bears the title *The Trouble with Islam*—a telltale title, to be sure, which, to me, betrays a form of back door orientalism.[30] To cut corners, is she aware of her bias, even though she cites the philosopher Ibn Rushd just to show that Arab-Muslims are anything but literal-minded (an act performed in good conscience, no doubt). Again, is she aware of the furtive and sly bias insinuating itself into her writings? I'm afraid she isn't.

Nor for that matter is J. Keegan either, who a year later pens his "masterpiece."[31] History aside, of all things Arab-Muslim, he speaks of "Muslim illiberalism." Whatever the phrase means, it surely throws you out of your stride, for it fits in no Arab-Muslim text or context. Where, then, does he find it? I'll tell you. In that pile of withered concept-mummies which orientalism, carrying away his mind and heart, scuffles silently, as it were, into the twisting corridors of his book. There you strain your eyes and ears to grasp its signification or that of its opposite, liberalism. He definitely implies the latter,

---

[29] E. Saïd, *From Oslo to Iraq*, pp. 264-65, particularly in reference to the Arab Orientalist Fouad Ajami.

[30] Irshad Manji, *The Trouble With Islam* (New York: St. Martin's Press, 2003).

[31] J. Keegan, *The Iraq War* (New York: Alfred A. Knopf, 2004), p. 54.

too, and is biased in favor of it.[32] (Today the term 'liberal,' and whatever its opposite may be, seem to be acquiring new ideological significations.[33]) Nothing doing. Finally, you shake your head, you condole him on his loss of the historical sense (at least Manji sprinkles her account with a dash or two of history), on his overlooking, consciously or not, the dark underside of liberalism in the history of the West.[34] And, by the same token, in the history of American politics of which Howard Zinn speaks most eloquently.[35]

Such books, and others like them, in which masked orientalism speaks in different keys, have a long history. Let's, however, limit it to modern history, beginning with Hegel. Hegel, you see, is the first modern philosopher of Reason, and, as has been said, the "great thinker of forgiveness and reconciliation."[36] But if so, it's most catastrophically ironic. Like the hurricane I spoke of a moment ago. Sure enough, it turns out this reason forgives and reconciles nothing when it comes to Orientals and Mid-Easterners. It does one thing, though: it goes in and out of any individual's body as if this body's mere diaphane, simulacrum, or the apparition of a shadow. What's more, I'm reminded me of someone who says, "so and so is bad." "Why bad, asks another?" "Well, because of his badness, you

---

[32] Keegan and Manji, among others, might want to study carefully the differences between Arab-Muslim traditionalism, Shī'sm, and Mu'tazilism. They can, then, realize the issue isn't a matter of illiberalism, liberalism, or what's the trouble with Islam. Each domain of thought is as valid in its own grid of premises as the other, and has nothing to do with the first being close-minded, the second less so, the third more open-minded. My point is that one must have historical sense.

[33] President Bush designates Senator Kerry as liberal—that is, out of the mainstream of America. I'm wondering if liberal arts would also be liberal in that sense.

[34] Keegan could easily have consulted M. Foucault's famous study, *Discipline and Punish: The Birth of the Prison* (New York: Vintage Books, 1979); or equally famous study, "Society Must be Defended," *Lectures at the College de France, 1975-76* (New York: Picador, 2003).

[35] See Howard Zinn, *A People's History of the United States* (New York: Harper & Row, 1980). It would have been a most invaluable source to consult for a counter- or parallel-concept to "Muslim illiberalism," such as "illiberal liberalism," which pretty much sums up the hidden history of the United States.

[36] I borrow this phrase from J. Derrida, *On Cosmopolitianism and Forgiveness: Thinking in Action*, trans. Mark Dooley and Michael Hughes (New York: Routledge, 2001), p. 34.

addle head." And now I suddenly recall who that someone is: Hegel himself. A strange spirit, to be sure, though I hardly blame him for it.[37]

13

To illustrate, imagine a grim-lipped, pop-eyed man and master of happy consciousness—that's Hegel in a nutshell, literally and symbolically. Literally, he speaks out loud and clear, and what he says symbolically morphs into the master-race ideology so dear to his nineteenth- and twentieth-century philosophical cohorts and progeny. Ali Mirsepassi sums up the whole thing succinctly. With zero experience in the Orient, Hegel fabricates the exotic figure of the 'Oriental'—Arab-Muslim included, of course—as primitive, savage, inferior. Why, he asks himself? Well, because of his primitivity, savagery, inferiority. This is a copycat of the question, why so and so is bad? and the answer in five words: well, because of his badness. So a fog in the head becomes an illness: let there be illness, and there was illness. The Arab-Muslim is, naturally, the corporality of this illness. Reason would, Hegel concludes, urge the West to rise to "dominate and enslave these Eastern cultures in order to emancipate them." 'Dominate' and 'emancipate' are loaded words.[38]

They weave a dense subtext that, paradoxically, reveals more than it hides. Which, to repeat, is essentially illness, or, in Hegel's mind, evil. And which, in turn, implies a double relationship: one of force between good and evil, the other of force between adversaries. The whole density of this subtext, you see, melds into the function of the West as at once a repository of Good and as redeemer. How does the West emancipate these 'evil' Eastern cultures from their clanking chains of primitivity, savagery, inferiority? It's simple: by dominating them militarily, then, to nail them "good", by enslaving them to the Christian Western Good. That, to sum up, is the whole baggage of orientalist semiotics. What's beneath or below this semiotics, you ask? The other, it goes without saying. The

---

[37] I don't blame him because other forces were traversing him at the time, of which, despite his consciousness, he might have been aware. See M. Foucault's discussion of the concept of rationality in his "21 January" lecture at the College de France.

[38] Ali Mirsepassi, *Intellectual Discourses and Politics of Modernization* (New York: Cambridge University Press, 2000), pp. 24-35.

other as much feared for his savagery as detested for his primitiveness and inferiority, as Hegel says without saying it.

14

Let's be reasonable for a change. Let's turn the tables to see what's going on here. Isn't it true that every great philosophy—Hegel's is a great philosophy—is the personal confession of its author and a kind of involuntary and unconscious memoir? Isn't it also true that the moral intention in such a philosophy constitutes the real germ of life from which the whole plant grows? I think, with Nietzsche, it is so on both counts.[39] Well, then, might it not be the case that this other—this savage, primitive, inferior other—of whom Hegel speaks is none other than Hegel himself, or at least a piece of him? I mean the other that unconsciously (if I may say so) reminds him of his own savagery, primitivity, inferiority—which, in a word, is that frightful evil inside? And I insist: inside himself, first of all?

My answer is, again, yes. Hegel is indeed the one in whose fantasy all three meld into the image of a dreadful, foul-smelling truth that he has just conjured up. Foul-smelling—and you can almost surmise how he, facing his stinking truth, holds his nose to dam up the vapors from rising from his lower depths. But by a sleight of hand he saves himself the trouble of doing so: the other, you see, is so handy, so exotic, so evil, so ribald that he can easily, that is, vicariously, bear the brunt. And so Hegel, wanting to be as solid as his own foundation of reason, seizes hold of the other—the Oriental, the Easterner—and saddles him with that stench and every negative element he senses in himself. This, to generalize, is typical of the brood of Western orientalists-imperialists, and Hegel's idealism is their modern mother.[40]

---

[39] I'm here adapting a couple of ideas from Nietzsche's *Beyond Good and Evil*, trans. W. Kaufmann, Section 6, p. 13.

[40] See Abdul R. JanMohammad, "The Economy of Manichean Allegory," *Post-Colonial Studies Reader,* eds. Bill Ashcroft et al (New York: Routledge, 1995), pp. 18-23. Though brief and no Hegel is mentioned, it's an illuminating analysis of the West in relation to the other. You may also want to review, in a different key, Terry Eagleton's creative tour de force, "Death, Evil, and Non-Being," *After Theory* (London: Allen Lane, 2003), pp. 208-222. This second polyvalent essay operates on different registers, though all converge upon a single theme designated in its title. I may have to cite it in a different context.

If my description stands the truth on its feet, it illuminates an interesting, though ironic, aspect of Platonic ontology: the other proves to be an eye-mirror, after all. But with this little twist to it: until he spins his fictitious and factitious yarns about the other, Hegel hardly deems himself savage, primitive, or inferior at all. This is a foregone conclusion. Only his own concoctions enable him to do so afterwards, and only through a process of "extrojection," or transfer from the self to the other. And when he recognizes himself as such, he reacts with disgust, blinding himself in the process to that other element in the other—the divine—in which he could have, otherwise, contemplated his soul. In a word, instead of politicizing difference the better to appreciate its value in the formation of Apolline selfhood, Hegel externalizes in the figure of the other the already implicit in his self—in order to dominate him.[41] In other words, Hegel understands Plato's ontology incorrectly as psychology, thereby seeing the other and his self as related parts of the same.[42]

After Hegel, all thought-ingredients brewing the semiotics of orientalism and its psychological motivation replicate his procedure. To this day, it remains, to use a hackneyed phrase, a vicious circle: cobwebbery cloaking Western self-alienation, itself giving rise to or displacing itself into greed, domination, and politics of imperialism. M. Rodinson and E. Saīd follow these racist-imperialist frill-tales and masquerades to their final conclusions. Their objective is to show the true color of savagery, not to speak of the primitive, ferocious freedom with which Hegel's jaw-squared idealism (so-called objective idealism) has been

---

[41] The Greek Apollo embodies the drives toward distinction, directness, and individuality as well as toward respecting boundaries and limits. He also teaches an ethic of moderation and self-control. See Moses Hadas, *A History of Greek Literature* (New York: Columbia University Press, 1965), pp. 44-46.

[42] This is a classic example of how Christianity—the ethic of the chosen—penetrates every nook and cranny of Western philosophical endeavor. Where Plato has no recourse to exclusivity except reason or science, Hegel has Christian valuation behind him of whose deep influence in his philosophy he seems unaware.

systematically carried out in the Mid-East.[43] Today, you look America in the face and wonder whether the G.W. Bush and allies campaign in Iraq doesn't, in a sense, fulfill or continue Hegel's idealist-objective program. But God knows best.

16

I'm slowly inching my way toward the questions I raised earlier, and I think I've gained some headway. I'd like to gain more headway now by looking at orientalism from a different perspective. You see, today orientalism adopts, as if proudly, a variety of different guises or masks, and still, so to speak, gets away with murder, not to speak of getting off with impunity, to boot. Therefore, I think it ought to be seen in total in order to appreciate its grandiose intellectual baggage, though, again, I wouldn't be saying anything new.

Needless to say, the Western view of Arab-Muslims differs from the latter's view of the West. I tried to put across certain aspects of that difference before. But now I see the former as an on-going mythic saga of imperialist family and its members the human sciences, while the latter, occidentalism or counter-orientalism, as I named it, stands as its antipodes—with the important difference that its agenda isn't so much for domination as for understanding and self-understanding. Allow me to explain.

17

How does this imperialism manifest itself? Well, I'd say, and it may sound strange, as a love affair. And it develops as a relation of force between beauty and the beast. Or, to interpret what Hegel has in mind, a relation of good and evil. For he, like many orientalists, is so enamored of Arab-Muslim East the beast he wants, "phallogocentrically," (forgive use of this pompous word[44]), to soften it up, to Westernize it or, as you now know, to "emancipate" it—that's to say, to tame it, and in doing so, to tame the beast in himself through it. In case of the former taming, however, assuming it's his immediate goal, the beast, to all

---

[43] "The Western Image and Western Studies of Islam," Eds. C. Bosworth and J. Schacht, *The Legacy of Islam* (Oxford, 1974); *Orientalism* (New York: Vintage Books, 1979).

[44] I borrow this term from Derrida. See *Acts of Literature*, ed. Derek Attridge (New York: Routledge, 1992), p. 57.

intents and purposes, seems to hate the procedure; it refuses to be tamed. What's more, it spurns every effort and prospect of being turned into a handsome prince—at least not the type of 'hand-some' prince called love of man that's perfectly tailored to Western moral specifications, conditions and qualities.[45]

The ambers of love start to glow anew in orientalism. Now orientalism is head over heels in love. And it doesn't really matter which love it inherits from Hegel. After all, love, any love—strait, gay, or otherwise—conquers all, especially when it comes to the imperialist desire to penetrate the other. Now the elect few, the penetrators, the orientalists, grant themselves the love-token. They're indeed the supreme lovers. And not only lovers, they're masqueraders as well. They call themselves world-redeemers, that is to say, universal intellectuals and pose as the consciousness/conscience of their public,[46] even if the latter gives not a fig for the Orient so long as the latter and the world westernize. Not so the orientalists, clearly. In fact, they do give not one but two figs or more. They believe in orientalizing first of all, and dub the practice new scientific studies or, in more pompous terms, human sciences distinguished in principle and goal (at least in their head) from all other sciences. For that they range, like hunters, like spermatozoa onto the oval surfaces of Orient and Mid-East in quest of objects and people to orientalize.

18

What do those surfaces yield them? Facts, of course. But facts devoid of the unique and wholly individualized original experience to which the culture of the other owes its birth. Indeed, most orientalists, intellectually un-Apolline as

---

[45] See Santha Rama Rau, "By Any Other Name," *Gifts of Passage* (New York: Harper-Collins Publishers, 1951). In this short story, based on actual events, Rau, reflecting on her kindergarten life, portrays the British, in the person of a headmistress, in a telling manner. Indian names are apparently too much for this headmistress; so she says to the two young Indian sisters, Premila and Santha, on their first day in a British-run school: "suppose we give you pretty English names. Wouldn't that be more jolly? Let's see, now—Pamela for you, I think. That's as close as I can get. And for you, how about Cynthia? Isn't that nice?" For the British elite at the time the other remains beyond their grasp if it isn't confined on their procrustean bed.

[46] For thorough understanding of this issue, see Michel Foucault's dense response to a question on the subject of the universal intellectual. "Truth and Power," *Foucault Reader*, ed. Paul Rabinow (New York: Pantheon Books, 1984), pp. 67-75. Though he refers to no Orientalist intellectuals, his meaning remains unmistakable.

they are, couldn't care less about cultural uniqueness or originality. If they do, it would certainly hamper their work of simplification (or "simplistification," if you will).[47] You see, their apparatus of knowledge is directed not at knowledge but at taking possession of things; ends and means are as remote from their essential nature as are concepts. With ends and means, they take possession of the process (they invent a process that can be understood); with concepts, they take possession of things that constitute the process. But they never take possession of knowledge. They can only think essences: images, representations, simulacra—or word-concepts with which the world is codified into the binary opposition between master and slave. They're the masters, it goes without saying. As such, they sit proudly on their destiny, tooting their horns, churning out one grandiosity after another—race, war, power, democracy, ideology, (il)liberalism. As proudly, too, they melt into their governments' functions and functionaries. Then under the name of lords and ladies, they strut off to liberate the savage beast. The beast, they've just learned, that doesn't know enough to understand things, least of all itself.

Orientalists, then, transform everything they touch or face into essential types. Just as the cuttlefish squirts its ink to protect itself, they obscure Arab-Muslim world, fixate it into an object which can be forever possessed, catalogue its riches, embalm it, and inject into reality some purifying essence which stops its transformation. Once fixated and frozen, this object becomes calculable, computable, hence subjugable. In a word, they perform a basic operation, more exactly, a weighing operation by which peoples' essences are placed in scales of which orientalists remain the motionless beams. In other words, to the naïve, uninformed Western public, they present an Orient, an Arab-Muslim world, fully encased in grandiose orientalized forms (simplified, falsified, artificially distinguished) ready for takeover.

---

[47] You can easily see this in the way others judge Othello: for Iago, for example, Othello is "an old black ram" and for Roderigo a "gross lascivious Moor." Of course, Brabantio, to whom these demeaning epithets are addressed (they think his daughter was abducted by Othello) echoes with his "sooty bosom," the curse he hurls upon Othello's head. This, in a nutshell, is the extent to which exoticism distantiates or "simplistifies" the other. See William Shakespeare, *Othello*, ed. Edward Pecher, A Norton Critical edition (New York: W.W. Norton and Company, 2004), pp. 6-8. Might it be the case that today's 'red necks" are the heirs to this portrait of the other? I wonder.

And what could the effect on the gullible, decent public be here? To begin with, consider the following. Western public exists in the most manipulative civilization human beings have ever experienced. From its daily awakening to its troubled sleep, this public bombarded with all kinds of signs, chimera, abstractions; all kinds of images transmitted by audio-visual media (news, movies, videos, ads about peoples and events of all types and colors—all rigged up for its control.[48] In addition, for a variety of reasons, this same public, so long accustomed to such numbing bombardments, is relatively deprived of the experience in the thoughtful reading of texts. What's more, it's sadly deficient in certain kinds of historical knowledge that might otherwise give it some perspective on the manipulations it continuously encounters.[49] To cut corners, too many decent people in the Western democracies succumb to a dangerously romantic view of the Orient (including Mid-East) perpetrated by orientalist technologies that blind them to its reality. The danger here is none other than political innocence.[50]

19

And precisely the kind of innocence that orientalism counts on. Orientalists, you see, like commercial advertisers, keep a watchful watch on the public. They know this public exactly as they know what sells it. The rebels, the atrophied types, the troubled sleepers, the drugged enlightened, the romantics whose libido is in constant search of some fulfillment which will deliver them from the anxieties of reality but which will, nevertheless, contain this reality—in relation to all such people (that is, the innocent, decent public) the orientalists

---

[48] See John Fiske, *Reading the Popular* (New York: Routledge, 1991). Especially pp. 149-217 in which news, history, and events are packaged according to the requirements of democracy.

[49] For an insightful study in this regard, see Roland Barthes, *Image, Music, Text*, trans. Stephen Heath (New York: Hill and Wang, 1977).

[50] As I write these words, a thought strikes me: To what extent orientalist propaganda today replicates that of the Soviet Union in the forties? Does history repeat itself? The manipulation and control of opinion of even the enlightened people conducted by Soviet surveillance machinery seems to me to parallel those conducted by orientalism against the decent people in the Western democracies. I realize the impropriety of making this comparison. But anyone reading George Orwell's *Animal Farm* and Aldous Huxley's *Brave New World* can't help seeing the parallel, particularly when they portray a heavily drugged society easily manipulated by politicians.

have the politician's instinct for trimming sails to the wind when it's expedient to tell it what it wants to hear. They select only the kind of perceptions which concern this public, now that it's been made into a clean slate ready for new writing, in order to give it a sense of security.

The same holds when the issue comes down to the Orient (also the Mid-East). Ignorant of what transpires in the dark cellars where orientalist perceptions and ideologies are packaged, the public, in effect, knows only what's given to it to know on the surface—truths, even if these are dressed up or illusory. And whatever evidence is adduced, it's still part of that illusion.[51] Thus Orient (Mid-East, Islam) is offered up to it, as it were, on a silver platter all trussed up, that is to say, reduced to an exotic object or spectacle.[52] In other words, the public, whose feelings are helplessly fettered to orientalism, takes in this pure fiction and sign language and enjoys this beautiful object without wondering where it comes from. Or even better, this object can only come from the mysterious Orient: since the beginning of time, it has been made for Western man—not to ignore or deny, not at all—but to come to it face to face in order to transform it, willy-nilly, into himself.[53]

In the final analysis, unable to imagine Islam, Mid-East, or Orient in itself (now you know why), Western public, this compassionate public, with dust in its eye and chimeras in its mind, can at least imagine the place to which orientalism relegates them: the confines of humanity where they don't threaten the security of the home. This is what's known in the West as liberalism, as it's practiced today,

---

[51] Consider Othello's handkerchief, the ocular proof which he demands of Iago that Desdemona is a whore. But you know, as Shakespeare dramatizes it, it's all based on a lie/ illusion. Even the concrete handkerchief is a tissue of illusion, that's to say, rigged up as real. And so you may, willy-nilly, conclude: isn't Shakespeare ultimately showing us that mankind loves, hates, does, says things, and adduces proofs under the unconscious truth that truth is an illusion and illusion is truth without which mankind can't live? Doesn't he choose Othello, the Moor, just to clinch that thought? Finally, isn't he saying to the public, "wake up"?

[52] See note 40 above. In his essay, Abdul JanMohamed discusses, among other things, colonial symbolism.

[53] Saīd, "What People in the U.S. Know About Islam is a Stupid Cliché," *Power, Politics and Culture: Interviews with Edward Said* (New York: Vintage Books, 2002), pp. 368-384. See also note 44 above.

a sort of intellectual equilibrium, if you will, based on recognized places. Orientalism, therefore, removes from sight both determinism and freedom of the other. And you can easily guess the ultimate effect of this removal: it sabotages all fruitful encounters between East and West, at the same time renders the Western public as much irresponsible as blissfully ignorant.

20

Now the big question: if Western public assimilates heart and mind with orientalism, if it nurses its chimeras, if even well-informed observers believe the most fantastic accounts of orientalism, then could this public spur democratic outreach in its own internal ecology? Could it look creatively beneath or behind the surface of things to recover its own five wits? Consider this phenomenon for an answer: except for the few who despise Saddam Hussein, the American public in general, always boundlessly optimistic, always bull-headedly buoyant, couldn't care less who or what manner of man he is. Or if it does, it simply, if not sheepishly, follows how and where the political winds blow. I mean when authority figures—state, media, academia and their symptomatology of images, words, concepts—program what it should know or think, what ethical recourse does this public have against its unconscious gullibility?[54] But if symptomatology says, "the sky's the limit," "never say never," "you can crack it if you have faith in yourself," etc., this kind of moral teaching is music to its ears.[55]

So the question may be re-phrased: will this public awaken from the kitschy optimism with which the state, media, and academia inoculate it? Or will it continue in its callow languor of afternoon? I wager on the latter case. Indeed, so long as it wallows in lack of will to power, hankering as it does after the base ideals of self-preservation, physical health, and comfort, it fails to see through orientalism's "hiremen" (historians, critics, interpreters), to think for itself, not to speak of transcending itself—which is the function of will to power on whose

---

[54] For an in-depth look at how stage and media influence people's thinking, see John Fiske, *Reading the Popula*, chapter 7.

[55] Of course, there are individuals and groups of individuals who leave no stone unturned in search of the truth, and they're courageous enough to declare it, too. See the immediately preceding note and the one immediately following.

presence and strength, after all, depends every enhancement of the human being. Rather, it remains slumping in a state of inertia, stuck with itself, going on amid the earth's stir and jar, passing through life but scarcely touching it, bearing on its brow the slight mark of a sublime destiny—a destiny set and sealed by the big corporations, language, media, and politics.[56] How depressing it is indeed to repeat the same life day in and day out!

In this context—and the point I'm trying to reach—you can now grasp what's missing from East-West scholarship: it shies away from an overview of the whole theme of Arab-Muslim view of the West. You see, scholars, as I tried to show earlier, prefer to fasten upon fragments of histories or texts and transpose what view or meaning they contain rather than interpret them and their subtexts. They do so because they unconsciously kowtow to orientalism's power of language and its manipulative concepts. More than that: not only they become victims of this fabrication, but, ironically, victims of their own ignorance as well. It's as if, in their slumbering conscience, orientalism, discerning their will-power (different from will to power), takes possession of their souls which it has swept clean, and purifies them for initiation into its highest mysteries without recourse. Which, I dare say, it does to this day by putting these "hiremen" at a loss to purvey alternatives.[57]

21

The love affair, the orientalist romance, the public's naivete—all this and more has been necessary to describe just to say this: it's an altogether different experience with the Arab-Muslim public. And for several reasons which I'll run through before detailing references to them. First, it has no cult, no enthusiastic veneration for occidentalism as does Western public for orientalism. As a corollary, Arab-Muslim public doesn't, as does its Western counterpart, thrive on catching glimpses of tantalizing phantasmagoria of exotic realities which

---

[56] For further insight into state and corporate manipulation of the public, see Frances Fox Piven, *The War At Home*, (New York: The New Press, 2004). And for insight into the role of language in politics and media—what's called framing—see George Lakoff, *Don't Think of an Elephant* (Vermont: Chelsea Green Publications, 2004).

[57] That's one good reason why Arab-Muslim cultural theorists, knowing this to be so, bracket orientalism, though without dismissing it out of hand.

orientalism dangles before public eyes in order to keep up the suave indolence and harmony of things at home. Nor, finally, does it possess mechanisms, supplies or tools that would make occidentalism serve as fuel for its will-power— namely to dominate or Islamize the West. These are irrecusable facts.

The same holds for Arab-Muslim view of the West, which we know about from the fifty or so medieval and modern writers. These writers are neither instruments nor functionaries of their governments. Even if they are, they lack the opportunist tactics and ruse of reason necessary for political and ideological manipulation of the public's thought and feeling. They're transparent to the public. As such, they also embody no hierarchy of intellect imbued with scientific knowledge and biased judgments, nor they set down any theories or ideologies suggesting or implying something or anything like Arab-Muslim imperialism. It's foreign to their ethos. They and the public are one and the same when it comes to viewing the West.

Perhaps I don't even have to say all that in the first place. But I'm compelled to it just to stress the point that occidentalism á la orientalism-in-reverse doesn't exist anywhere in Arab-Muslim thought and feeling. I mean that hyper-intellectualized simplemindedness so typical of orientalism which falsely advances the view that concepts can tell Westerners something about the essence of the Orient, that the Orient is composed of identical cases that can be correctly subsumed under general concepts, and so on—this naïve and wrong view is quite foreign to Arab-Muslim ethos. Arab-Muslim view of the West is a peculiar lookout which hasn't yet been seen for what it truly is.

22

Arab-Muslim view of the West or, if you will, occidentalism (should we still want to call it that), seeks to grasp the world, the West, and itself all at the same time. It does so through a down-to-earth mode of heuristics—reading books, observing, traveling, in a word, experience. But the experience isn't the same for every writer or region: different Arab-Muslims from different regions take their bearing and realize each their singular identity by describing the other and themselves through the other. Put otherwise, each society—individuals, or

28

groups of individuals—Egyptian, Syrian, Iraqi, Saudi, Jordanian, and so on—
evolves and has evolved its own peculiar view of the West independently of the
other. This multiple perspective, that is, a plurality with one sense (the West),
never coalesces into a concept identifying or underscoring one view or essence of
the West. True, here and there certain aspects of it copycat or repeat each other,
but that's because plagiarism (if that's what it is) is a venerable traditional
practice among Arab-Muslims. In any event, the view, as I try to show in the
following chapters, remains on the whole a plurality.

You see, plurality is an inherent quality of Islam and causeful in part of
that multiple view. It lives and has lived dispersedly in many hands, and every
school of thought, of theology, of law, in short, every society sings it differently.
Yet one resplendent truth shines through: Arab-Muslim ethos—embodied in
social justice, in ethics of equality, and in non-violence (this last may sound
strange)—remains underneath it all singularly constant. I mean, though this ethos
appears adversely divided from within, it persists as one and indivisible in origin
or in essence.[58] These two aspects of Islam, then, plurality and singularity, should
be kept separate. And for two reasons: they help to identify the nature and quality
of Arab-Muslim view of the West; they could be found more easily reconcilable if
one day some Arab-Muslims become leaders (not autocrats) and happen to
comprehend them as such. If only for the sorely desired peaceful coexistence
among Arab-Muslim nations and for better quality of life.

23

But plurality or, if you will, diversity of lookout, gets more complex
because it has a history. In fact, a long history. To cut corners, it's rooted in pre-
Islamic tribal establishment of Quraysh. More specifically, in a rivalry between
members of familial kinship: between the house of Umayya (later the Umayyad
dynasty) and the house of Abbas (later the Abbasid dynasty). Beyond that, it

---

[58] A good example, I think, may be found in the Quranic Sura number four, which is "Women."
Essentially it states this: "if you hear God's revelations being denied or ridiculed, you must not sit
and listen to them until they engage in other talk." That's all there's to it. This is the Arab-
Muslim way—the gentle way, the merciful way, the effective way of dealing with people like that,
and not the way of death threats. See *The Koran*, Sura 4, Verse 140, trans. N.J. Dawood (New
York: Penguin Books, 1993).

may even structure the very moral fiber of pre-pre-Islamic tribal societies. At any rate, it survives into and beyond Islam, and all but scuttles Muhammad's fragil attempt to put together the *ummah* (community with a juridical base) from his tiny following.[59] A few decades after his death, however, the *ummah* comes to a head only to come apart at the seams: different splinter groups vie for power and prestige, thus pushing Arab-Muslim history back to the old system of internecine tribalism.[60] This last, let me quickly add, could have become, despite difficulties, a socio-political unity without Islam. But, alas, tribal leaders fail to seize the most opportune day for the purpose.[61]

And so diversity of lookout endures and constitutes, as if from time immemorial, the internal ecology of Arab and Arab-Muslim peoples. Difference eternally inhabits it.[62] Of course, it morphs into fresh forms of political turmoil based in differing religious pieties, and these continue unchallenged into the medieval period, through colonialism, and up to the present. At present, it puts in place still a new breed of discrete, motley, shrewd autocrats and Islamists who, like their ancestors the Umayyad and Abbasid rulers, exploit religion for personal and political ends. They install themselves in power on the backs of their peoples and, being under internal pressure and external market forces, they can't help but play footsy with the West, which the West gladly reciprocates. And the game goes on. To sum up, plurality in Arab-Muslim history evolves before it becomes

---

[59] This is further discussed in first chapter below.

[60] See Omar Faroukh, *Tarikh Sadr al-Islam wal-Dawla al-Amawiyya* (Beirut, 1983), pp. 35-56.

[61] This is a long history the upshot of which is this: the battle of Dhu Qar is a famous moment in the national life of pre-Islamic (Arab) warring tribes who for the first time unite against a common enemy, Persia. Certain Arab tribes join the Persian forces against other Arab tribes, but then the Persian King Kisra reneges on promises made to the former. At which point, when one day he orders the allies to attack the invading tribes, they refuse. They then secede and join their brethren at Dhu Qār, a valley between Baghdad and Damascus, against the king himself. But that moment itself, the great opportunity for establishing a permanent political unity among all tribes, and right after the defeat of the king, is never exploited for the purpose. See Ali Ibrahīm Hasan, *al-Tārikh al-Islāmi al-'Ām* (Cairo, 1965), pp. 68-85.

[62] Perhaps Derrida's concept (which isn't a concept) of *différance* finds support in this history. A great insight, I think, by which to enlighten Arab-Muslims in their history.

(which it finally does) an element in the modern ideological and dogmatic struggle among those very Mid-Eastern societies.

24

Political fragmentation aside, let me now consider occidentalism from another vantage point. Arab-Muslim view of the West, to repeat, is neither a product of relations of force (love/hate, good/evil), nor a fabrication of universal intellectuals with agendas for domination. Already Lewis, Maalouf, Abdel-Malek, and Hillenbrand, among others, have abundantly demonstrated the fact.[63] Indeed, if 'universal intellectual' signifies some master of truth for all time and place, then no one in the Arab-Muslim world, past or present—Muhammad, Ibn Rushd, or Khomeini fits the category or claims such mastery.[64] This is so, philosophico-theologically speaking, despite Islam's claim to universality.[65] What's more, no socio-political soil has ever been tilled for the growth of the universal intellectual.[66] This is as it should be. For one thing, unlike Christianity, Islam has never morphed into an organized religion; for another, though it bans no books or learning, it's as much pristinely as ethically an egalitarian faith. Politics-as-*realpolitik,* then, isn't precisely what underlies Arab-Muslim plurality; nor is it what wedges and has wedged Arab-Muslims apart historically. Something totally different is at work.

---

[63] If this view isn't based in theoretical knowledge, then something else motivates it, as I try to show in later chapters. For now, however, let me offer this metaphor which I think might best describe this occidental view as a whole: imagine the state of someone's gorge rising, the tide of pain and anger swelling within the blood—but soon it dies away as quickly as it came. Such a metaphor suggests that the matrix of Arab-Muslim feeling about the West is an oscillating emotional state of ebb and flood as pain and suffering and the memories associated with them swell and bate—no more, hardly more. Having said that, let's not forget the influence of the affects of egoism, selfishness, and self-centeredness in the structure of East-West relations.

[64] Let's just take the example of Khomeini, which also points to plurality in Islam. He certainly was a charismatic figure. But that's not just because he was himself charismatic, but because of the role he played within the theology of Shi'ism, which Sunnism doesn't have: imams for Sunnis are imams: they lead the prayers; and there are the Ulama who are very knowledgeable, but they don't have a direct line to divine messages. So the politico-theological reality will be very different in the two cases. In a word, the universal intellectual doesn't exist anywhere in Islam.

[65] See *The Koran,* 21: 105-112.

[66] Only outside the Mid-East could something like an intellectual flourish.

It's religion as belief or, if you like, as ardent piety. The very stuff as anger and friction are made on in Arabia. Think back to six-century dispute of who controls the tribe of Quraysh, sons of Umayya or sons of Abbās? Again, who, besides minding finance and law, provides food and water for the pilgrims visiting Mecca's black stone each year? Think also if the dispute is sprinkled with seasonings of greed for wealth and power. Finally, think of Islam entering the fray only to add its own coal of fire to flaming passions. Well! The result's inevitable: the whole tribe, including Islam, gets embroiled in deadly factionary wars. Abbās and Umayya each, now that Islam is in, vie for piety with the other, while Islam splits up between them. And so in its name wars rage on until the Abbasids, claiming to be the true Muslims, oust the tribal (though Muslim) Umayyads from rule in mid eighth century. But the most ironic outcome of all is this: in such atmosphere of ardent piety and ferocious war Islam loses its simple-spiritual ethics, its center of gravity, to hairsplitting dogma.

25

The loss is unfortunate, to say the least. For after the ascension of Abbasid dynasty, Islam soon breaks up into little Islams, with their little pieties and their little moralities and their little dogmas.[67] These religious fiefdoms (as I'd call them) are still with us today, I mean in their hard-core way. They and not the Crusades (whose success is an effect of this long-coming dissolution) constitute the history of the present.[68] A present we've come to know in its factious and factionary forms of autocracy and Islamism and the latter's splinter groups. A present, too, we've come to see as the arena where a new critical dawn battles with the nightly ethos of old-new tribalism—and the battle, incidentally, hasn't finished, while a terrible sense of failure makes the already troubled former tremble with fear.[69] A present, finally, when for all Arab-Muslims there's yet no

---

[67] See note 60 above. The entire book referred to has to be read in order to understand how this religious rivalry plays out politically through the eighth and ninth centuries.

[68] As you can see, Hillenbrand misses the point in her account of the Crusades. See note 27 above.

[69] See the new sense of anxiety as expressed by none other than Djait himself: a brief passage cited by Mernissi, p. 46.

promise, vague or clear, floating in the future, like a golden fruit suspended from a fantastic tree.[70]

The question may now be raised: how in the absence of a political template, in a world of clashing pieties and without center, could a large-scale intellectualism or even a bevy of ethically-minded leadership develop? I ask the question because I want to make a cautionary remark: though no answer is forthcoming as yet, the absence on both counts ought never, again ought never to be construed as giving license to wild or smug speculations. I mean nothing short of ignorance or prejudice would induce anyone to conclude that Arab-Muslims are either narrow-minded or backward for founding no political institutions or ideologies, for breeding no intellectuals, and for developing no historico-political discourse linking relations of truth with relations of force—a discourse deemed in the West the root and matrix of nationhood.

26

Islam, you see, remains, underneath it all and despite its checkered career, a spiritual force in its essence. It begins as such in the very teeth of Mecca's six-century material and egotistic world. Power, anger, and greed (the hallmark of that world) are all alien to its simple ethic of social justice and egalitarianism. By a stroke of fate, however, it gets caught in the meshes of bloody hostilities it can't control, and has to defend itself, even with blood. They all but break its wings. Its distinctness (or rather distinctness conceived as such[71]) stands outside their (hostilities') realm. Still its essence remains intact, though on the surface its school for spirituality, as you saw, turns into controversial doctrines: that is, it learns to set itself up to a form of semi-state organization, to wage war and, psychologically (more of this in next chapter), to isolate itself into the bargain by

---

[70] In 2002, fire breaks out in one of the girls' schools in Mecca. The girls run for their lives, the religious police forces many to go back to seek their robes and head-covers. As a result, fourteen girls die, and triple the number are critically injured. Does this situation make room for the exercise of intellect and leadership ethics? I wonder.

[71] It's interesting to compare this with Arkhoun's remarkable work. I think he's quite right to argue that neither Christianity nor Judaism ever makes the gesture to accommodate Islam's originary idea of Abrahamic moment as the nucleus of all three faiths.

creating its two imaginary entities, among others—*Dar al-Islam* (House of Islam) and *Dar al-Harb* (House of War). But, and this is the important point, it never develops, past or present, any political and social institutions urgently necessary for the building of a nation.

Hichem Djait, one of the few Arab-Muslim thinkers to be discussed later, puts it elegantly: Islam, past and present, he says in effect, rests on no political base; if there's any political element in it, this is neither a conception of power nor that of power itself, nor the search for a principle to organize society as a political body. Islam, unlike the Church in Western Christianity, has had and has no ideology with institutional framework to sustain it; rather, Islamic politics, if you can call it that today, is not just a failure; it's actually no more than pure nostalgia for the primitive era together with a need for defensive military might.[72] Given this picture, you can easily understand why Islamists and autocrats, those factious powers, have evolved at all today: they're precisely the kind of prosthetic, bromidic elements substituting for what may be referred to as a political desideratum, a what-might-have-been, that is, a political void without recourse.

27

Once again, Djait's words corroborate Islam's essence throughout history: give to Allah what's Allah's and to Muhammad (his messenger) what's Muhammad's—a patently unpolitical faith in every part.[73] A faith, in short, in which Islam tallies itself and its spiritual interests with those of Christian and Judaic faiths in one single originary instance: trust in God as the underlying reality of the world. And it's this very instance, to come to the point directly, that

---

[72] Take, for example, the Ottoman empire of the sixteenth and seventeenth centuries. Whether you speak of sovereignty, law, or politics or of whatever system of power representation you may think of, this empire has no such things in place, neither a political system, an ideological framework, nor even relations of power—technology, knowledge, science, the play of superstructures and infrastructure—to enable it to develop anything like an organized military or society. And so when it invades Western Europe, it does so not with any intention of enlightening or emancipating the West from ignorance or evil. The invasion is spurred by sheer, blind faith in its military might which itself is goaded by sheer ideological non-being called fundamentalism, no more, hardly more.

[73] See Hichem Djait, *Europe and Islam*, trans. Peter Heinegg (Berkeley: University of California Press, 1985), p. 148.

informs the view of the West it promotes since the ninth century. Indeed, even today's seemingly Islamist and autocratic politics and power fit the same bill: they're as much motivated by religious as by tribal ethos—ethos, to repeat, that's all but political, as you saw, and that by the same token gets manipulated by the oil-hungry West. Yet just such manipulation, in turn, constitutes no politics in the proper meaning of the term. Rather, it's a case of rub-my-back-and-I-rub-yours, a mutually secretive East-West flirtation, no more, hardly, though it frequently overshoots the mark.

Finally, Islam qua faith also applies to the idea of plurality with one sense. For one thing, Islam, to say it again, is inherently plural; for another, it has no politico-legal center of gravity, no cult of theoretical reason, no mega-philosophico-hegemonic schema á la Hegel or orientalism with intent to dominate the West in order to emancipate it. In a word, such megalomaniac view of the West is as much alien to its religious, even tribal ethos as capitalism is to the spirit of egalitarianism.[74] An ethos, to be sure, barely conscious of itself as a central power capable of putting its political "imaginary" (if it has one[75]) in the saddle for instructing or compensating the West for what it lacks, namely, to put it in Mirsepassi's words, though in reverse order, "the human and cultural qualities necessary to attain freedom on its own."[76]

28

So seen, you may now ask: if it's religiously grounded, what form, then, does Arab-Muslim view of the West ultimately assume? My answer, hopefully, comes in final and clear: that of the affects. I mean this view modulates and fluctuates: now it sounds indignant and dazzled and resentful, now meager and weary and fickle—affects framed (to some extent still are) in a grid of defeats, victories, alliances, assassinations, failure or success of rebellions, failure or

---

[74] See notes 37 and 60 above.

[75] I borrow the term from Arkhoun, p. 6. However, he uses it in a different context.

[76] Mirsepassi, "Islam and Democracy: Two Centuries after the Persian Letters."

success of conspiracies, and so on.[77] What's more, all societies, both individuals
and groups (educated politicians, diplomats, thinkers, authors, poets, theologians),
have a stake here, though no society matches another in the degree or quality of
those affects. The only exception to this rule is that of the second half of the
twentieth century, in which case, as you shall see, the view takes on a critical
function or role.

Put otherwise, Islam's multi-faceted view of things shows that though
Arab-Muslim eyes have gazed at the same target (West) since the ninth century,
no pair of eyes sees or interprets it in the same way. Consequently, any attempt to
reduce this view to a simple form of binary opposition—of the type, for example,
if they don't love us, they hate us—fails. It fails because it's made out to be as
something issuing from that other misleading binary division of the world, as you
saw, into *Dar al-Harb* and *Dar-al-Islam*. Again, this division is religiously
motivated and so must be cautiously interpreted in any study of Arab-Muslim
view of the West.[78] (I take up this point in the second half of first chapter.) In
the final analysis, this view, allow me to rename apolitical occidentalism, has
been, to return to the point I started with, a daunting enterprise for most scholars.
Daunting, largely because it's too sentimental, too emotional, too psychological,
too religious and too moralistic to confine on the procrustean bed of so-called
scientific discourse.

Finally, apropos of this daunting enterprise, I just wish to mention two
things: modern Arab-Muslims and their synchronically many-sided experiences
with the West; over and above that, Islam and its diachronically multifaceted
content: Islams (in the plural), their divergent schools of theology, their individual
experiences with the world and the West.[79] If this proves insufficient, let's
imagine Kamal Abdel-Malek's micro-text blown up into a macro-text with all

---

[77] See not 63 above.

[78] See Ahmad Khalīl, "Dar Al-Islam and Dar al-Harb: It Definition and Significance," [online
document], 2003. The article draws on many sources for the purpose of illuminating this difficult
though simplistic concept.

[79] See E. Saīd, *Covering Islam* (New York: Vintage Books, 1997), pp. 37-79.

Arab-Muslim views of the West recorded there. You can see the difficulty, if not utter impossibility, of fitting everything into a unitary, univocal, or fixed structure. You can also see that no scholar alone, no matter how extensive his or her knowledge might be, could command, or even dream of commanding, the totality of these details. However, that doesn't mean a scholar ought to settle for what our four scholars each have done—produce fragmented, limited accounts or books about Muslim and Arab-Muslim view of the West. But it does mean that totality could be achieved either by different specialists collaborating on different aspects of the Mid-East and Islam, or by individual effort exerted cumulatively over a period of time and in one direction: that of Arab-Muslim history. The latter hasn't been attempted until now.

29

Therefore, it's quite possible, based on Arabic documents in plenty, to develop a rounded picture of Arab-Muslim view of the West. I mean as rounded as objective, so that no chinks, no lacunas, but also no blind spots (in the form of prejudices, biases, fragmentations, or detractions) slip into my work unattended. Hence the need to exercise caution with respect to a number of modern studies contiguous or contemporary with others I plan to deal with. For example, there are studies on the rise of modern Arab-Muslim thought which might contribute to the crystallization of Arab-Muslim view of the West, albeit in an indirect way. Such studies, unknown in the West, are mentioned, though without authors' names, in Saīd's 1992 interview.[80] I intend to verify them, then to use them, among others, only if they happen to redouble or enhance the matter of my work. As well I intend to verify the assumption that modern Arab-Muslim thought is no more than a shadow, a repercussion or reaction to that launched by the West, or, at least, to the positivistic thought through which the West has come to dominate the world. In a word, the assumption, particularly in this context, that Arab-Muslim thought is reactive and not proactive. This is quite a serious assumption,

---

[80] Some of these are mentioned by Saīd. See "What People in the U.S.A. Know..." and his lecture on the intellectual, "Gods That Always Fail," *Representations of the Intellectual* (New York: Vintage Books, 1996).

I think, since it reduces that thought to a mere dwarfling capable only of mining or metalwork.

On the other hand, a further distinction, perhaps equally significant should, I think, be underlined at once. Studies of Arab-Muslim thought by such Arab scholars as Albert Horani, Fahmi Jad'ān, among others, or by such Western scholars as Charles Adams, Gustave Von Grunebaum, and H.A.R. Gibb,[81] among others—all carried out in the latter half of twentieth century—differ markedly in their trajectories from those mentioned by Said. They also differ in their aims from others studies having to do primarily with East-West relations, mine in particular. Kitschy or not, these studies give to the category of mentalities and evolution of rationalism (Eastern and Western) the lion's share; whereas the view of one people by another is scarcely limited to this kind of one common rubric, but rather transcends it to other fields as well.[82] Even so, these studies might still prove to be an invaluable grid of reference for highlighting certain points in my work.

Part Two

30

Now a few words regarding my personal relation to East-West relations are in order. Well, first of all, I deem it one of the formative forces behind the present work; perhaps also one of the cornerstones in my humble attempt to build a bridge between East and West. For that, I take cues from the few Arab-Muslim cultural theorists (discussed in last two chapters) as well as from four other

---

[81] Horani, *Arabic Thought in the Liberal Age 1789-1939* (New York: Oxford University Press, 1962); Fahmai Jad'ān, *Usos al-Taqadum 'ind Mufakīrī al-Islam fi-l 'Ālam al-'Arabi al-Hadīth* (Beirut: Institute of Arabic Studies, 1987). ("Principles of Progress in Islamic Thinkers of the Modern Arab World"); Adams, *Islam and Modernism in Egypt* (New York: Russell and Russell, 1968); Von Grunebaum, *Medieval Islam* (Chicago: University of Chicago Press, 1954); and Gibb, *Mohammadenism* (New York: Osford University Press, 1962).

[82] See Alfred W. Crosby, *The Measure of Reality: Quantification and Western Society, 1250-1600* (Cambridge: Cambridge University Press, 1997). The entire book is based on this concept of mentality: "We should examine that mentalité in the 1500," says Crosby. "It is the effect, and knowing it, we will know better what to look for in the ways of causes." I'm in doubt about Crosby's thesis, for the simple reason that certain historical conditions, which he doesn't go into, are the presuppositions for Western scientific progress. Foucault's lectures of 1975-76 are an invaluable source for understanding this issue.

important writers (whom I mention in a moment). This relation rests on two arches: unhappy, dark, or shadowy experiences (though not in any religious or moral sense) before my emigration to the USA in 1967; and reading four magnificent works in 2003. Allow me to profile these arches with a few solid details.

East-West relations have a long history.[83] They're conflict-ridden relations. So gory, so anguished and anguishing they make you shudder to know how brutal certain humans can be. But then you think: this is downright enslavement to will-power, isn't it? And those of us who are gentle humans (the majority) really suffer. Such is the way of the world. At any rate, my point is simple: these relations fetter and afflict us locally and globally. Globally aside, locally (Syria), I live through it first hand, a decade of afflictions the like of which has rarely been seen on earth. A trivial thing, I recall—say, an English word spoken in public, even the word America, most often mauled by a trumped up charge into "what! the son-of-a-dog here, a spy for the West!"—such a trivial thing could send a person to dark, stinking dungeons where he or she would be heard of no more. I could tell you horrors, topped only by early German torture methods, about what transpires down there. But I spare you the ordeals of such atrocious spectacles.

However, I can evoke a broad-brush portrait of horrors through the effect that a description of them would have on you. Such horrors are and have been endured by thousands upon thousands of innocent men and women. The secret tortures, the slashed flesh, the gush of blood, the mutilated corpses, the incarcerations, the tyrannies, the power games, the psychic damages, the raping of male and female—all endless, horrendous nightmares, in their most singular, abominable, and concrete forms have been perpetrated by successive autocratic governments (one or two annually) against docile, responsible, law-abiding citizens. Saddam Hussein's crimes against his people, now become visible, known, and named, come to mind here. Yet he isn't alone in this, of course. Other autocrats, as in my country, for example, perpetrate copycat atrocities as

---

[83] C. Northcote Parkinson, *East and West* (Toronto: The New American Library, 1963).

well. Of which, to conclude, my family—brothers, relatives, including me—have been unable to break free. Today, unpurged images of pain and rapine still rattle in memory: I still hear the bursts of suffering and cries.

31

Once again, it gives me no joy to make parade of my pain or to stir up melancholy emotions in you. I'd sooner smile the smile of mute melancholy than pour out my suffering into plunging tears. I'd have it no other way, believe me. This is not because pathos interests me no longer; after all, it's a basic human need, and, no doubt, also an infinite fount of language.[84] Yet other needs, other founts, equally basic and boundless, form language's life-spring; they work in tandem with pathos as well.[85] Their name spells the will to live—the will to forgive and to forget, the will, in short, to roll time into a ball of high spirits and free spirits and triumphant gratitude and joy in the world. As for me, I shouldn't know how to live if I weren't, in like manner, a cheerer for that which must inevitably come: a new dawn, a new birth, and—a new democracy. A democracy, let me quickly add, not for power (power of itself would come uncalled for) but to live by freedom's law which can lay down the law. In a word, a democracy of solidarity and will to responsibility.

32

Reading four magnificent works. I still grieve, and would be far inhuman to deny it. Yet I hold on, as it were, to the umbilical cord of time and love of mother country all the same. I forget and forgive. Then I push on, looking up in order to rise higher, to understand more. In doing so, I dare to do more: that is, to look for a new self, long scattered as it's been among all things and accidents of a strange land (U.S.A.). At last, one day, out of courage and uncertainty, of courage in uncertainty, East-West nexus looms before me like a bright, golden horizon. I reach out to grasp it and imbibe its delightful light. I read avidly, still more avidly after 1975, the year I complete my doctorate. And not only read. I

---

[84] The best discussion of this issue may be found in Nietzsche, "On the Genius of the Species," *The Gay Science*, trans. Walter Kaufmann (New York: Vintage Books, 1974), pp. 297-300.

[85] See Michel Foucault, "Language to Infinity," *Aesthetics, Method, and Epistemology*, trans. Robert Hurley, Vol. Two (New York: The New York Press, 1998), pp. 89-10.

receive grants for research. Above all, I write on certain aspects of the subject: papers at conferences, Masters Thesis ("Oriental Elements in J. Joyce's <u>Ulysses</u>"), Dissertation ("Troubadour and Arab Love Lyrics: A Comparative Study"), a book on pre-Islamic poetry (translation and criticism) published in 1993. [86] All attest, you see, to the cumulative efforts exerted on behalf of the subject—which, like tributaries, eventually flow into the present work.

After 1993, I start reading many more good books, though none, I admit, stirs my hands and feet to tackle the theme. A decade later, however, one experience, as if willed from on high, clinches all. In 2003, I encounter Saīd's, *Orientalism* (1979), Hentsch's *Imagining the Middle East* (1992), Arkoun's *Rethinking Islam* (1994), and Mirsepassi's *Intellectual Discourses and Politics of Modernization* (2000). How to describe this priceless, moving encounter? How to phrase it? Let me say I feel spellbound almost instantly, captivated beyond recall, and this without being aware of it. My eyes see things in a plastic way, together with their pure, honest delight in color. I'm in the garden and vineyard of intellectual delight. I read and re-read these books, ruminating over their content like a cow chewing the cud. They deliver me from all nooks, brushing dust, spiders, and twilight off me. They even teach me what to find in them: the chance to find myself—so as not to die.

33

Obviously, I'm not dead, but plan to die at the right time. This is because I find myself in 2003. Not before. You see, we humans, slaves to will-power or not, come into being with a cry, already a sign of suffering. We grow. We go on with the business of life, laboring, suffering, though, unknowingly, disgusted, for diverse reasons, with living, perhaps even ready to give up. What for, asks one half of us? And the other half counters: must we die for suffering? Deny this world, and cease wanting to want any more, cease seeking knowledge any more? Giving in to suffering—doesn't that occult the one sustaining morality that remains untapped, the morality of development? For this morality says living

---

[86] *Translation and Critical Study of Ten Pre-Islamic Odes: Traces in the Sand* (New York: The Edwin Mellen Press, 1993).

also means growth. More, it holds up a mirror to us to say pain and suffering is worth it, after all; the whole world of agony is needed so as to compel us to generate the redemptive vision. Only then do we appreciate suffering Job who rebukes his wife when she says, "curse God and die." "You speak," he answers, "as one of the foolish women would speak." Job, you see, wants to live, to seek to want to know. For ever curious, he's like his Greek counterpart, Odysseus who, in Tennyson's words, wants to "drink life to the lees." The upshot is that Job and Odysseus each construct a self by challenging suffering.

Pep talk, you think? But wait! Don't rush to conclusions! Let me tell you something about our other morality, superego. For I descry him, if you don't, shaking his head in dissent. He really believes we're neither Jobs nor Odysseuses, but merely lonesome, dismal, cheerless, self-less, forlorn beings in need of holiness, incorporeal spirituality; in a word, self. So he, unbeknown to us, swings into action in our most desperate moments, and speaks to us unctuously without a voice: "cheer up! You have a self. Or even better: you know you have a self because I gave you one. Don't go off the lonely, hard way. Loneliness and hardness is guilt." So we gullible ones drink up those words like our very milk and honey. We think sentimentally, "Since we have no recourse to a self, it must come from our dear old Father Morality." Armed with that lofty thought, we go on living, having learned to refer to ourselves, insouciantly if you will, as knowers of ourselves. Thus we introject society's self as our own.

34

Someone else, though, knows better. He knows we humans are no knowers of ourselves. What's more, he suffers, as many of us suffer, and turns that suffering into a beacon to cheerfulness. The kind arising precisely from the knowledge that he can have no self unless he invents one.[87] Nietzsche, a no-nonsense philosopher, bears out this truth. "We "are unknown to ourselves," he says, "we knowers, we ourselves, to ourselves, and there is a good reason for this. We have never looked for ourselves. So how are we supposed to find ourselves?"

[87] See F. Nietzsche, *The Gay Science*, trans. W. Kaufmann (New York: Vintage Books, 1974), pp.32-38.

He finishes by affirming that "we are not knowers when it comes to ourselves."[88] After this, you wonder: have things changed since those words were penned? Not really. The proof? Well, we don't have a self to grasp or know because, despite society's disclaimer and our introjected, ingrained belief, no self has been given to us as identity in space and time.[89]

With Nietzsche's words truth wakens for me: I've got no self to know. My own society, too, it dawns on me, has never given me a self in the first place, let alone one to know or to be responsible for. And that's not from negligence or malice; after all, it has taught me good and evil, all the shalt's and shalt-not's of things that I need to know; it's been solicitous of my welfare and kind to me as well. And yet such teaching and kindness, I hasten to add, is at a high cost: for my society's instruction, like every society's, goes by subtle coercion, overhung and disguised with thoughts and precepts which, if you look closely into them, do no more than a bellows: they puff up and make emptier. I mean the more society puts into me, the more it empties me out. I've come to know that quite well. And thanks to this knowledge and my devotion to truth, I've shooed off my emptiness. I'm about to reached *my* goal, to grasp it with my fingers. So I push on, saying to myself: I'm going to look for myself, I'm going to find myself, to know myself, now more than ever. And if I couldn't do that, I'd have to invent it. And when I have it, I shall never cease monitoring, testing, improving, and transforming it. Otherwise, I die.

35

To gain foothold here, I consume, so to speak, my old self, the suffering one, in my own flame. How else to become new unless I first become ashes? Indeed, how else to overcome myself, the sufferer? Suffering, as Nietzsche teaches, isn't something to give in to; rather, it's a stimulus, a way, in the Confucian sense, to new dawns. By its light I see reason, and reflect on reason in

---

[88] For these thoughts I'm indebted to Nietzsche, *Genealogy of Morals*, ed. Keith Ansell-Pearson, trans. Carole Diethe (Cambridge University Press, 2000), p. 3. See also "Preface for the Second Edition," *Gay Science*, trans. Walter Kaufmann (New York: Vintage Books, 1974), pp. 32-38.

[89] See Foucault, "The Ethics of the Concern of the Self as a practice of Freedom," *Ethics*, Vol. One, pp. 281-301.

reality. So I bring my ashes and fire to bear on my relation to the history of East-West relations. This is my new dawn. I'm reborn. First, I forgive my country its crimes against my family and me. Next I go outside of myself, outside the limits of myself, the better to discount that which my society's foisted upon me, the self that hasn't been the product of my own work. Finally I take command of myself, thus confirming, without knowing it as I learn later, the very core of genome theory, namely—and this is the moment of my double triumph—"the brain is capable of awesome feats of self-organization, and equally impressive feats of experience-driven re-organization."[90] In a word, I become, politically if you like, a cosmopolitan.[91]

By the same token, I accomplish more things, as I further learn how the brain forms a template for more recursion. I try out my own work; I give myself my own valuations and hang my own will over myself as a law. In doing so, I'm able to clear the space proper to it for an encounter with the other (the West). There in this other, now my mirror, I contemplate my soul; it's the eye in which I see myself. And from that reflection I come back to myself and begin once more to direct my eyes toward myself and to reconstitute myself where I am.[92] The four critical-historical books I discover in 2003 dissipate shadows and help me arrive at the truth of myself: they enable me, as I watch every step I take, to perform my self's commands. Commands to monitor, test, improve and transform. In a word, the performative I-and-me-are-always-too-deep-in-conversation becomes my mantra for life.

36

In another sense, these four books are a resounding gift. Not only they invite me to go farther, to develop a thirst to go farther; they also rekindle my instincts, making me choose, instinctually, what's advantageous for me. As if to say, "go on, do something different, something not done before; or, if it were (as

---

[90]See Gary Marcus, *The Birth of the Mind* (New York: Basic Books, 2004), p. 148.

[91] See Derrida, *Ethics, Institutions, and the Right to Philosophy*, pp. 1-17.

[92] See page 5 and notes 10 and 11 above.

if to remind me of or warn me against those four writers I mentioned earlier), it remains cursory, fragmented, prejudiced, superficial, off the cuff." And I chew these words like the good grains they are; my teeth grind them and crush them small till they flow like milk and honey into my soul.

A few months later, I find my theme and title embedded, as it were, in my four heroes' garden: *Arab-Muslim View of the West: A Historical Revaluation.* This thematic is more than just revelatory. True, it reverses their trajectories, yet it extends their works; more than that, it complements them precisely by putting itself, by embedding itself in their context, the better to cover the ground and background of all things Arab-Muslim and the West. From the same garden another thought wafts to me on the wings of the wind. This time it whispers to me some of the uncharted regions to explore. For example, how Arab-Muslims think and feel concerning the West through time; how their worldview, rooted in a peculiar, specific ethos, gives impetus to such feeling and thinking; how, finally, a few Arab-Muslim cultural theorists, from the second half of 20th century on, attempt to open up new avenues of thought, and to study the space in which that thought unfolds, its conditions and mode of constitution. Their aim, you see, is to overcome Arab-Muslim ignorance of both history and the West in the same gesture of overtaking. And conversely, through juxtaposing East and West—the very space that defines the grid of their thought—they demonstrate Western ignorance of Arab-Muslim culture and history.

I'm now doubly ready—ready to explore those uncharted regions and ready to launch my work, my mind ranging far as an additional sense of possibility seems at hand.

37

This is the possibility of bridging the age-old gulf between East and West. Or, to put it in S. Rushdie's words, between the "Muslim polarized world of honor and shame, and the Christian world of sin and redemption."[93] Is this possible today? Better, is it desirable today? If so, how? And wherefore? The

---

[93] See *Fury* (London: Jonathan Cape, 2001), p. 11. Quote slightly modified.

latter question I leave to you to ponder, watch, and sleep on for a while.[94] The former is my concern here.

Briefly, that possibility or desire can be realized if no one tries to ordain, prophesy, or prescribe solutions. I for one certainly don't and won't. For one thing, I'm no politico, theologian, or Hegelian. And therefore, such possibility or desire, thank goodness, comes not under law, theology, or philosophy, nor belongs in history either. It exceeds them all; it's all. For another, I don't think this possibility is possible under the current form of politics understood as war or domination.[95] Though I know it's been so understood for a long time, which explains why East-West stand-off continues to drag out.[96] It must, then, be a different kind of politics: a sort of creative effort or, if you like, an invention integral to the new democracy to come. You see, times have changed, and a new dawn is on to lift the self from gloom to bloom. Formerly, this self's a fruitless fallow; now it quickens to life once more. It takes sides with life, and wants to go far: it wants to invent its own virtues, to gives itself laws as conditions of its own life and growth. What's more, it sees through the inveterate mendacity and manipulation of ideology, fundamentalism, and Orientalist metaphysics. It spurns them all to seek its own truth and corporeal spirituality in its very earthly body.

Given this light after death's shadow, what is to be done? What first step to take? What bridge to invent where West and East look each other in the eye? Well, already some social sciences—psychoanalysis, anthropology, and analysis

---

[94] Apropos of this, I'd like to recommend Terry Eagleton's book, *After Theory* (London: Allen Lane, 2003). It takes you up to the verge of a new human necessity: namely after post-structuralism and postmodernism, how to imagine new forms of belonging and of coexistence.

[95] This is, of course, M. Foucault's contribution to political discourse. Though he's right in so far as Western political systems are concerned, I think politics as he sees it develop and acquire meaning in history may not after all be the way to operate in effecting East-West rapprochement.

[96] See F. Saigh, *Arab Unity* (Beirut, 1958). Saigh believes and I agree with him, that polemics (ideological, religious) denies gaiety in human exchange, while politics (zeitgeist, factious power games) threaten boon solidarity of cultures. Both figures are parasitic on the joy of discussion; both are obstacles to the search for truth; above all, both sap the energy, blunt the genius of Arab-Muslim culture, and militate against its merry unity, even against its integration in the world at large.

of history—are allowing this confrontation to take place.[97] Already, too, a few Arab-Muslim cultural theorists (in a moment I return to them for a brief review) are paving the way for that encounter as well. But there's a fourth that I deem urgent, though it consists of no more than initiatory acts of grace pointing to that bridge: I'm thinking of the two most potent and healing means on earth—forgetfulness and forgiveness.

38

Forgetfulness: Why must I learn to know how to forget? Well, it helps to cut off the Moloch's head of abstractions and essences, which often happens to be the bane of human existence. Permit me to digress briefly.

You see, there's a species of man other than the suffering one. It's the priestly species (autocrats, mullahs, puritans) that posits and has always posited, among other dogmas, a whole imaginary world of psychology, of revelation, of conscience, of moral purposes. In doing so, it squares religion with moralism as if religion needs moralism); what's more, it feels proud, honored, chosen for this association just the same; it even attaches great importance to not being considered at all as individually inspired, but merely as a mouthpiece of some beyond. This hyperbolic fiction only sets aside the concept of natural course of events; it cold-bloodedly conceives a Janus-faced design both to increase its fascistic constructs of domination and make them binding on you and me. You can guess the ultimate but troubling effect here: it mutilates, belittles the sublime moral states as something willed, as work of the individual. In a word, the debasement of the concept "man" is complete; life itself is transformed into a defamation and pollution of life.[98]

39

You may ask: how does this species of man do all that? Well, being Orientalism's handmaid, its notary and votary, it projects its religio-moral and

---

[97] For example, the four magnificent books I referred to earlier. I'd also like to cite Alī Zay'oūr, *al-Tahlīl al-Nafsi lil-Dhāt al-'Arabiyya* (Beirut, 1982). This work is a psychoanalytical study of Arab-Muslim self, its past and present, its evolution and demise—and, let me add, it possible resurrection from the dead. Let me not forget Fatema Mernissi, *Islam and Democracy.*

[98] In today's world, Mid-Eastern religious autocracy and Western religious McCarthyism are two peas in the pod.

psychological constructs into the essence of things. It lays them down to found the true world of grace according to its own image: a narrow, abbreviated, simplified world for the happiness of the greatest number. And calls it democracy to which the majorities of Western and Mid-Eastern publics can be trained to adapt themselves easily. But let's face it: this fascist-minded species of man can do so no longer. Why not? Because the awakened self, the morality of development is catching on; actually, it sees through the falsity and mendacity of this so-called world of democratic happiness. As well because it sees through the priestly nihilism as decline and recession of the strong will, as negation of the individual's good, great, true work. Finally, because it unveils a deadly paradox inherent in that nihilism: just as this fascism perishes without its phantoms, it also perishes by generalizing them. In either case, these phantoms lose the name of truthfulness and authority.

To return to the point, I say forget it. Let this fascist species of man go. Let it keep its phantoms to itself and to others like it, but not make of them duty and obligation in general. Otherwise, it fails fatally, as has happened in the case of Arab-Muslim *Ummah*. Sure enough, by mid-ninth century, having spread its wings by force of religion and war almost to infinity, this community suddenly ceases to exist as a coherent whole. For one thing, it waxes too ambitious, too ecumenical; for another, ostensibly it acts as protector of others, actually it lords it over them, and over their religious discourses. Such ambition, you see, supersedes better judgment and eventually, backfires: the *Ummah* disintegrates beyond recall. One constitutive element after another crumbles: religion, Arabism, ethics, knowledge. Where are these pillars of culture that cost Muhammad so much blood? What swirling vortex has sucked them in? The answer is simple: Arab-Muslims lose their soul and sense of ethos, their original ethics, namely the matrix of Greater Jihad.[99] Which Muhammad himself at one

---

[99] See *Rudolph Peters, Jihad in Classical and Modern Islam (Princeton:* Markus Wiener Publishers, 1996), pp. 1-17. These precious few pages are devoted to *Jihad* of the pen and *Jihad* of the tongue—in short, Greater *Jihad*. The thrust of the book is this: although *Jihad* has come to be equated with "holy war" in the West, most Arab Muslims and Muslims would argue that military action is only a small part of *Jihad* (The Lesser *Jihad*) and that this form of *Jihad* should

point abandons in the interest of politics of conquest. Currently, you see an atavism of this will-power everywhere in the Mid-East

40

To repeat, today's Arab-Muslims must learn to know how to forget in order to restore their glory. After all, forgetting exhorts and keeps away grave thoughts which bloat the heart. This is the first step toward acquiring knowledge. Secondly, they're to see to it that they look into the other's eye. There, they contemplate their soul and recognize themselves as different, needing no fictions, ideology, or metaphysics for their survival. Rather, they need real common sense. For that, they're to look back and, paradoxically speaking, idealize in the direction of past ugliness, perhaps even embrace it, and at the same time be unfaithful to its memories: this is called active forgetting; it allows these bad memories to drop, lose their leaves one by one. Thirdly, as a corollary, Arab-Muslims should learn to breed for themselves more opportunities than ever, to gain strength to posit for themselves, productively, a goal, a reason, a faith. That is, to invent for themselves a healthier, brighter beginning or re-beginning. One so radical, so sovereign it faces up to the production of knowledge and of science. Finally, they must have more than they have in order to become more, above all, in order to displace their ignorance of history both into self-awareness and a new democracy to come.

What I just said about the morality of development, someone else says it much better. In his article "Islam and Democracy: Two Centuries After the Persian Letters" (2003), Mirsepassi stresses, among other things, what deportment Muslims and Arab-Muslims should adopt so as to empower themselves to think differently and with freedom: "Fear of democracy in the Islamic countries," he says," is indeed a product of becoming alien to their own history and culture; and to achieve self-awareness, to re-gain insight into the most important aspects of their repressed history and culture, they have to face the West, walk through it,

---

be undertaken only in self-defense or against injustice. They see the internal struggle to attain self-mastery and lead a virtuous life as far more important (Greater *Jihad*).

get to know it first hand, and then look back."[100] Though Mirsepassi doesn't explicitly mention the word 'forgetfulness,' he, nevertheless, implies it. For it resonates within the folds of his tone-words. Forgetfulness, to sum up, forgets shortcomings and deficiencies, which then clears the ground for Arab-Muslims not only to recapitalize on past glory, but also to attain and retain their spirit, their clarity, sobriety, and coldness of spirit so as to protect themselves from withering.

41

For the West, too, active forgetfulness is no less significant. It performs at least two functions: it gets rid of the monotonous self-justifications and self-criticism which the West constantly lacerates itself with. It also actively displaces the self-conscious "why they hate us" into an attitude of self-correction: namely terrorism isn't a far-fetched reality but as much a piece of it as of the very civilization (a far cry from culture) by which the West imposes itself and will upon the Mid-East. Both circumstances are rooted in the West's ontological failure to communicate with the East, its cultures, institutions, states, habitats—in a word, its ethos; that is, the culture and living will to invent new values so as to replace old ones, on the one hand; and in the incommensurateness between the West's responsibilities and the powers to implement its judgments, on the other. Forgetfulness puts aside or beats down these failures, and gives room for the West to step forward and shore up Arab-Muslims confidence through psycho-social education, not through imposition of democracy.

That said, there's a new book in the market (others like it may be on their way to print as well). This book, *America the Vulnerable: How Our Government is Failing to Protect Us From Terrorism* (2004), unfortunately can go quite far to scuttle the work of forgetfulness, not to speak of negating its cause; more than that, it can bar the way to mutual understanding and cooperation between East and West. In point of fact, it's symptomatic, I think, of that ontological failure I just spoke of, and perhaps constitute a relapse into it. Or even better: not only it endorses, underhandedly, subterraneously Orientalism's phantomship—that which mobilizes and has mobilized Western public for wars in far-off places (for

---

[100] Mirsepassi, p. 4.

unclear goals), and calls it terrorism; it also promotes the West's cruelty against itself and, by the same token, cruelty against others. This is the danger of dangers in that it ministers to hatred of all who think, live and act differently. And does so at a time, precisely, when ethics signifies cosmopolitical exposure to difference; I mean alone of all Western foreign policy problems is one for which the West bears responsibility of acknowledging—difference of the other.[101]

42

Once again, such a book compels me to ask: must we kowtow to its diktats (it has many)? Must we, given its prescriptive morality, be Hegelians or Orientalists through a bogus backdoor romance? To put it another way, must we be anti-realists, fearing politicization of difference which might otherwise lead us to embrace cosmopolitanism, that is, the recognition of the values of difference and their influences in the formation of selfhood? In a word, doesn't one, today more than ever, have to look into another's eye as in a mirror to contemplate one's soul?[102] After all, bloody twentieth century is over, though the American invasion of Iraq at the beginning of the new millennium shakes this certainty a bit. Still, I wager America won't repeat the mistake again. In fact, everyone knows it's a mistake, even if unspoken. At any rate, we live, like it or not, in a new epoch, a time that calls for invention and change. Forgetfulness is an invention of nature, and helps right wrongs or failures by giving them over to new thoughts, to new relationships to self, to the other, and to modernity—as Mirsepassi says. Only then can we invent a new spiritual language to formalize a new kind of power relations. Finally, let me add this on behalf of forgetfulness: how little ethical or spiritual, indeed, would the world appear without forgetfulness! You could say that nature has placed forgetfulness as a doorkeeper on the threshold of the temple of human dignity.[103]

43

---

[101] See Stephen Flynn, *America The Vulnerable: How Our Government is Failing to Protect Us From Terrorism* (New York: Harper Collins, 2004).

[102] See page 5 above and notes 10 and 11.

[103] See Nietzsche on forgetfulness, *On The Genealogy of Morals*, pp. 38-41.

As I set down these thoughts on forgetfulness, thoughts of forgiveness come hot on their heels. And no sooner the latter resonate with me than I hear something uncannily beautiful—a melody on earth which, as I cock my ears, eases to a duet between East and West: "How do we put it Right"? And the question resounds as much in my mind as in the world's. Echoing: "Yes, indeed, how do we put it right?" Then a certain truth of life comes to me like a whiff of fresh air: life isn't a permanent valley of rifts, though humans live on its broken mirror, and fresh cracks appear in its surface every day. There's, then, I conclude, some continuum, some succession of things out there, and I wish to recognize it, if not capture, it. I'm thinking of the first initiative step taken by certain Western institutions and their representatives toward global peace and amity.

You see, the West now slowly awakens to the crude and gruesome acts of oppressions it has perpetrated against the other (Arab-Muslims, for example) since The Middle Ages. But Arab-Muslims, too, particularly Arab-Muslim cultural theorists, reflect on injustices inflicted, in turn, upon the other (the West). More and more the latter show in an unprecedented, daring way, as documentary proof lies before them, just how Islam, like the West, has founded its institutions violently or atrociously in history. That East and West are equally guilty of colonial brutalities: to say nothing of the fact that rights, laws, even peace are in each born in the blood and mud of battles. To sum it up in Derrida's words, "all states, all cultures have their origins in an aggression of the colonial type."[104]

44

Of course, such acts or similar ones of violence, I hasten to add, have been committed by other generations at other times. Which means no institution, no individual or groups of individuals today can in any way be held responsible; besides, those other, past generations have been driven by drives whose underlying cause or conditions, thanks to the wheel of change and becoming, no longer obtain. And yet these same institutions, individuals, or groups of individuals, or their representatives today, though heirs to their ancestors' crimes, are innocent, pure and simple. Even so, and that's the melody I've heard, they've

---

[104] *On Cosmopolitanism and Forgiveness*, p. 57.

come forward today to express their responsibility for those atrocities. In so doing, it seems they've heeded the words of Vico's: the world of nations is made by people, so people can unmake or remake it.[105] Or those of Nietzsche: of all evil I deem you capable; therefore I want the good from you.[106] The second "you," being the first's double, commands atonement from it. This gesture of atonement, which, with Terry Eagleton, I christen self-reflection, attests to the highest nobility human beings can reach.[107]

I believe such a free-spirit nobility to be motivated by the same dialogic question East and West pose to each other, to their societies and to the world: "How do we put it right"? And their responses to it may herald, perhaps even also fulfill the promise inscribed in the book of life, nature, or earth, namely the unity of East and West—one day. Who knows? After all, Kant may have hit the truth on the head when he says, "all human creatures, all finite beings endowed with reason have received, in equal proportion, common possession of the surface of the earth on which, as it is a globe, they cannot be infinitely scattered, and must in the end reconcile themselves to existence side by side."[108]

45

These responses are expressed in the form of apology or forgiveness. So many signs that say, we are sorry. For example, in 2000, Pope John Paul asks forgiveness for sins committed by Roman Catholic Church, including the Crusades and the Inquisition; he also apologizes for inaction during the Holocaust upon his visit to Jerusalem. Earlier, Jacques Chirac of France refers to the crimes against the Jews under Vichy. France that day performed the irreparable, which is precisely, according to Derrida, what forgiveness forgives.[109] Thus the Japanese

---

[105] See page two, note 3 above.

[106] See Thus Spake Zarathustra, Part Three.

[107] See Terry Eagleton, " The Path to Postmodernism," *After Theory,* pp. 59-73.

[108] Quoted by J. Derrida, *On Cosmopolitanism and Forgiveness*, trans. Mark Dooley and Michael Hughes (New York: Routledge, 2001), p. 21.

[109] Ibid.

Prime Minister asks forgiveness of the Koreans for past violence as do the white oppressors of their black victims in South Africa.[110] In 1996, the Southern Baptist Church apologizes to African Americans for slavery. Even President Bush's recent remarks upon his visit to Liberia, though falling short of apology to the Liberians for slavery, carries the day when he says, "Slavery is a crime of history." A quasi-noble gesture all the same. Finally, though I hope it never stops there, Prime Minister of England, Mr. Tony Blair, has been contemplating an apology to the Iraqi people for bogus information in connection with WMD.

Once more, Derrida's short book, *On Cosmopolitanism and Forgiveness,* may be invoked at this juncture. He demonstrates the extent, though still narrow (but hopes it widens), to which the West, at least a segment of it, as we just saw, gradually embraces change in its attitude and in its democratic outlook in general. The significant point he makes is this: he cites the Abrahamic tradition as a grid for reinforcing the change: "As enigmatic as the concept of forgiveness remains, it is the case that the scene, the figure, the language which one tries to adapt to it belong to a religious heritage (let's call it Abrahamic, in order to bring together Judaism, the Christianities, and the Islams. This tradition—complex and differentiated, even conflictual—is at once singular and on the way to universalisation through that which a certain theatre of forgiveness puts in place or brings to light."[111]

That said, Derrida never ever makes, for forgiveness behalf, any appeal to any monotheism, though he respects them all. In point of fact, since forgiveness or apology is slowly becoming more and more global, no such institution is needed anymore. This stance, of course, poses a challenge to us today: Could we, while respecting the tradition, employ reason as a means for abandoning savagery and entering a society of nations? My honest answer is—yes, particularly if we take into account some of the recent findings of the genome theory (section 22 above, first paragraph and note).

---

[110] Ibid.

[111] Ibid.

46

Right at this answer's heels the thought comes to me: isn't it time Western Christianities, since they're heirs to the Abrahamic tradition, owed Arab-Muslims an apology? Time they pitched in as much spiritually as educationally (i.e. opening their institutions to the best Arab-Muslim minds)? Time they asked forgiveness for all atrocities inflicted by the Crusades and colonialists? For such atrocities—traumas, socio-economic regression, brutalities wreaked upon Arab-Muslims in the name of the chimerical notions of emancipation and civilizing programs, among others—still rankle, though Arab-Muslim cultural theorists do in fact strongly desire to transcend them. Certainly, Western Christianities can do all that easily enough as a gesture of good will: one that might, directly or indirectly, help to reinforce the current experience of ridding themselves of long-time tormenting pangs of conscience. If anything, such a gesture would surely go a long way toward affirming, solidly, a common future, a shared higher ideal whose name is friendship. One pregnant with creative promise that defines us all in our global, mature modernity as doing, saying, thinking human beings—human beings in a process of constant (re)invention of ourselves while still guarding, preserving, promoting our politico-cultural differences.

I, for one, believe this historical meeting of minds, this friendship, let me say, this intersubjectivity, to be most urgent. Not only does it hark back to the Abrahamic tradition, as well it lays the ground work, the social and cultural conditions, for a cosmopolitical way of life as Derrida and Mirsepassi envision it. Must I say the world's in dire need of this way of life today?

47

You see, the roots of cosmopolitics reach back to the ancient East, the site where the Abrahamic tradition, now a universal tradition, first sees the light.[112] East and West, then, that is, Islam, Christianity, and Judaism are constituent parts of that tradition in seamless, equal measure. This means that Abraham, the cornerstone of the tradition, is neither Jew, nor Christian, nor Muslim—at least

---

[112] Ibid.

not yet. To that extent the Qur'an is accurate.[113] Before the tradition rolls on, Abraham is a Chaldean and descendant of an idol-worshipping family. But, being sensitive, upright, perceptive of life around him, he spurns idolatry and finds it tasteless, unreasonable for anyone to pray to a piece of wood or stone. Thus a free spirit, he inaugurates a custom and a ceremony in which innocence and beauty are born. This is the worship of one God. Judaism, Christianity, and Islam are, therefore, undifferentiated, originary branches of the same tradition before each puts its own interpretation upon it shortly afterwards. But as soon as this 'afterwards' arrives, every branch rushes headlong and stamps what it likes to think its indelible interpretation upon it. Thus begins the religio-political conflict as we know it in history.[114]

But I'm not here to resolve problems. I'm not a troubleshooter by any stretch of the imagination. The truth of the matter is that all three religions derive from the same tradition—which remains originarily undifferentiated. Well, if that's the case, how, then, does it help us today? Actually it does only if this originary origin is treated as a kind of double *rond-point* mirrors, so to speak. I mean each monotheism, standing between the double mirrors, at once sees itself and sees the other and sees itself seeing the other, so that all at once converge unto the same point again and again no matter which round path each takes.[115] This circular specularity seems to me to constitute the socio-historical condition of possibility of intersubjectivity or, if you will, of cosmopolitanism. Arab-Muslim cultural theorists are acutely aware of this truth. Which explains in part why the question "How do we put it right" becomes especially a poignant one for them; in part why the idea of the mirror, symbol of intersubjective experience par

---

[113] The Koran, 4: 51-55.

[114] See F. E. Peters, *Judaism, Christianity, and Islam : The Classical Texts and their Interpretation* (Princeton: Princeton University Press, 1990).

[115] In order to prove I'm not a troubleshooter, I'd like to offer this contrasting theory: since each monotheistic religion puts its own differing interpretation on the same tradition, then that tradition doesn't exist. And yet we humans (Jews, Christians, Arab-Muslims) insist that it does. Well, obviously we're caught, willy-nilly, in a double bind. But isn't that what life's all about—being in a bind and in difference?

excellence, is the only means by which to deliver their Arab-Muslim societies from the swampy miasma of self-laceration; and, finally, why critiques of East and West are juxtaposed in their texts—a practice which not only takes the latter out of their contexts for a change, but also provides the political strategies toward reconciliation. That's not all.

48

Watch-dogs of their societies' best interest, Arab-Muslim theorists subscribe to universal history as another means to displacing the question "How do we put it right" into a form of apology. One that's neither a boneless generality nor a good-natured idealism that wants merely to affect noble gesture, voice or both. It's rather an apology infused and suffused with the heart-felt embrace of cold, dry reality, but also with whole-hearted passion, temperance, and skepticism. On the other hand, this apology isn't expressed for a sustained harm inflicted by Arab-Muslims upon the West. Rather it concerns a reflection on self and history in a positive way. It thus takes on a symbolic meaning without losing sight of what exists. Actually it expresses a kind of regret for what partially and historically exists, as if to say: how could we, Arab-Muslims, have done this to ourselves? More specifically, how could classical Islam have allowed such imperious forces as Umayyad Dynasty with tribal structure and Abbasid Empire with inability to fashion a State ideology and a polity—how could this crude, ignorant species of humanity become possible at all? Again, Hichem Djait, hits the nail on the head when he says: "Muslims believe they have recovered their Islamic identity; well and good; the question now is, what will come of it? Not, assuredly, a new Abbasid Empire, but some kind of feeling of solidarity, a rediscovery of values, an examination of self and the world, with a lesson for everyone."[116] A year later, William El-Khazen develops this remark into a full-scale study: al-*Hadāra al-'Abbāsiyya*, 1985 ("Abbasid Civilization").[117]

---

[116] See Hichem Djait, *Europe and Islam*, trans. Peter Heinegg (Berkeley: University of California Press, 1985), p. 38.

[117] See El-Khazen (Beirut, 1985).

Djait's performative clearly urges Arab-Muslims, not to rebellion, but to revolution: that of self-discovery—the very essence of *Jihad*. He importunes them to explore Western cultures or, in Mirsepassi words, to get to know them, at the same time to look to themselves, to look to see, as it were, the mote in their own eye for a change. This specular and speculative revolution, Djait implies, may reveal a terrible but healthy truth which they ought to acknowledge in their backyard, now more than ever: namely neither Umayyad nor 'Abbasid empire, has succeeded in molding Arab-Muslim society—politically, militarily, and, more significantly, psycho-socially.

49

In addition, Islam can't do so today either. Not only it's too late; there are no institutional bases for it; at least Islam is yet to developed or put in place such institutions. What Islam can do, though, is a preliminary three-fold operation: to cease its polemics against the West (even against those locals who are pro-West), to affirm itself as politically different, and to seize the opportunity, not to engage in critical one-upmanship, but to gain insight, beyond the Qur'ān, into the other two constituent religions of the Abrahamic tradition. This operation, for Islam, amounts to one thing: precisely the will to change, to turn in on itself, to examine itself, as Djait suggests, in the mirror of universal history in order to learn how to count itself a sharer in the world's patrimony.

Once again, without naming him, Mirsepassi confirms Djait's performative as an instrument for change. Constant face-to-face dialogue, constant emphasis on self-other relations—which ultimately redounds upon Islam's restoring spiritual leadership relative to Christianity's and Judaism's—is such an instrument. Also, without referring to them (Abdullah al-'Urwī or Abid al-Jabirī, as we shall see), Mirsepassi's brilliant idea of knowledge-as-strategy illuminates the nature and quality of their thought. For one thing, like Djait, they spurn all concepts, but advance intelligibility (culture, ethics, art) as their mechanism to account for it. For another, they don't saturate their mind with piety toward everything Islam is, leaving no room for new goals. Rather, they look to reason fused with imagination as guide. For it helps rob sentimental obscurantism off their backs; teaches gratitude for nature's having created them naturally, above all, for imbuing them with a philosophy that's not, like Hegel's, a personal confession but a means to inoculating culture with art, the surer to make its seeds blossom. They're thus the genii of the new Mid-East enlightenment— that which wants to bear the whole of society's wishes along with its flood.

Chapter 1
Arab-Muslim Traditional View of the West
Part One

50

What might the traditional view of the West be? Conversely, what might the modern view be? Some say the one's closed, narrow and resentful, others the other open, enlightened and rational. Still others think the two views seem somewhat inter-tied, in that the first paves the way for the second. I, however, say all of these views at once.

So let's be unprejudiced for a change, and let things, as it were, unfold as they please. The traditional view may be the first flush of joy into which some medieval Arab-Muslims plunge us by breaking away from a seething religious ambience. The aim is to blaze a trail for new goals, horizons, powers, impulses, and above all ideals and phantasms of the modern Arab-Muslim soul; and, beyond that, for an ontological view of the other, of the world and the West, leading in the end to knowledge of self with the broader, pragmatic view, as a side-shoot, to the interests of social and political intercourse.[118] This, as you can see, is a multi-faceted statement calling for a piece of perspective, the better to escape the simplistic opposition "either... or" which has shackled scholarly hands and minds for some time.

The piece of perspective I have in mind is a detour into the history of Arab-Muslim's rise to and fall from power. That way, the statement's facets get grounded and, at the same time, the opposition eitherorism scuttled. Otherwise, everything would stay the same, and prejudice and ignorance, grinning with delight, would keep the field. For this history I shall dip into secondary sources,

---

[118] Intercourse is here understood to include the influences of the outer world and the reactions they compel on the part of medieval Arab-Muslim geographers, historians, travelers, no less than modern cultural theorists.

with the aim of filling out certain gaps left between the words or statements of their texts.

51

To take our bearings, permit me to present a broad-brush view of Arab-Muslim traditional view of the West. Also a miniature of what I plan to do. Since the ninth century, Arab-Muslim historians, geographers, explorers, portray the West in various colors and forms. (Initially the West refers to Western Europe, and later includes USA). This portrait, however, alters somewhat in the wake of the decline of civilization. The West then becomes the butt of almost every Arab-Muslim's anger and frustration. Later still, the portrait, perhaps as a reaction against such resentful interpretation, further mutates into, as it were, a ball of fire in the eyes of its viewers. One more mutation and it serves as a positive tool: Arab-Muslims begin to contemplate their soul in the eye of the West, thereby letting their mind unfold and culture regain its the center of gravity: its values (ethics, spirituality) and goals (solidarity of all Arab-Muslims), which have been presumed lost in the hierarchies of medieval maze of scholastic erudition.[119] This presumption, however, isn't accurate, actually.

To do justice to both texts—portrait and its transformations—I shall do what I do in "Instead of an Introduction." Just as I probe ideas for East-West rapprochement in a high-minded, ethical context, I treat those texts in the historical context in which they logically belong. At the same time, naturally, I raise questions of truth in relation to them. For example, these texts, contrary to certain scholarly prejudice, reveal no intellectually deficient content. Rather they breathe fresh air into a world (in Iraq) totally ruled by Sunni orthodoxy, a world become supreme for five centuries after a short-term ebullition of Arab-Muslim genius in the first half of eighth century.[120] In a word, these texts, and the

---

[119] On the distinction between civilization and culture, see note 117 below, p. 67.

[120] See Vali Nasr, "Iraq's Real Holy War," *New York Times*, March 6, 2004. "It is virtually unthinkable to many Sunnis that one of the most important Arab countries—the seat of the Abbasid Empire from the eighth to thirteenth centuries, which established Sunni supremacy and brutally suppressed Shiites—would pass from Sunni to Shiite domination. In militant Sunni circles, it is taken as proof of American conspiracy against them and against Islam as a whole." signifies different things at different levels, all pertain to what I'm trying to set down in this work.

enlightenment preceding them, suggest, in effect, a way out of the inertia of an entrenched dogmatism. For they introduce something new into Arab-Muslim thought: change and development.

I trust that my plan sets off my revaluation trajectory on its historical course. After all, truth belongs (to) in history, doesn't it? It's also said to be of this world. I agree. But truth is shy, too, and perhaps won't readily unveil its face unless it's coaxed and cajoled. One way of doing so is to use a seductive tool: stylistic brevity. That I do. I treat each stage, event or text in history not too heavy-handedly or too ponderously, but, like a cold bath, quickly in and quickly out. Come to think of it, I use this stylistic economy throughout my work. That way, I suspend judgment, go around and see each individual case, each "thing" from all sides. The upshot, you see, is to kill two birds with one stone: to enlist as much of your sympathy and appreciation as I can, and to ensure you from error and mistakes in your judgment of both Arab-Muslim ethos and character.

52

One more cautionary word: context always presupposes another that defines or sheds light on it. I mean an effect (text, law, event, thought, philosophy, religion, morality, etc.) always follows from another effect before it, and this one, in turn, from still another before it, and so on. History (and the truth embedded in it) is a process of a manifold one-after-another, that is, a series of effects (though it happens that sometimes an effect is mistaken for a cause, and vice versa). Arab-Muslim view of the West falls within that genealogical description. It's a link, or better, a series of effects linked together, not in a cause-effect form, but a manifold one-after-another. For me this is the surest, least arbitrary way to describe how we become what we are precisely and, therefore, to understand ourselves better? I mean as atavisms of past cultures and their powers? Yes, I believe it. With that in mind, let me, then, start from the beginning.[121]

---

[121] I add these cautionary remarks for the benefit of my Arab-Muslim readers to whom this work is ultimately addressed.

The first quarter of the seventh century is a busy time for Arab-Muslims. For one thing, they're hard put to it to defend their lives; for another, they want to organize themselves into the *Ummah*: an ethical or juridical, not a territorial or political entity. This is as it should be, for no fixed territory is yet in hand on which to frame or forge a state. Though more lands are conquered, it never really materializes. In fact, by the end of the eighth century, what semblance of politico-religious structure the *Ummah* has had or to which it aspired comes apart at the seams. In the final analysis, at the beginning of the seventh century, the *Ummah* is the initial spark of Arab-Muslim culture fulminating against the capitalism of Quraysh, the tribe that holds price over value and the material over the spiritual.

In the second quarter of the century, the star of this idealism shines more brightly as it rallies more believers from all sides. Meanwhile the *Ummah* finds itself caught between two fires: its enemies increase numerically, and starvation looms menacingly beneath, behind, and all around the desert dunes. The situation worsens daily, gradually boiling down to a matter of life or death. But, as fate (Arabic *qadar*) would have it, the balance tips in favor of life. And death must die. Thus obeying the desert ethic in what may be described as a pyrrhic effort (in a moment you'll understand why) to stave off death, Arab-Muslims led by Muhammad ambush caravans and carry out raids for food. They engage in battles as all nascent peoples do before them (Greeks, Romans, Franks, and so on). And miraculously they win each time. They conquer, and they conquer more, gobbling up faster than the wind one territory after another. In the end, the experience enhances their sense that something tremendous happens and has happened to them.

This something links up vertically with Allah's guidance and gains value there. How so? It's a paradox, actually. What I mean is this: When, as a result of conquests, the hearty, vigorous community is suddenly suffused with the feeling of power, this circumstance and the concomitant feeling of power raises in it doubt about its own human efforts: it doesn't dare now to think itself the cause of its staggering accomplishment, and so it posits a stronger force, a divinity who doesn't lie, to account for it.[122] It thus belittles itself by separating the two sides of itself—one very paltry and weak, one very strong and astonishing—into two spheres: human and divine. That's why, at this very point, the Qur'ān comes down to shore up self-confidence; it displaces the weak, human sphere into an astonishing, divine sphere. Which explains the sweeping victories: after all, a correctly guided community prospers because it conforms to Allah's laws.[123]

Knowledge and truth and faith, on the one hand, weakness and strength, on the other, all form a chain ensuing upon war; war gives rise to these figures which, in turn, through their centralizing power-effects, lead a people to form a nation. In the case of Arab-Muslims, they help to make the *Ummah* step by step functionally coherent and systematically organized. New precepts, new rules, and new ethics declare that things shall be different. And they are. A new species of Arab-Muslims is born. And this, as a corollary, would involve a critique of everything, of every way of life and thought up to that moment—even if the entire accomplishment is indeed merely up to that moment, that is, temporary.[124] Temporary here suggests that the *Ummah*—because it ceases to believe in its own human strength and will, its moral states, its chain of knowledge, truth, and faith—this *Ummah* soon disappears, though faith and ethics remain. But then faith itself, once conditions of war come to an end, eventually dissolves: it turns from practical goodness grounded in ethics to the quest as much after the

---

[122] For what it's worth, there's an analogue of this in Western culture: the Greek dramatist Euripides and the French philosopher Descartes reach the same conclusion as Muhammad and his *Ummah* do: they all prove the reality of the empirical world by an appeal to the truthfulness of God and his inability to lie.

[123] The term "prosper" implies all kinds of prosperity: to prosper by conquering land, to prosper by conquering oneself, to prosper by struggling for a cause, to prosper by feeding the poor, and so on. All of which frame the Qur'anic message. And what I'm trying to do in these few pages here is to separate one kind of prosperity from another, with emphasis placed primarily on self-conquest and ethics. And the way to do so, at least as I understand it, is to give a quick review of each kind of prosperity.

[124] Arab-Muslims fail to organize themselves into a definite system of power or state. See above, pp. 32-34.

supernatural and marvelous as after selfish religious excitement. In a word, it becomes orthodoxy and orthodoxy becomes fundamentalism.[125]

54

To backtrack a bit, shortly after the *Hijra* (migration) from Mecca to Medina in 622, Arab-Muslims lay down the initial underpinnings of a polity. After which they now long to re-take Mecca, the original hotbed and plinth of Muhammad's divine mission. They do so, and this is most important, peacefully, not militarily. Not a drop of blood is shed. That, of course, is due mainly to Muhammad's conduct. The very site from which Arab-Muslims today can draw food for thought, principles of behavior, and intellectual strength for recapturing their dignity among the nations again.

How does Muhammad do it? Well, you see, he's a man, first of all, not son of Allah. Besides, he may be a prophet, but he has no political function, nor does he aspire to it;[126] better still, he sees and declares himself a *mundhir* (a warner[127]), moral leader of men, no more, hardly more; one who stands for social justice, his mission's central virtue. A downright hero combining ethics and justice, idealism and wisdom which, to say it again, are worth emulating in the Arab-Muslim world, now more than ever. And doing so not by imitating the details of his external life, his expedient raids or conquests, and certainly not by reproducing the way he eats, washes, loves, speaks and prays (that would be superstition or fetishism, pure and simple). But rather by acquiring his interior attitude of kindness to the poor, to the orphans, to women to animals, as much as by adopting his mode of courteous and refined behavior towards all—in short,

---

[125] The way I see it is this: when faith becomes a matter of submitting to the authority of circumstances under which an individual or groups of individuals flourish or gain power, it loses its center of gravity, its ethical basis and plunges into the opposite extreme, as has happened in the case of both Arab-Muslim community and faith.

[126] The first Muslim and Arab-Muslim philosophers, al-Fārābi and Ibn Sīna, for example, disagree with this. They believe a prophet's function is political. See Horani, pp. 17-18. The irony here, however, which Horani doesn't seem to perceive, is that orthodoxy itself rejects this notion of prophecy's function. This is just another instance confirming Djait's point of view with which I myself agree, namely Islam is unpolitical through and through.

[127] *The Koran*, 74: 1-5, 8-10; 88: 21-2.

only by assimilating his practical goodness and ethical practice can Arab-Muslims today recoup the glory that's Muhammad's.

To put it in more specific terms, or at least in terms that might mean more to you, let me say this: Muhammad, a pious leader, has or develops a relationship with himself. That implies the practice of constituting himself as an ethical being. To accomplish this end, he delimits that part of himself that forms the object of his moral practice. And this requires him to act upon himself, to monitor, test, improve, and transform himself. Which he does: he, so to speak, inverts himself. An anal-expulsive raider, looter, and conqueror at first, now, despite threats of hunger, he comes to realize the insidiousness and moral turpitude of such a behavior. By means of this agonistic education, vigilance and struggle, he abandons the Lesser Jihad (will to power as lust for power, transgression, war) for Greater Jihad (will to power over himself); or, what amounts to the same, by following the diktats of his ethical vision, he displaces the one into the other, the desert ethic of raiding and conquering into the ethic of moderation and self-control.[128] This, you see, is what enables him to recover Mecca without shedding a drop of blood. Under his leadership, the *Ummah*'s edifice receives a new, stronger bulwark: Arab-Muslims destroy all idols then Islamize the *Ka'ba* (holy shrine). That accomplished, the divine mission, the *Ummah*, in effect, seems more assured than ever of its complete triumph over the odds.

55

Well, not quite, I'm afraid. For both mission and triumph are already cankered since Muhammad's birth, if not before, as you saw.[129] And now this atavistic necrosis proves them short-lived; I mean tribal division or intertribal warfare of old, returns with a vengeance: Arab-Muslims, as if by necessity, unconditionally, split into warring factions—after all, the pre-Islamic desert ethos is still operative and holds power over them. (Had I time and space, I'd have

---

[128] See Adil Salāhi, *Muhammad: Man and Prophet* (Boston: Element Books Limited, 1998). The entire book deals with these aspects of Muhammad's life and works. See also C. Zurayk, ed. *Tahdhīb al-Akhlāq* (Beirut, 1967). The book is translated into French by Mohammad Arkhoun, *Traite d'Ethique* (Damascus, 1969).

[129] See above, pp. 29-32.

liked to show how, instead of depending on the divine alone, as they still do now, Arab-Muslims could have conjoined the human and divine elements to establish the *Ummah* on firmer bases and so safeguarded it from disintegration. Is it too late now? I wonder.[130]) The effect, needless to say, is disastrous: the bond between the forces of knowledge and truth ruptures, while the *Ummah*'s edifice seems about to cave in.

Soon enough, it does. After Muhammad's death, the disease spreads: most tribes secede from the *Ummah* only to reassert their former tribal independence. Originally, you see, they espouse (if that's the right word) Muhammad's missionary cause not from religious conviction but for personal gain (wealth, land, power, vendetta, if you will). Now that he's dead, the contract's work is up and fighting and in-fighting, known as wars of *riddah* (apostasy), resume as has been the case in pre-Islamic Arabia. And so overnight, as it were, the starlet of Arab-Muslim culture, so brightly burning with blood almost to extinction, begins to recede; everything embodied in Muhammad's ethical inversion—respect of boundaries and limits, of distinction and individuality—gives way to sheer lust for power. Arab-Muslims rally for more conquests, more in-fighting, more strife: Arabs fight against Muslims, and Arab-Muslims against non-Muslims, with no end in sight.

This time it's indeed pretty bloody and merciless. Where one or another faction conquers, it collects taxes, as it must, to allow it to carry out its military functions; sometimes it resorts, as it later does, to mercenaries—non-Muslim Arabs (as in Umayyad dynasty), Persians or Turks (as in Abbāsid dynasty)—to aid it in holding on to or preserve its military might. These two fanatic, tribal dynasties are the final straw that breaks the camel's back: by the end of ninth century classical Islam ceases to exist, and these dynasties, ignoring the original ethic of *tawhīd* (unification), disperse into independent, though unvassalized, fiefdoms, precisely the antipode of what the seventh-century small community of Arab-Muslims once attempts to found, namely the politico-spiritual and religious unity (or *Ummah*). And so Greater Jihad, that art of self-discipline and personal

---

[130] See above note 61.

struggle for the sake of preserving the *Ummah,* buckles to let the ethos of Lesser Jihad (gory strife) rule once again both mind and spirit.[131] By the twelve or thirteen century Arab-Muslim culture comes to a complete halt, and the last glimmer of its light is extinguished.[132]

56

To backtrack once more, let me say this: after Muhammad's death, Arab-Muslims burst full force into Iraq, Syria, Egypt, Persia, achieving more sweeping victories (perhaps in an attempt to neutralize or countervail *riddah* wars. In the aftermath, as time ticks away, a certain character trait resurfaces, which, let me quickly add, already has roots in the Qur'ān,[133] but which now crystallizes into what I'd call, to cut corners, an elitism of sorts. War, you see, at least sometimes, if I may say so, is the great revealer of things concealed, isn't it? Anyhow, this character trait, despite the passing away of onetime glory, is prevalent today and sustained, as it has been formerly, by some divine element, guidance or control. Whether or not it crops up consciously in time is still a mystery; or, if not a mystery, at least an atavism, a force of nature or, if you like, an unconditional obedience which could easily, that is to say, consciously and rationally, be rooted out for ever simply by confronting, identifying, analyzing it as such. I'm inclined to think, though, that at the time of their wide-ranging conquest Arab-Muslims aren't as yet aware of it. They will be, particularly during the intellectual brilliance coruscating in the first half of the ninth century and a bit beyond.

The character trait in question, or at least one aspect of it, concerns the other: in all their conquests, acquired by victory, Arab-Muslims barely get to know or assimilate into the conquered peoples; they don't even confess to an interest in knowing their manners of life, their cultures, styles of living, or modes

---

[131] For an in-depth view of Greater Jihad and Lesser Jihad, see Rudolf Peters, *Jihad in Classical and Modern Islam.*

[132] However, as a metaphysical concept, *Ummah* still hold, though, politically speaking, it has never been a unity or a community in the sense of nation. Muhammad has had no such political conception in mind in the first place, simply because he never sees himself as a prophet wielding power.

[133] See above page 48.

of doing things, and so on. Sometimes they actually make heavy weather of a respect for the other—for example, Christian dogma, Judaic teaching, as the Qur'ān makes abundantly clear. And yet, such character trait, an elitism of sorts as I just called it, underlines a certain behavior quite distinct from that of other conquering peoples (some of whom I mentioned earlier). A behavior, paradoxically speaking, which, underneath it all, may be too conscious of itself to be aggressive

True, like the Franks, for example, who conquer Gaul in the fourth century, Arab-Muslims simply, unequivocally dominate, like a force of fate. But, unlike the Franks—and this is quite interesting—they don't, being wielders of power, behave dualistically; they don't separate ability to help from ability to harm. They possess both. For that reason, which, paradoxically, marks off another ethical aspect of the trait in question, they choose not to harm or inflict atrocious brutality of any kind.[134] Besides, and this is equally important, their domination is never a relationship of force as that between enemies either.[135] Again compared to the Franks, they're no barbarians and never put on blinders or impose a burden on the conquered peoples. If they sideline certain individuals and groups of individuals, if they keep themselves at due distance, this is prompted by an elitist or a group feeling (religious 'asabiyya') rooted in fear of losing their control of things, which ultimately derives from divine authority. This is a moral-ethical imperative that's quite understandable, of course. But they never install a policy of humiliation by forcing these groups to act or behave in any way against their will. And this, incidentally, isn't just in connection with Christians and Jews.

By the century's end and in the next 150 years, to finish the narrative line, Arab-Muslims calm down a bit. During the lull, two groups, already long time

---

[134] The killing of several hundred Jews in 625 is an anomaly and can only be understood by not applying the standards of modern times. It is a form of what may be described as primitive freedom, the kind that says: this is the law of the desert and I exercise this right only for purposes of domination and self-defense.

[135] For further information on brutality of the Franks, see Foucault, "Society Must be Defended," pp. 141-165.

foes or rivals, emerge formidably on the scene, the Sunnite Muslims and the Shiite Muslims. The former outsmart the latter, their will gradually constitutes itself the new leadership in Arab-Muslim world. A very long story. In any event, to clinch the operation, and acting under the impress of all-round religious fervor, they gather up the major traditions and script them. They compile 114 long-to-short revelations (*Surahs*) into a Holy Book, The Qur'ān. This Book becomes, along with *Hadīth*, the matrix of the orthodox tradition (*Sunnah*) which tends to depend on it for continued power, for survival, and for salvation of Arab-Muslim soul, whether Shī'i or Sunnī. They then consolidate the various traditions of Muhammad that are additional doctrinal pronouncements and moral precepts attributed to him, including a vast complex of religious, moral, and social law deriving from the Qur'ān and the semi-canonical traditions. All these traditions come together and function as regulatory principles in the affairs of everyday life.[136]

57

In the early part of eighth century this body of traditions is launched into history. Great expectations hinge on it, of which the most important would be the Arab-Muslim world resonating with joy at the prospect of renewing its community solidarity. But rivalry gains the upper hand and squelches every slight effort toward that noble goal. It's as if a certain active force, like a rolling machine (earlier I called it atavism), dispenses of events one way or another with no conscious subject behind the act or event.[137] In effect, the *Ummah,* once again,

---

[136] For further information on this second half of the century and the period of 150 years in question , see Omar Farroukh, *Tārikh Sadr al-Islam wa-l Dawla al-Amawiyya* (Beirut, 1983), especially pp. 35-124; 196-222. ("History of the Rise of Islam and the Umayyad State"); also Ali Ibrahim Hasan, *al-Tārikh al-Islami al-'Ām* (Cairo, 1986), pp. 169-475. ("General History of Islam"); finally, Karen Armstrong, *Islam: A Short History* (London, Phoenix Press, 2000). In my account here, I'm trying to fill in what I consider important gaps left open by these and other historians—for example, elitism, binary structure of the world, Sunnite blunders, among others.

[137] This echoes what J. Derrida calls "Différance." It follows the lines neither of philosophical-logical discourse nor those of empirical-logical discourse. Rather it's "the concept of play [that] keeps itself beyond this opposition, announcing…the unity of chance and necessity in calculations without end." See *Margins of Philosophy*, trans. Alan Bass (Chicago: University of Chicago Press, 1982), p.7. Arab-Muslims can endlessly reap to their heart's content the humbling fruits of this historical development of things and events, of thought and religion. It's indeed the one and only tool of understanding.

runs head-on into another paradox as devastating as the divine-human divide surrounding its conquests half a century before. What actually happens is this: no sooner these traditions are launched into history than they edge it out altogether. At first history, stunned, as it were, by this abrupt turn of events, gives way, perhaps in all deference to them. Soon, however, it gets displaced, stripped out of commission; in the end it evaporates from top and toe when Sunni Arab-Muslims, in a metaphysically rash judgment, declare it to be neither useful nor exemplary. That precipitate behavior, however (and I'm schematizing here), is an excusable, if unforeseen, perhaps because unconscious, Sunnite blunder. Nevertheless, it would be the same blunder repeated time after time in a network of thought stretched over most of the Arab-Muslim world. And this multifarious repetition of blunder remains unrecognized by the greater majority of Arab-Muslim public even today. [138]

Why unrecognized? Well, Islam, its red-hot fervor in the heart, and emulous traditions in the mind, comes in time to assume the potency of a tranquilizer that saps the public's strength to struggle, to dare, to seek the high seas. (This struggling and seeking has to await the development of *Ijtihād*, personal initiative, as we shall see in a moment.) It's as if fear of a life that has lost one charm takes hold of all Arab-Muslims, tying off the veins of conscious understanding and creative thought from other means of growth and enhancement of life. I think the point I'm trying to make is this: when religion, along with the morality it gives rise to, no longer finds anchor in history, or, what amounts to the same, when religion becomes systematized as a finished sum of historical events under the severe, intellectual gaze of orthodox dogmatism, it then dwindles to a mere perspective illusion, a kind of apparent unity that encloses everything like a horizon. In other words, when religion's votaries no longer share its ethical presuppositions, it ceases contact with the text of reality—and dies.

---

[138] See Ibn Khaldūn, *The Muqaddimah*, trans. Franz Rosenthal, ed. N.J. Dawood (Princeton: Princeton University Press, 1969). If Arab-Muslims would only take trouble to study carefully this philosopher-historian, they would then recognize what they're capable of achieving precisely by unlearning radicalism in thought and behavior and relearning advocacy of religious pluralism, a.k.a the validity of all true religions, since they're symbolic representations of the same truth. In this respect, see also Youssef M. Choueiri, *Islamic Fundamentalism* (London, 1990).

Islam dies toward the end of eighth century, though something of it remains. What is it? Perhaps a metaphor may help visualize my answer. The major traditions (*Sunah, Hadith,* Qur'ān), now that history's out of sight and mind, take over and function as a kind of ideal servant. It prepares all things Muslim, brings them, lays them out, and then withdraws. All that's left for the pious believers to do is to enjoy this beautiful object that comes from eternity (Allah, His Laws, His paradise); since the beginning of time, it has been made for Arab-Muslims. What's more, peoples of the entire earth, whoever and wherever they may be, should enjoy it in tranquility as well. After all, Arab-Muslims' Islam deems itself, intrinsically, I might say, the originary ecumenism emanating from heaven itself and uniting all monotheisms into a single religion—Islam itself. Not only it's "the only true faith in God's sight"; it's eternally embodied in the one and only Holy Book: Qur'ān: "a transcript of the eternal Book in Our [God's] keeping, sublime, and full of wisdom."[139]

58

(Here I open parenthesis. For five centuries orthodoxy converts a means to life into a standard of life. Well, that's its prerogative. But the conversion sets little by practical wisdom. Instead of discovering the standard in life's enhancement itself (i.e. in the problem of birth, growth and death, which is philosophy's sole reason for being), orthodoxy rejects philosophy and employs religion as sole means to a distinct kind of life, excluding all other forms of life— namely to criticize and select life. Consequently Arab-Muslims, heirs to this lack of foresight, espouse wholeheartedly the means for its own sake and forget that it's a means, so that it enters their consciousness as an aim, or as a standard for an aim. In other words, they treat a condition of existence, the one their orthodox ancestors imagine for themselves and for those like them, as the condition which ought to be imposed as law, truth, or faith—in a word, as perfection—on everyone. It is the kind of perfection whose historical conditionality, even

---

[139] *The Koran*, suras 43: 1-3; 56: 74-75. It's easy to understand why Islam dies: when a later monotheistic religion claims to possess the only key that unlocks the world of the spirit, thus riding roughshod over other monotheistic systems of faith, it logically, if not naturally, asks for trouble. And it gets it right in its own backyard.

relativity to other groups (Jews and Christians, but also pre-Islamic peoples in general), they fail to perceive.

It's possible for Arab-Muslims today to think and do exactly the opposite. First, to learn to become what they are—inclusive, as they've always been. To learn, in addition, to emulate Muhammad's ethical conduct, and to exploit this ethic in order to cut through the tight swathes of their historical ignorance. Finally, to do what Djait and Mirsepassi suggest: study all historical events diligently—for example, how the faith morphs from one stage of history into another—and, in doing so, apply rationalist principles in conjunctions with eternal truths. After all, they've got all the brilliant philosophers, historians, and exegetes of the Qur'ān in their backyard.

Take the Qur'ān, for instance. Since it professes earthly egalitarianism, it also affirms as much the horror of existence as delight in it. And it does so through revelation, Muhammad's greatest feat. But since Islam is also a way of life, revelation is insufficient for the historical-spiritual edification of the *Ummah*. That's why Muhammad enjoins the *Ummah* to struggle for self-cultivation. He wants it to probe behind the words of the Qur'ān, behind revelation into that other reality, the mythical precondition of the Qur'ān, which isn't objectified adequately in the words, and without which there would be no faith. This is the *Ummah's* only choice if it's to resume its glorious place in history.[140] Put otherwise, the Qur'ān's teaching isn't content with the words' literal meaning; its deeper philosophy shows that struggle to learn is as much a part of life as delight is. The sole means to grasp this fact is for Arab-Muslims to insert themselves in the web of historical knowledge, so that they can become a force once more, and, by the same token, establish themselves as the subject of their history. After all, an individual, a group of individuals, or a nation consists of the whole course of

---

[140] See Boulares, pp. 112-119. The struggle for self-cultivation, for learning in general as enjoined by Islam is no where more clearly presented. I agree with Boulares that there's no other way but self-cultivation through which Arab-Muslims can become a member of the world's community. But isn't it what Mirsepassi has abundantly made clear as well? If I'm right, Mirsepassi's central concern in East-West scholarship is to find ways and means to help Muslim and Arab-Muslim spirit to return to itself, to reunite with its own being after the Muslim spirit, which has been living hopelessly but which has also been tyrannized for too long by a vast invading force—ignorance.

evolution and not, as religion would have it, only of something that begins in the seventh century or at birth. I close parenthesis.) [141]

To resume my narrative, let me say this: a tradition may at first appear minor, but it may also carry weight quickly, even acquire as quickly a certain magnitude. And Arab-Muslims, being at the time and for the most part least attuned to the aleatory nature of evolution of human thought, may be quite baffled by it. But history, you see, has its own quantum of force, giving rise to events most often impossible to trace to a specific source, consciousness, or subject. Or, if there's such a source or subject, it lies within the folds of distant time, perhaps within the old atomistic system of tribalism. It's hard to know. But one thing is sure: it resurfaces now and then under different guises: this time in the form of a division among different schools of theology. Be that as it may, this minor tradition's unprecedentedly inventive, daring, and comes to piggyback other traditions, causing their votaries (the 'Ulamā') no small trouble, mostly big fear that they will be destroyed by it. [142]

I have in mind the tradition relating to the binary structure of the world. It's attributed to the great Arab-Muslim theologian and first-rate intellect Abu Hanīfa Nu'mān Bin Thabit (699-767 A.D.) of Kūfah, Iraq. Though he himself writes nothing, his teachings, quite innovative for the time, are recorded by his admiring pupils. [143] I'm here reminded of what M. Foucault's description of the

---

[141] In presenting my brief analysis and suggestion, I'm addressing only an internal problem which has nothing to do directly with East-West relations or rapprochement as I profile it in this work. Ultimately, however, when that problem is resolved (and I hope it will be soon), the result should smooth the way for a better, more successful encounter between East and West.

[142] Allow me to repeat briefly: everything I've narrated so far—victories and defeats, short-lived glory, character trait, ethos, ethics, and a good deal more—everything said so far constitutes the wider historical and cultural context in which Arab-Muslim view of the West, in both its traditional and modern aspects, must be seen. Indeed, without such context, no intelligent appreciation, no comprehension of that view is possible. I insist on this truth. I go further: I put it forward as a challenge to any scholar, working on a similar theme who thinks otherwise. Finally, the innovative tradition I'm speaking of might very well be the chance or necessity or opportunity underlying or perhaps prompting the work of medieval historians and geographers, which consolidates the initial steps towards that view and the later modern view as well. See above, page 60.

[143] See El-Khazen, pp. 143-158.

hypomnemata of classical Greek education: account books, individual notebooks, public registers serving as memoranda. Among other uses, such as guides for conduct and meditation, the *hypomnemata* also constitute raw material for the writing of more systematic treatises containing arguments and practical models which an individual can use as tools to struggle against some defect or to overcome some difficult circumstance.[144] This is precisely the case with Abu Hanīfa's recorded teachings whose overarching method of argumentation can be called deductive reasoning. The upshot of which is that you can overcome a defect or a difficulty, or conclude a judgment by reasoning from the facts of a determinate source, namely the Qur'ān and *Sunnah* (the exemplary behavior of Muhammad, consisting of statements, deeds and judgments). I shall return to this in a moment.

According to his pupils, who apply the method for tackling legal and social issues, Abu Hanīfa introduces the concept of the binary structure of the world in his new discipline of jurisprudence (*fiqh*), which has an immense impact on Arab-Muslim piety, and which becomes the main discipline of higher education, a.k.a. theology, in the Arab-Muslim world even today. In this *fiqh,* he differentiates Muslims from non-Muslims in the form of two diametrically opposed categories: *Dar al-Islam* (Abode of Islam) and *Dar al-Harb* (Abode of War). Further, he refers to any non-Muslim domain, which would include Arabs, as *Dar al-Kufr* (Abode of Unbelief) or *Dar al-Harb* even if there's no current or on-going war between them and the Muslims. In addition, a country or territory becomes *Dar al-Islam* if Muslims are able to enjoy peace and security, on the one hand,[145] and if the territory has common frontiers with some Muslim countries (other *Dar al-Islam*), on the other.

60

---

[144] Foucault, "On the Genealogy of Ethics: An Overview of Work in Progress," *Foucault Reader*, pp. 363-369.

[145] As happens in 1055 when Arab-Muslims, having lost to Seljuk Turks, live with the latter in *Dar Al-Islam.*

Let's pause here for a moment. Abu Hanīfa equates *Dar al-Harb* with *Dar al-Kufr*. The latter, if I'm right, would, first, refer to the non-Muslim wealthy and worldly Meccan unbelievers who spurn Muhammad's spiritual mission out of hand. And secondly, to non-believers in general, Arabs or not— for example, Christians, Jews, among others, who, though people of the book, not only oppose him, like the Meccans, but also doubt the authenticity of the mission.[146] Thirdly, the concept extends to non-Muslim groups of Asia and Africa, who are technically considered part of *Dar al-Harb* as well. Even so, in no way does the concept designate or, just the same, instigate wars of aggression against these peoples. For one thing, Arab-Muslims, despite arrogant feelings having to do with conquest and divine aid, have always coexisted amicably with non-Muslims, those surrounding or those subdued by them. For another, the Qur'ān, though born of war, doesn't sanction warfare at all. Certainly it endorses the notion of just war when necessary, but only as a tactic in self-defense or as a means of protecting decent values. On the whole, however, it vociferously condemns killing and aggression.[147] Finally, Arab-Muslims have reached the limits of their expansion by the end of eighth century.

These details should further help explain from another perspective what I earlier described as evaporation of history at the hands of Arab-Muslim (or Sunni) orthodoxy. If anything, they prove these Arab-Muslims to be low on political instincts to the point of indifference, actually, precisely because of their overarching religious fervors and fears of extinction. I seize this opportunity to underscore the following important point: this is the aspect of Arab-Muslim history that the West really, seriously ought to take account of, now more than ever.[148] And to do so for no other reason than to re-interpret its views of and,

---

[146] See Adil Salāhi, Muhammad: *Man and Prophet* (Boston: Element Books, 1989), pp.274-298; see also F. E. Peter, *Judaism, Christianity, and Islam: The Classical texts and their Interpretation* (Princeton: Princeton University Press, 1990).

[147] The Koran, 2:194, 252; 5: 65; 22: 40-42.

[148] I think it would be most helpful if the West in general ceases to concern itself with questions of margins and minorities in the Mid-East, also with sects and factions, fundamentalists and terrorists, and so on. Rather a more urgent in-depth analyses are called for—for example, analyses of the kind that show a certain educational policy or religious architecture or cultural degeneration,

thereby, mend its relations with the Mid-East. The mending might take the form of a run-up to discussion, not imposition, of democracy.

61

You see, Arab-Muslim culture, made from a definite perspective with the sole purpose of preserving the *Ummah,* is, to say it again, a profoundly religious culture. What's more, it produces the Qur'ān's entrancing cadences and articulates them upon God's unity as the ultimate authority that speaks them as if from on low. And the whole is framed in a schema of moral values and duties constituting the very condition of its existence. It's, therefore, a religio-moral culture or, if you like, a religion of life integrated into its every aspect, though a culture absolutely withdrawn, unpolitical, egalitarian, uninterested in formal philosophy, pragmatism, or philosophical theology.[149] For these reasons it resonates with Arabs—tribal or Muslim. For example, not only it presents its view as necessary for all; it also generates in them the feeling that their reward for espousing its cause shall be self-preservation and prosperity in the face of all adversity. In fact, it raises their soul's temperature, so that they come to believe the most wretched, aleatory life can become rich and inestimable through a rise in temperature. That's why, like the artist-people they are, they experience religion as something sacramental, as revelation and dream-figure of real divine presence in their daily life.[150]

Not at all as something, and this is my point, giving rise to socio-political institutions. Arab-Muslims' all-divine, hence real mind, you see, bars any study

---

and so on, that neither the West nor the East are quite enlightened about or conversant in. When they are, it would be, needless to say, of untold mutual benefit to future generations.

[149] You realize that I don't include ethics here. Well, this is because I distinguish between morality and ethics. The latter constitutes the real behavior of individuals in relation to whatever rules and values that are advocated to them by morality; they may obey or resist these rules and values depending on the object of their ethical behavior.   Self-control (anger, aggression, incivility, etc.) is such behavior, as exemplified by Muhammad when he turns aggression into peace through he wins back Mecca. For those reasons I can safely say that this culture is quite different from the new critical culture that would develop in the second half of twentieth century.

[150] For further information on this important aspect of Islam, see Wilfred Madelung, *The Succession to Muhammad: A Study of the Early Caliphate* (Cambridge: Cambridge University Press, 1997).

of how conquests can provide principles for instituting political power, sovereignty, or even a schema for interpreting political power in terms of war, struggle, and confrontation.[151] Muhammad or the Qur'ān isn't of much help here either. Unlike Jesus or St. Paul, Muhammad isn't raised in a world imbued with Hellenic-Roman science and political philosophy; even if he is, he wouldn't or couldn't, given his small modicum of biblical knowledge, resist it just on ethico-religious grounds.[152] Similarly, the Qur'ān invites no political investigations of any kind, while its ethics is too personal for that; besides, it hardly contains anything like politics or rules of right.

What of the dream of world domination, you ask? Doesn't that sufficiently stimulate political thought? Well, that dream of fantasy turns into another or a different kind of dream. After Muhammad's death, Arab-Muslims, forlorn, turn in on themselves, with the sole goal of solidifying the *Ummah* against all-out threats. In time, this goal rubs off, though eventually it rubs the wrong way: they become like artists: they look away from horrors of existence, something strikes as being not as real as the religious dream-figures of their imagination. A few decades later, they come believe that a thing's value resides in only one secure kind of reality—Sunna or tradition. These developments are a far cry from what the Qur'ān, as you saw, teaches. Hence reflection on politics or on political institutions gets nipped in the bud; philosophers get ostracized from the community (Ibn Rushd, for example), even theologians, those who deviate, albeit slightly, from the traditional norm, get imprisoned (Abu Hanīfa, for example). All in all, it seems that orthodoxy, on the one hand, philosophy and philosophical theology and politics, on the other, remain unreconciled; at least so far no effort has been exerted to reconcile them. Could this be the educational role of the West?

62

---

[151] See earlier reference to Hichem Djait, p. 40.

[152] Christianity, so steeped and profoundly influenced by Jesus's idea of separating God's ways from Caesar's, applies the ethics of resistance against ideological domination.

By the same token, the concept of *Dar al-Kufr* can't but be religiously motivated. It refers neither to war against Westerners (Arab-Muslims are already in Christian Spain, whom Abu Hanīfa never mentions) nor to war against anyone else. It would be a bad mistake, then, to separate *Dar-al-Harb* and *Dar al-Kufr*, construing the former, as does B. Lewis, a blanket concept subsuming the entire Christian world. The case is otherwise. First, Abu Hanifa hardly possesses such a far-reaching conceptual armature. His intellectual, or rather, philosophico-theological purview, though significantly creative, remains attached to the inherited traditions. Secondly, his binary opposition is an experimental morality of sorts put forward before Arab-Muslims learn anything about the West and the world, even though they've reached certain regions of Byzantium and Spain. To that extent, the two concepts *Dar al-Harb* and *Dar al-Kufr* merge into one, thus installing an imaginative moral boundary between Arab-Muslims, on the one hand, non-Muslims and Arab unbelievers, on the other. The same moral boundary applies to non-Arab-Muslims residing within *Dar al-Islam*.

That brings up their peculiar attitude toward neighbors. Arab-Muslims are barely gregarious. The reason is simple: their ethos, confined to the concept-dwelling *Dar al-Islam,* pulls them apart, now more than ever; fear of being swept aside even more so. Both attitudes are due less to feelings of enmity than to esteeming themselves of higher moral value. If you consider their bluffly commonsensical style, they hardly get to know the peoples they've fought or conquered, not to speak of getting familiar with as much as the latter's proper or countries' names. Jews and Christians are peoples of the Book; Franks "Franj"; Europe "Urûfa;" Byzantines "Rūm," and so on. This isn't because they're dumb or autistic; they're just not interested in establishing socio-political relations. In fact, after Islam's come to an end (i.e. as a power), they feel no compulsion to sweep across the plains of western Christendom. Besides, Europe, as we shall see, though offering a few opportunities for commercial relations and profit, seems quite unattractive, and the climate is most terrible.

You can see why the concepts *Dar al-Harb, Dar al-Islam,* and *Dar al-Kufr* feature nowhere in the Qur'an and *Sunna.* The latter, the core of Islam, have, as you saw, pressing issues at stake: *Ummah*-building, solidarity, piety, duty, social justice—which purport to structure Islam as a polity. And they do, though the polity, unhappily, comes apart in the eighth century. Nevertheless, the issues remain very much alive, but in dire need of reinforcement, or better, of re-interpretation if they're to remain Islam's ethical legacy. Are those concepts, then, a way towards that re-interpretation? If so, how do they originate? What, if anything, do they signify about Islam as a faith? Three questions in one.

Truth to tell, they signify Islam's capacity to develop or adapt to new life exigencies from within. That means one thing: the concepts themselves are a consequence of this capability. To put it in terms other than those expressed a moment ago, they're neither war-based nor emanate from a state-power or caliphal sovereignty which exist no longer. Rather, they take off from a different kind of war, one without weapons, without warlike poses, without pathos and strained limbs. This war's *Ijtihad,* private initiative or intellectual contest, carried out within the walls of *Dar al-Islam.* The term, therefore, designates religio-moral endeavor to exercise personal judgment based on the principles of Qur'an and the *Sunna* only. Even so, *Ijtihad's* a daring feat, an audacious performative of independent reasoning geared to steering Arab-Muslim legislation into new directions. In a word, an agonism whose practice mirrors a regulative idea of the time: not only does it give rise to theological innovation; it also paves the way for a development not possible before: philosophical speculation.[153]

64

Obviously I'm schematizing for reasons of space. Still, an important point must be made clear: *Ijtihad,* no doubt is a great event or, if you like, a turning point in eighth-century Arab-Muslims' intellectual life; it raises them, though without being aware of it, above being just morally horizontal. It complicates their lives in all aspects, giving them depth, breadth, height; what's more, it adds a

---

[153] See Mernissi, pp. 22-41; see also F. E. Peters, *Aristotle and the Arabs* (New York: New York University Press, 1968). The period is brimful with intellectual activities which actually require a separate study.

pragmatic dimension to their thought, allowing them to apply in a significant way the principles of the Qur'ān anew to the problems of the time. In short, it makes them potentially more interesting, more adaptable to contingencies. For the first time, thought acquires a modicum of freedom.

But, and this is the other face of it, this great event, by creating the binary division, brings it about that Arab-Muslims insulate and isolate themselves from others, which adversely affecting their view of the latter. And yet, I repeat, in no way does *Ijtihad* originate in a vision of some political Mid-East order or organization by any stretch of the imagination. This fact ought to be frequently repeated in order to assess matters accurately. Otherwise, a notion or rumor like "Islam versus infidels" can nowadays be dangerously misleading. What's merely a conceptual residue of the binary division motivated by the psychological need for self-preservation is understood and misunderstood as an adversarial political formalization. Yet the West still sees it as such, that is, either as signifying war or hatred, which means it doesn't grasp the concept or the great event for that matter at all. In either case, the West not only is a victim of the either-orism opposition (as is usual with it), but also forgets what makes Arab-Muslim thought complex yet simple.

65

What makes it so is, again, this apolitical, theological performative called *Ijtihad*. Though it itself is no more than a simple effect of the evolution of human thought. Even so, Arab-Muslim public, like Western public, fails to grasp its import or give it the attention it deserves. What Islam and the West in general ought seriously to begin to do is this: they must study how thought evolves—for example, to grasp that something not specifically human, call it nous if you will, some cosmic mind or soul, can be as much productive as causative of differences and at the same time produces mutations in human thought, taste, and behavior. You see, it's not a matter of a subject or consciousness or God that brings about division or difference, though God does divide the waters from the waters. But no one knows who or what God is. At any rate, there's always something external to human agency gestating in the womb of time or history. I wish that Arab-

Muslims and Westerners would give this truth ample mind instead of resting contentedly attuned to the dogma of the moment, or to the politics of the moment.

If they do, they'd find something quite interesting: apart from human intervention, a thought, a word cuts open a space in the human intellect itself, in which two parallel discourses come into being, as if everything in the past leads to them: critico-religio-moral discourse, the one I've been outlining here, and critico-philosophical discourse which, again for reasons of space, I can't pursue further. Suffice it that the former branches out into several discourse or at least four different theological schools, and the latter into several philosophical ones: Mu'tazilism, Qadirism, Sufism, and so on, which other scholars have studied most thoroughly.

You see, things really get more and more interesting. These discourses reach full fruition in tandem, so to speak, in the ninth and tenth centuries. Today, at least the two main ones, theology and philosophy, exist side by side, even in a state of on-going struggle or perhaps because of it. Isn't that what keeps Arab-Muslim thought alive and kicking today, especially in the domain of East-West relations? In the final analysis, *Ijtihad* and the concept of binary division of the world it gives rise to—as Abu Hanīfa determines it, though without predicting or anticipating its adventitious effects—ushers in what may be called the climate of Arab-Muslim "democratic" thought. The word deserves quotation marks, first, because it's a borrowed word and inadequate as a description of that intellectual event (except for *shura*, Arabic has no equivalent word, naturally); secondly, it's no more, hardly more than an innovation in some sort. Even so, a very significant innovation, I dare say.

66

This is because it's an agent of freedom of thought. You see, for a time, *Ijtihad,* given its intellectual integrity, dissociates itself from religion so as to do its own thing, so to speak, in the face of opposition. That is, to argue for its behalf, as it were, or to allow Abu Hanīfa to destine it for freedom to make new laws or clear the way for new ideals when these couldn't be *Hadīth-* or a Qur'ān-based, though without undermining the latter. In other words, Abu Hanifa, perhaps unwittingly, yet prompted, as you can imagine, by the joy of this intellectual fellowship, puts forward a form of "syllogism" as a tool for supplying or inserting thought missing in a traditional text. Obviously the move is a daring performative not too many Arab-Muslims are prepared to accept. Which gives Abu Hanīfa the sense that if *Ijtihad* abandons the faith altogether, going far afield on its own, the community's solidarity would be at risk. Fear and anxiety mount. To stem the tide, Abu Hanīfa, in his innovative foresight, invents a double leveling-off agent or, if you will, a counter-agent, hoping thereby to temper *Ijtihad*'s force and appease agitated spirits. But the die's cast, fear and anxiety peak, causing orthodoxy to put him in prison where he eventually dies.[154] The entire innovative spirit then follows suit: it dies with him. Now what precipitates this demise is rather very interesting in itself.

The two other magnet-forces or counter-agents Abu Hanīfa invents for the occasion are *Qiyas* (analogical thinking) and *Ijma'* (consensus); they lure *Ijtihad* back into the orthodox fold for a time, forcing it to stay the course of Qur'ān-*Hadith* tradition. Meanwhile, however, something else occurs, as if in a sort of irony of situation. An ensemble of three discourses fused into one come into being, forming in their own way an Arab-Muslim version of Greek *hypomnemata.*[155] The three-fold discourse brings Arab-Muslim thought to bear on answering, arguing, or explicating not just knotty moral problems, but also legal, private, public, and philosophico-theological issues whenever, wherever, and whatever conditions these arise from.

This time, you see, things are really getting out of hand for orthodoxy. Soon this leavening of thought induces intellectual responses in kind. Three more schools of jurisprudence each develop their own perspective interpretations of the same data; consequently, competition and debate, as the network widens, wax keener. Particularly in view of the presence of Christians and Jews, among others, whose sometime dialectical skills outweigh Arab-Muslims'. The latter, at

---

[154] See al-Khazen, p. 150.

[155] Only Allah knows how much of Greek thought secretly slips into Arab-Muslim thought. See Badawi, *al-Turath al-Yunani fi-l Hadara al-Islamiyya* (Beirut, 1980).

all events, their differences notwithstanding, confront them right in the eye. As if to sharpen their own wit therewith. Which they do. And to vanquish them, they even dare to call upon the critico-philosophical discourse to join in the new polemics. In doing so, they perform a double function: while each school tries to justify or reinforce its own conclusion, they all join forces to edge these other peoples out intellectually. This is the moment of the great "democratic" joust.[156] Whether or not it's meant to shore up the tottering *Ummah*-building hardly matters at this point in time.

67

What matters is the "democratic" hot ember in Arab-Muslim archival memory. True, the flaming glow of *Ijtihad*, philosophy, *Qiyas*, and *Ijma'* may vanish under the impact of orthodoxy. But it all but dies at the time. I say "all but" and "at the time" because this democratic ember still smolders today, waiting, as it were, to be fanned to flame again when Arab-Muslims muster up courage and will to acquire historical sense and knowledge necessary to start a new lease on life. I hope for their sake they do so as to recoup that lost summer of flaming glow again.

Until that happens, however, it's winter at the time. And this is how it sets in. The clouds move in and the bright "democratic" skies darken. One innovation after another begins to lose its luster as the orthodox body of traditions takes shape and takes hold. Eventually, this body puts up a fight and dislodges philosophy, *Ijtihad* and *Qiyas,* barring them from any productive function. *Ijma'*, though, remains for a time, since it directly links up with the traditions. Yet it, too, having just been used to establish *Hadith* (a tradition of Muhammad), ironically, gets ousted in turn by *Hadith* itself; that is, *Hadith*, to avoid bloodshed, doesn't kill it but converts it, so to speak, into a scorpion that turns in on itself and bites itself to death. And so law, dogma, tradition—in a word, *Sunnah*—rules the day. To this day things remain the same or relatively unchanged.[157] In fact, if it's

---

[156] Mernissi presents a brief but very interesting and scholarly assessment of this "democratic" ambience.

[157] Fazlur Rahman, Islam (New York: Anchor Books, 1968), pp. 75-95.

true, as people say, that in certain cases history repeats itself, then frequent reversions of *Sunnah* bear that out: for example, eighteenth-century Wahabism of Saudi Arabia, and now Hezbollah (The Party of Allah).[158]

Despite that depressive history, I'm optimistic. I even wager this, too: Arab-Muslim culture, the highest art attained in democratic thought and faith in eighth and ninth centuries, will come to life again. Indeed, it will be reborn when Arab-Muslims recognize in these centuries a treasury of ideas to searchlight what's going on now, and to change it; also, and most importantly, when they learn to weather the consciousness of the hardest, yet necessary defeat, without suffering from it, and so embrace with gusto the cause and continuity of life on earth. This is a tough call, I know. Yet it can be accomplished. I'm, again, thinking of the decline of classical Islam, and with it the *Ummah 'Arabiyya Islamiyy*, at the end of eighth century. Yes, these are historical facts that must be dug into with rigor, understood thoroughly, or better, interpreted accurately with the aim of paving the way for a democracy to come. The outcome of this endeavor is two-fold: it shows Arab-Muslims that the decline of Islam is absolutely irrelevant to the smoldering democratic embers; and it leaves intact both Muhammad's ethical conduct and ethos of the community. These two forces, ethics and smoldering embers, are waiting to be conjoined in a work of renewal, now more than ever.

68

And there will be renewal, certainly. Allow me to elaborate. *Ijtihad* and *Qiyas,* though give way to orthodox *Shari'a* (dogma and law), still, to repeat, smolder with life; they wait patiently to be quickened to glowing heat once again. The proof? Well, for one thing, Abu Hanīfa's inventions are an indelible part of Arab-Muslim archives, and can't be denied, ignored, or distorted. For another, his binary division, assuming it's still alive (though I doubt it), barely signifies, as I tried to show, the reemergence of Arab-Muslim *Ummah* as a force—one

---

[158] See Judith Palmer Harik, *Hezbollah: The Changing Face of Terrorism* (New York: I.B. Tauris, 2004, especially pp 7-39.

deeming itself fundamentally supreme, and for that reason isolating itself from or pitting itself against the world. After all, *Dar al-Islam* is no longer a single homogenous community governed by a single state, headed by a single sovereign. While *Dar al-Harb* has never borne the common rubric that all mankind will accept Islam or submit to its rule lock, stock, and barrel. How could this be indeed if no cohesive unity exists? In fact, given current historical events, no one, Arab-Muslims in particular, can in good conscience negate the evolution of thought—whether to the good or bad. Islam, again as I tried to show, has always already been broken into pieces, even before it rolls into being.

Lest I break with my note of hope, let me say this: Abu Hanīfa's *Ijtihad,* including his concept of binary division, is innovative enough, it's true. But let's not at the same time forget the performative innovations of other peoples surrounding Arab-Muslims: the Greeks, for example, divide the world into Greeks and barbarians; the Hebrews into Jews and Gentiles respectively;[159] and the Christians have always made a boundary between themselves and the world (in all the senses of the word). Besides, each of these peoples construes life after its own image, as if it's the meaning, the salt, the measure, and the standards of all the rest. This, to put it in a nutshell, is an erroneous psychological presupposition that makes no sense any more.[160]

Indeed, today or yesterday, no society can stamp the world according to its own image. If it does, it fails, despite appearances.[161] That's the great lesson of history. In any event, if Arab-Muslims (Abu Hanīfa and others) are influenced by such peoples, I mean Greeks, Hebrews, Christians (and I think they are), it certainly unveils an aspect of Arab-Muslim readiness to emulate and surpass: their ability and willingness not only to learn from others, but also, as you saw, to

---

[159] See Bernard Lewis, *The Muslim Discovery of Europe* (New York: W.W. Norton & Company, 2001), p. 59.

[160] I don't deny, however, that certain drives—will-power, fear, greed, love, compassion, pity, etc.—unconsciously determine human action. But these are now gradually being brought out onto the surface, perhaps even also controlled as well through an all-out study of religious morality in relation to will-power.

[161] As is the case in Iraq today. Also as is the case of Arab-Muslim *Ummah.*

compete with, perhaps even outstrip them intellectually. How else do Arab-Muslims get intellectual stimulation if not on their own turf, in their own home? This is what *Ijtihad,* and on another level *Dar al-Harb,* too, signifies—namely the abode of internal war whose essence is intellectual agonistics, not the abode of external war as lust for power and conquest.

Ijtihad, then, seen with the advantage of hindsight, performs two functions: it engenders the binary division which tells us who Arab-Muslims are: different, pious, traditionalists, but also thinkers, creative, daring, who do their possible to start up "democratic" ideas as debates, discussions, arguments. At the same time *Ijtihad,* almost invisibly, as it were, restores to the word j*ihad* (from the same root *j-h-d,* effort), its original import: to recall Arab-Muslims to the work they must perform on themselves as ethical-religious beings.[162] This is the historical meaning of *Jihad* or *Greater Jihad* (self-cultivation) predating that other *Jihad* or *Lesser Jihad* (aggression) and opposing it term by term.[163] If you join these two functions, you then end up with something like this: it teaches you how culture and civilization, historically, have a sort of a healthy wedge between them.[164] Where culture generates democratic-philosophical-thoelogical discourse in the first half of eighth century, civilization "degenerates" them into a decadent course of history—650-850—spanned by Umayyad and Abbasid dynasties.

That's why I urge my fellow Arab-Muslims to delve into the bottom of this history, I mean to tunnel, mine and undermine, in other words, to analyze why and how that magnificent culture has given way to civilization, also how to see to it that the latter or similar one never develops again.

69

I'd like to sum up all this by highlighting certain aspects of Arab-Muslim multi-faceted background which, epiphenomenally, may reveal hidden currents of

---

[162] See Dwight M. Donaldson, *Studies in Muslim Ethics* (London: S.P.C.K., 1953).

[163] See Rudolf Peters, *Jihad in Classical and Modern Islam.*

[164] Nietzsche, *The Will to Power,* trans. Walter Kaufmann (New York: Vintage Books, 1968, p. 75, sections 121and 122. A whole study of the difference between the two terms in Arab-Muslim history is worth undertaking some day.

thought and behavior leading through *Ijtihad* to Arab-Muslim view of the West.[165] For this view in particular must be contextualized if it's to be fully appreciated. What's more, by means of this contextualization I might (who knows?) be able to alert Arab-Muslims in general to the dynamic force bursting through traditional bounds in the ninth century, taking to the high seas.

To recap briefly, Arab-Muslims, as you saw, grow up in Mecca, the thriving urban stronghold of the pagan tribe of Quraysh. The city's ambience isn't only already rich in local color; it's actually a beehive of commercial activities as well. An ambience that, naturally, gives rise to local friction, even among members of the same family—for example, sons of Umayya and sons of Abbās squabbling about who should preside over commerce with the flux of pilgrims each year; a squabble that eventually proves fatal to the solidarity of Arab-Muslim *Ummah* in the seventh and eighth centuries.

In this hub of pagan business life, Arabs and soon later Arab-Muslims rub shoulders with a splendid array of cultures and moralities: Christian, Judaic, Magian, Sabian, Zoroastrian, and so. The tribe of Quraysh (of which Muhammad's early followers are members) has for a long time been carrying on business relations with Persians, Byzantines, Ethiopians, and Indians, among others. Muhammad himself imbibes dutifully the mercantile spirit: he first becomes a business agent, then a keen-eyed traveling merchant working for his sober and senior future wife Khadīja. In the busy course of his career he meets various peoples and learns about their different deportments and modes of life. On the dark side, Arab-Muslims undergo onerous experiences during the early years of their divine calling. For example, local wars, struggle for survival in the harsh desert, hostilities directed against them by Meccans in cahoots with certain Medinese Jews, not to speak of starvation, poverty, and search for food, also of the occasional side roads and wrong roads, the delays, modesties, seriousness wasted on tasks that are remote from the task, namely fulfillment of a promised faith.

---

[165]For further information, see Donaldson.

Such multiform experience, good and bad, foster in Arab-Muslims critical eminence which enable them to outdistance Quraysh ethically and intellectually. While Quraysh remains the affluent, bubbly enclave, confined horizontally to desert life, Arab-Muslims who secede from Quraysh acquire a new perspectivism—one that takes them far afield, even if they seem as yet unaware of it. But it's there, like a silent undercurrent coursing through their sinews. Gradually, it promotes capacity to transcend the average, the desert, the old ways quite significantly. This sense of expansion, of self-enhancement, eventually leading to self-overcoming, starts in the eighth century on their own turf, then receives added impetus in the ninth century when the hitherto unknown western world emerges before their eyes. In time, it grants them a fresh eye to see beyond the mere *Ummah*-conditioned perspective. If there's a single word or phrase to define this state of awareness, it may be what Arkoun calls "presupposed political space" or "imaginary."[166] This in another sense is Abu Hanīfa's contribution to the new perspectivism.

70

As I now see it in hindsight, this presupposed political space or imaginary is more than personal. Like a genius, it awakens in certain Arab-Muslims political reverence of themselves and no longer pangs of conscience and drives them to become the creators of their own ideas of what their society should be now that it's entering a new stage. For example, as you saw, it steers them in the direction of intellectual reform: I mean that which enables them to develop better interpretations—better for themselves and better than those of paganism (*asabiyya* or group feeling) and even orthodoxy, which, until then, has kept the Arabian mind outside the orbit of world cultures, that is, outside the larger and more complex societies surrounding it, even though it maintains business relations with them. Once again, it's a new phase in the life of Arab-Muslims. To that extent, you can say they feel that the old cult, with its scowl and cowl, its

---

[166] Arkoun, p. 6.

absurd rigidity, its vacant expression, its stiff false hair to be no longer appropriate, no longer adequate to quench their thirst for a new, inclusive culture.

The imaginary also brings Arab-Muslims closer to Christians and Jews. In point of fact, it links them to the same originary site as do Christian and Jewish imaginaries: Abrahamic tradition. In other words, it inspires oneness of faith which, Christian and Jewish opposition or apartness notwithstanding, Muhammad never tires of affirming: my faith is the faith of Abraham, of Moses, of Jesus.[167] As such, it forestalls any coercive measure to espouse Islam or make it binding on all. If it aspires to universalism, if it insists on being universal, this is because it belongs in the same Abrahamic site. And it says so when Christianity and Judaism don't. Hence the word 'Muslim,' signifying less a religion than a common, undifferentiated tradition. All three religions, then, according to Islam, are Muslims, and so feelings of superiority felt by one over another vanish.

That's exactly what on another level distinguishes Islam, the all-inclusive faith, from today's fundamentalist thought. The latter, like Christianity and Judaism, believes itself to be apart, outside human history; a belief that has steered Christianity and Judaism each to counter it and to re-examine their own positions relative to it and to each the other. But, again like Christianity and Judaism, it never affirms a heritage common to all three. Which leads me to conclude that fundamentalism lives as a parasite on Islam. At any rate, the fact remains that the common tradition is there, even if it's an imaginary. And this tradition enjoins all three faiths to perform some creative, ethical work that may help them cease being mental nomads, one people or faith exercising one-upmanship over another, and to live instead side by side.[168] In the case of Arab-

---

[167] There's a sense in which Christians and Jews point to a certain pathological condition in Muhammad's emotional experience of seeing visions. I counter that seeing visions is a vehicle to new ideas, which break the spell of venerated usages and superstitions. How else society is supposed to advance in matters of faith and intellect?

[168] See Dan Cohn-Sherbok, ed. *Islam in a World of Diverse Faiths* (New York: St. Martin'e Press, 1997). The book explores the diverse ways in which dialogue between the three monotheistic faiths can help bridge their differences.

Muslims, many Qur'anic *Surahs* actually refer to this urgent political settling, so to speak, upon the lees.[169]

71

And not only in the Qur'ān. After all, the Qur'ān takes its bearings from actual events. Events showing Arab-Muslims have always already been a part of this world. I mean they coexist, among others, with Christians, Jews, Magians, Sabians, Zoroastrians, all of whom are dear to their heart. What's more, it's historically the case both before and after Arab-Muslim conquest.[170] For example, prior to *Ummah*'s flight to Medina, where it's welcomed even by Jews,[171] it flees persecution by Meccans to seek and find a safe haven in Christian Abyssinia.[172] If anything, this event underscores both Arab-Muslims' wholehearted embrace of Christianity and their rejection of paganist Quraysh, the very tribe Muhammad himself comes from. (It's interesting to note here that the binary division of the world is still far from Arab-Muslim purview.) More than that, the incident, the flight along with the gesture of welcome, has a far-reaching and decisive effect on Arab-Muslims' later view of themselves and the world. Ultimately it becomes, if unconsciously, as much a model to follow in terms of organizing relations with other peoples (conquered or not) as a measure of the perspective view of Arab-Muslims of non-Arabs as well as of non-Arab-Muslims down the centuries.

---

[169]See The Koran: for example, 2: 39; 2:129-32; 3:58-62.

[170] From the very beginning of Islam, from the time when Muhammad is in Medina, the first thing he does after establishing the masjid (mosque) is to create a constitution, known as the constitution of Medina, where not only the new Arab-Muslim community, but also the Zoroastrians, the Christians and the Jews, as well as non-religious people, could cooperate together, to meet the needs of the city state. See John Bowker, *What Muslims Believe* (Oxford: Oneworld Publications, 1998), pp. 24-30. In another sense, this is Dar al-Islam, an amalgam of peoples.

[171] This picture gets a bit complicated not too long after this initial welcome. To cut corners, what happens is that once Jews begin to realize the new threat (but this realization is perhaps exaggerated) they try to conspire with Meccans against Muhammad. The Qur'ān explains it this way: "Have you not seen those who were given a portion of the Scriptures, and yet they believe in sorcery and digression, and assure the non-believers that they are better-guided than the believers. It is those indeed whom Allah has cursed. Whomever Allah has cursed shall have help from no one." The Koran, Surah 23: 21.

[172] See Salāhi, pp. 118-134.

The same ethic of coexistence (though not with pagans) is manifest in the aftermath of conquests. In Syria, Egypt, Persia, parts of India and Spain, Arab-Muslims, despite differences, live side by side with all the various conquered peoples. True, they observe, no doubt prompted to it by arrogance, certain defects, faults, or distortions in one or another faith and criticize them; they nevertheless accept the faith as it is, even though they wish it to be otherwise. In fact, they allow it freedom of choice in matters of worship and socialization without interference on their part. They go further. They try to keep their due distance both to ease up their authority over non-Muslim peoples and to ensure the latter's rights to self-government.[173] All in all, perspectivism based in the ethic of coexistence is an integral part Arab-Muslim ethos.[174] Two additional instances help illustrate this: first, Muhammad's endorsement of the attitude that "one doesn't express pleasure at the misfortunes of one's enemy";[175] Secondly, an anecdote (though of a later period) has it that Caliph Harūn al-Rashīd warns his fool Ibn Abi Miryam of a frivolous remark he's just made: "beware of the Qur'ān and Islam. Apart from that, you may do and say whatever you wish."[176] Both instances have one thing in common: tolerance and the readiness to straddle both worlds—Islam and the other.

72

To return briefly to Abu Hanīfa, his binary division of the world into *Dar al-Islam* and *Dar al-Harb*, is, to say it again, at once significant and fertile. It shows Islam wrapped up in history, constantly differing from itself one moment

---

[173] See Murad Wifried Hofmann, "Muslims As Co-Citizens of the West: Rights, Duties, And Prospects" [Online Document], [Cited 2002, Apr 27].

[174] And this perspectivism and ethos of coexistence, it should be immediately emphasized, is never founded on hostility prompted by ideology of coercion or domination of any particular group. Rather, it's a perspectivism erected on a religio-ethical base. After all, Arab-Muslims are conquerors who nevertheless make certain that others are protected. But when they make trouble, the former are forced to keep their distance. Thus the Qur'ān has it: "Believers, do not make friends with those who are enemies of mine and yours. Would you show them kindness, when they have denied the truth that has been revealed to you and driven out the apostle and yourselves, because you believe in Allah, your Lord?" *The Koran*, Surah 60:1.

[175]See Salāhi, p. 703.

[176] See below note 214.

after another: now a culture (first half of ninth century), now a civilization (second half of ninth century). Both, in turn, eventually decline, morphing into other forms—Wahabism, Hezbollah, fundamentalism, among others. Islam, you see, without someone seeking any intention in it or having intentions, I mean without a subject, a doer, or a consciousness, undergoes modifications since its early history. And for that reason it grows more complex, more diverse. *Ijtihad*, four schools of theology, diversity of denominations (Sunnism, Shī'ism), variety of thought (philosophy, Sufism, Mu'tazilism, Qadiriyyism)—all these and more lend Islam the pluralism that's proper to it. They also, let me quickly add, constitute a treasury of ideas, concepts, precepts, procedures that can be used as a tool to understand what's going on today—and to change it. No wonder Islam resists subsumption into one general word or concept—Islam (which is an irrecusable historical fact);[177] rather, it thrives only on its built-in capacity to re-produce, re-invent, or modulate itself according to changing circumstances.[178]

A fact and process that shakes orthodoxy's foundation to its very core, dwarfing it into a part of the whole, undermining its monopoly on faith, thought, or interpretation of sacred texts. This is a salubrious outcome, actually, reminding orthodoxy where it belongs, and, truth to tell, saving it at the same time from total extinction. As if to say, let history teaches it a couple of things, perhaps even also promising things: first, orthodoxy's rigid piety originates in an illusory fear for its hegemonic status, itself arising from a misunderstanding of Arab-Muslim history. Secondly, its deployment of eternal law and dogma is but a reactive measure to this illusory fright, and most ineffectual precisely because these texts are, by its own admission, always subject to different interpretations at different times by different groups. Mightn't orthodoxy, then, re-learn at once to demolish this, that, and the other illusion it erects without recourse and to refurbish its

---

[177] See Said, *Covering Islam*.

[178] This is what Mernissi attempts to do in her book, though the attempt remains, I think, incomplete due to other issues she must deal with first.

waning strength it tastelessly disguises as belligerent Islamism or fundamentalism of one sort or another?[179] It's time to do so.

Part Two

73

Part One is a backdrop for Arab-Muslim view of the West. Without it, this view, which hasn't yet emerged on the scene, would lose its psychodynamic force (if I may say so) which otherwise helps us discover signposts of possible East-West rapprochement over time. Put otherwise, in somewhat stronger terms, as a history, Part One, along with "Instead of an Introduction," constitutes the principal dynamo behind Arab-Muslim view of the West. I say this in order to ascertain that what I present is a rounded and thorough revaluation.

A propos of that, I should add a cautionary word. The historical events and thoughts I relate follow no such formula as *post hoc, ergo propter hoc.* For example, there's nothing, stated or implied, in the innovative practice of *Ijtihad* that indicates that the "discovery" of the West directly stands in the after-effect of this innovation. The same holds for the philosophy and the philosophico-theological schools of eighth and ninth centuries. Even if they embody new forms of thought, call them "enlightenment" if you will, these schools contain no special departments or sessions designed to train Arab-Muslims in international relations or how to view the West; besides, those scholars who do express or father that view don't even refer to this enlightenment.

However, what you could say is this: all these forms of enlightenment are like forces mutually engaged in intellectual jousts in which the stronger tries to subdue the weaker, in so far as the latter can barely assert its degree of independence. At the same time each strong element, the winner, as it were, tries to run *Sunni* orthodoxy into the ground, as if, in so doing, it expresses its need to expand, to assimilate new forms of life and thought beyond its narrow confines. In this circular agonistic combat the air, then, gets charged with new ideas and

---

[179]See Harik's entire book.

consciousness that, in turn, engender new interest in a world other than the Mid-East. In a word, the expanding atmosphere that's now gradually forming has as its nucleus the regulative and seminal idea of innovation.

That's why Part One and "Instead of an Introduction" as a whole are significant for this project. They show, particularly the former, how the historical unfolding of ideas, events, thoughts, things structure history as a mode of interpretation, not of cause-effect relationship. If you appreciate history as such, then what I plan to tell you next consists of certain quantities of force, in addition to those already discussed, that might have given the impetus to, though not caused, Arab-Muslim view of the West. More than that I can't say, otherwise I'll be accused of the very error I'm trying to avoid.

74

Arab-Muslims, as you saw, attack, invade, or conquer many lands (in some instances only parts)—Byzantium, Persia, Iberia, Syria, Egypt, among others, in the seventh and eighth centuries. Curiously, though, they seem to exert no effort to know the peoples they subdue, their cultures, ways of life, or modes of doing things. At least, historians say there's barely a clear-cut, objective indication that Arab-Muslims do or have ever done so.[180] But some historians, as usual, like more than just to split hairs; they like to cavil: they quickly get hold of certain texts, or quickly analyze certain events, and, instead of interpreting them, they transpose them, and as quickly have done with them. To put it another way, they often make petty comments or pass superficial judgments without due regard for understanding the real meaning embedded in and around said texts or events. In a word, they denaturalize the latter, tearing them from their turf or mode of conditionality in which they've grown and alone possess any meaning.

Take, for example, early seventh-century formation of *Ummah*. Recall how the tiny community must, against its will, fight tooth and nail not only to

---

[180] To this day, I dare say Arab-Muslims haven't really attempted to study rigorously and to understand well what the Western culture is all about, what makes it tick: its successes, its failures, its mythologies, its manipulative powers, but also its contributions to the advancement of humanity in all aspects. There are thousands of books written by Arab-Muslim and Muslim scholars alike on Western politics in all the senses of the word; but there's hardly a book, in so far as I know, on Western literary or philosophical achievements, in short, on the inner workings of Western mind and psyche.

keep its ideals alive and kicking, but to keep body and soul together as well. Recall, too, how hardships of all kinds dog it everywhere, even after its emigration from Mecca to Medina. There, in the midst of the din and hubbub, Muhammad, unfazed, searches for one or another way to end hostilities. He in good conscience calls on the diverse groups to beat down pagan *asabiyya* (group feeling) which seems to him, and rightly so, to be the root of hatred and war and in which one group lords it over another. He never tires, every time you read the Qur'ān, of inviting the world to coexist as one *Ummah*, whole and undivided.

The call, given Islam's inherently basic attitude of live-and-let-live, would have rallied in a multi-cultural, "democratic" community if that *asabiyya* has been rooted out once and for all. But envy, jealousy, hatred, in a word, group feeling, both internal and external, prevails over every shred of idealism and new practices. Almost instantly, the community finds itself on the defensive, jettisoning one little ideal after another—which in the long run dooms it to extinction. Meanwhile danger, death or starvation follows it, or whatever lefty of it, like its shadow. And yet Arab-Muslims, no longer an *Ummah* in the proper sense of the term but a mighty fighting machine, continue their conquests. As if this seems the be-all and end-all in life. Well, then, how could they, now tunnel-visioned and bent for war (though still idealistic) find time or freedom to get to know others? Put otherwise, what's there indeed to know about those others? In fact, the Persians, ironically enough, as if waiting to be delivered from some dire evil, give up everything and espouse Islam the moment Arab-Muslims subdue them. What does that tell you?

75

And now consider Jews and Christians. Arab-Muslims know these peoples to revere and worship the same scriptural figures as they. What's more, they all share certain taboos—*riba* (usury), to give a prominent example, is a common abomination, though neither faith bats an eyelid about practicing it today. If it does, the entire world economy would topple down in a minute. Finally, Arab-Muslims, though conquerors in the past, respect the customs and religious rites of their Abrahamic coreligionists, even protect and defend them if and when necessary, as has been the case historically.[181] This, to say it again, is their ethos, pure and simple, a regulative and regulating ethical instinct with which nature has endowed them.

Besides, let's not forget all three faiths belong to one indivisible tradition: they're all "muslims." Though the word's Arabic, it means neither Arab nor Jew nor Christian, but whoever happens to be one or other without the exclusive belief attached. To that extent, it names a gesture, not a separate race or creed. If Christians or Jews had a similar word, Arabic language would probably assimilate it. All in all, it seems there's little or nothing new for Arab-Muslims to learn about Judeo-Christian cultures or ways of life. At least, and significantly, at that time. Conversely, Jews and Christians have equally little or nothing to learn about Arab-Muslim culture or way of life. Ultimately, all of them are identical; again, all share the same history, the same ethico-religious tradition.[182] If you review what Romans do to Christians and Jews, to give a contrasting example, if you consider the atrocious manner in which the former treat the latter, as reported by New Testament writers, even by Roman historians themselves no less, you'd have to admire the genuineness with which underneath it all Arab-Muslims treat Jews and Christians. [183]

76

---

[181] See Ali Ibrahīm Hasan, pp. 551-597.

[182] So what's the big deal? Why can't they communicate? Or perhaps the question is: do they really want to?

[183] How to bridge differences between East and West? That's the question. I find it interesting that this question comes to me at the precise point at which I'm trying to draw certain parallel lines of thought and attitude between Jews, Christians and Arab-Muslims. Well, it seems to me the question is both simple and complicated. Ethics' essence, as I understand it, may be defined as desirability for change and that, consequently, things among the three faiths ought to be different. Well and good. Now this desire can be satisfied either by death or by discussion. Suppose discussion is given a chance, what then? Well, the content of this discussion would be something like this: each faith attempts to understand itself, first, as a natural growth, as a plant having grown in its own soil; secondly, if each faith does the same in regard to the other faith (since it too is a plant having grown in its own soil), then all faiths come to realize their foolishness for taking things out of context, out of their natural presuppositions which, willy-nilly, they have in common. It seems to me that such a realization might lead to some sort of mutual understanding, perhaps the sign of possible bridge-building to come. If humans can't give discussion a chance, well then, it's definitely death.

And yet there's a flip side to this picture. Historically, Arab-Muslims treat all subdued peoples as a master a slave, keeping him at due distance, even if he should adopt his master's ways. They thus rarely, if at all, assess the effects they produce upon the perceptions of those they coexist with and from this learn to look back upon themselves objectively—that is, to contemplate their soul in another's eye and, thereby, accede to fresh mental and emotional domains of knowledge. They miss out on that fertile experience. Perhaps they deem theirs a permanent condition of war, of survival tactic; in which case they think they have a right over the vanquished, albeit they must fight for and protect them. Well and good. But for that sort of tunnel vision they pay dearly. Fate, to cut corners, turns the tables on them. Gradually they lose ground, faith, authority and all. In retaliation, they lash themselves into a fury. You could see them bristling with fright almost to a catatonic state, as they charge their enemy hordes head on. Such livid aggression is, of course, of all time and place, and takes various forms.[184] Today, Arab-Muslim extremists, inheriting the same symptoms, behave no differently.

Already the older symptoms and their after-effect are quite obvious: Arab-Muslims, given their circumscribed activity and rigid rules, paralyze their better mind, bringing, in effect, boredom and misery to themselves and others. They wax so wretched indeed that they lose all sense of solidarity. The condition eventually propels them to the edge of disaster, and soon enough hurls them into the dark abyss. Gaps thus develop in the *Ummah*'s fabric. Non-Arabs on standing order carefully monitor such developments: the masters down in the dumps, they calculate, weakened by their own hands. And so they waylay Arab-Muslims, then wiggle their way into the inner arteries and clog them. Finally, they wreak havoc onto the waning *Ummah*, hacking it off into pieces. This, you see, is as much the story of the fall of Abbāsid dynasty as the story of the fall of Umayyad dynasty at the hands of the former. A double wham whose long narrative can't be told here.

---

[184] St. Paul, for example, proclaiming Jesus in the synagogues, so incensed the Jewish community that it plots to kill him. My point is that self-preservation at any price, needless to say, is a normal human feeling when it comes to external or internal threats.

All of which, again to cut corners, is rooted in Arab-Muslims' unconscious behavior: catatonic, imaginary fears, and in particular pessimistic judgments as to their own better nature and the world. They act according to such judgments and thus translate idea into action through attacking, robbing, mistreatment and bloodshed. I don't condone such behavior, though I know it betrays a law inherent in all peoples on the alert for enemy attacks, a law laced with a contingent prerogative a conquering people gives to itself: think of Greeks, Romans, Normans, North Americans, and so on. Arab-Muslims are no different. In the last analysis, their attitude toward the conquered may be described, if you like, as haughty, supercilious, hubristic, or murderous. Yet it's no reason at all for scholars in cahoots with popular culture to blow it out not only into all sorts of demeaning images and epithets, but also into something containing some dubious or insidious agenda, some secret metaphysical horror of seismic proportions. There's absolutely no reason for that at all.

(Muhammad's ethical work on himself is a model to emulate. Recall that he abandons war in favor of peace with the Meccans. In fact, as a result of self-cultivation and self-discipline he wins back Mecca, the city so dear to his heart, peacefully. Let this metaphor bring my point home: formerly, Muhammad prowls around angrily like a captive animal, watching the bars of his cage and leaping against them in order to smash them down; but then he is happy when he through a gap in them he sees something of what is outside, of what is distant and beyond, and dashes off to grasp it. With that ethico-ontological model in mind, then, today's Arab-Muslims can look beyond themselves. That's to say, they can relearn to discharge their pessimistic judgments not through bloodshed and war but only through words and thoughts. In such benign option they become each the poet of his or her life.)

77

Everyone knows, I presume, that the human world's anything but a solid matter of fact. there are also no facts, no things, no reality, no being, and no knowledge for its own sake. Ours is a world of perspectivism, a world we arrange for ourselves in which we are able to live by positing this, that, and the other thing. In a word, it's a fabric of diverse conventions amounting to subjective fiction, and nothing else besides. This truth, if it's one, is as much dismaying as it's unsettling, to be sure. And yet, when contemplated fully, quite a sobering one, to boot. And so an individual, a people may bend reality to their desire, adapt or transpose it into any shape or form they see fit. Put otherwise, in human hands the world or reality becomes mythologies. Which, of course, doesn't mean it's untrue.[185]

My point is this: Arab-Muslims, like other peoples, interpret and have interpreted life according to their image. Just as they fight and conquer, they also have it in them, based on their experiences, to develop new ways of thinking. Some do so theologically, others philosophically, still others morally or ethically, even some quasi-scientifically, though not objectively. What's more, these differing subjective interpretations often of the same data lead to or instigate atrocious infighting. But they also accumulate, store up, or perhaps alchemically change in time into a whole treasury of ideas, concepts, techniques, insights, a whole intellectual activity beyond *Ummah*'s original purview or expectation.

So without consciously targeting it, Arab-Muslims, throughout the first three centuries, despite a busy fighting schedule, make room for the pursuit of knowledge after their own image. They do so instinctively, I think, which, again, is itself a subjective fiction. It's what cognitive scientists call the cognitive unconscious—structures in the human brain that a person can't consciously access, but knows by their consequences. In other words, Arab-Muslims introduce something new without knowing it, to wit, this necessary perspectivism through which every center of force, every interpretation construes Islam from its own viewpoint—for example, it measures, feels, or forms the faith according to its own viewpoint or center of force. In effect, and to repeat what E. Saīd already

---

[185] See Roland Barthes, *Myth Today: A Barthes Reader*, ed. Susan Sontag (New York: Noonday Press, 1982). A remarkable work illuminating a fact that people are either embarrassed or frightened to admit themselves: namely reality is not what it is but what one thinks or interprets it to mean or be according to one's own perspective. Barthes gives a good example: "A tree is a tree. Yes, of course. But a tree as expressed by, say, Minou Drouet is no longer quite a tree, it is a tree which is decorated, adapted to a certain type of consumption, laden with literary self-indulgence, revolt, images, in short with a type of social usage which is added to pure matter."

says, there has never been, never is, and never will be one Islam. Such is its greatness.[186]

To appreciate this point, you could say, though it sounds banal, that without the Qur'ān, no *Sunnah* would have been possible; without *Sunnah*, no *Hadīth*; without *Hadīth,* no *Ijtihad*; without *Ijtihad*, no *Qiyās* and no *Ijmā'*; and without these, no philosophy, and so on, in a chain of endless one-after-the-other, each time the one differing and deferring the other, but also each time the one depends on the other contiguously and concurrently. And this chain, in turn, seems to take off by force of another chain of one-after-the-other, namely Arab-Muslims' early exposure to difference—different peoples, different cultures, and so on, throughout time and up to the present. Finally, you could also say Islam is impossible without differences (in) of viewpoints. Let's call that built-in *Ijtihad.* To this extent I believe the impossible may be possible, after all.

78

Another manifestation of the cognitive unconscious seems linked to further functions or enterprises. I'm thinking of translation from Greek and Syriac languages, beginning in ninth century. At first, it appears completely cut off from other former or contemporary interests. That's not the case, actually. This hankering for knowledge wouldn't have been possible without the philosophico-theological initiative, and I don't imply the *post-hoc- ergo-propter-hoc* fallacy either. In point of fact, the Caliph al-Ma'mūn, essentially a Mu'tazilite, has something to do with it. And, to follow the one-after-the-other chain to the end, without both activities of translation, Mu'tazilism and *Ijtihad* there would have been no Arab-Muslim historians and geographers. Those few savants, as I like to dub them, put foreign peoples and countries on the map, and make Arab-Muslim culture a part of the world. In other words, their work isn't only a new experience for Islam; it confirms the latter's immanently malleable character as well.

---

[186] This doesn't mean that Islamism can exploit the idea of Islam's plurality to justify its way of doing thing. True, it portrays the dogma or *sharī'a* after its own image, but it would be a violation of *sharī'a*'s spirit and ethics to translate or transpose that interpretation into bloodshed. If this truth means nothing to Islamism, then I don't know what does.

These savants open a new chapter in the history of Arab-Muslim intellectual venture beyond *Dar al-Islam*. From which, let me quickly add, hundreds of thousands benefit immensely. You may ask, what manner are these individuals who apply their intellect without preconditions? Well, they're daring, curious, and creative; they go far afield to adapt material, though not of their invention, to fit their differing interpretive interests. In this as in everything else, they're truly free spirits: they don't impose their interpretation on anyone. Rather, they investigate and criticize things (texts, events, ideas, conditions) as no one has done before, then they leave them there for anyone to learn from or admire. Ibn Battūta (fourteenth century) is an apt example of this amalgam of freedom and curiosity. His insatiable appetite for learning covers seventy-five thousand miles and forty-four countries.[187] Though not a philosopher but traveler, he, like many free, curious spirits before and after him, opens up a small window onto new worlds and peoples for the instruction, enrichment, and enlightenment of Arab-Muslim society at large.

Specifically, these savants get down to business: they learn about the world. Some visit Eastern Europe, others Western Europe or West (at the time called land of 'Franj'), still others read about both. Consequently, a picture of Western peoples and countries (assumed part of the fantasy of moral sublimity *Dar al-Harb*) gradually begins to emerge.[188] This picture is double-faced: disinterested and egoistic or cognitive and emotive. Therefore, a complex picture with one simple truth: to understanding and self-understand—with certain discriminative tendencies set forth to extol climatic and spiritual aspects of *Dar al-Islam* (the other side of that fantasy). And the materials purveyed for this

---

[187] Briefly, Ibn Battūta was first moved to leave home at age twenty-one in order to perform the hajj. This major journey through northern Africa and the Arabian Peninsula only whetted his curious appetite, however, and fate had much more travel in store for him. So, in fact, a prophetic man tells him as he is first going toward Mecca: he predicts that Ibn Battūta will eventually meet several of the wise man's relatives in distant India and China. He further instructs Ibn Battūta to give greetings to each of them. Which he did.

[188] I believe I've said enough about the untenability of the binary structure of the world: about the fact that it should be clearly understood in its essence before any hasty judgment is made about it. For further information, see the very interesting few pages on the subject in John Bowker, *What Muslims Believe*, pp. 75-78.

picture from translations and visitations are first cobbled together then revised or retouched to give birth to the discipline of Arab-Muslim geography. Ibn Khardadhbeh, Ibn Wādih al-Ya'quūi, Ibn Rusteh, Ibn Fadlān, al-Mas'ūdi, ibn Hawqal, and al-Istakhri are its stars.

79

We must, then, try to understand the specific branch of geography these stars are interested in and why. Initially, they don't blindly follow Ptolemy in everything he hands down to them. Surely, they admire his genius and are grateful for it; nevertheless they work selectively. They focus, for example, on regional geography that deals with climate and landforms, also on urban geography that deals with cities and other urban areas and their populations. Now and then they sprinkle such accounts with observations concerning certain effects that one or another climate has on the character of a people. Does this selectivity mark them as true or scientific geographers? Of course not. Yet it implies a method, and perhaps for a very good reason, to boot.

Ptolemy's geography fascinates them because it touches off a streak of curiosity in them: it offers a way of classifying the world into seven climate zones. In such classification, they concentrate on patterns of climate such as temperature, precipitation, and humidity. They also discuss climatic change, ranging from extreme heat to extreme cold. The fourth climate, for example, in which the Muslim world is situated, is characterized as moderate (in all the senses of the word). Suddenly, it seems, they recognize their own preference for such a climate. Later, Ibn Khaldūn would think it's the seat of culture.[189] Perhaps the thought, with hindsight, clinches that recognition, helping them to understand their own climate in more depth and detail. Perhaps they also feel lucky to find in a Greek source both that which teaches them what to think and that which they've always suspected but never tapped into. Now that they do, their jubilee is even greater when they see the contrast between their moderate climate and Western

---

[189] See *The Muqaddimah*, p. 54.

Europe's whose various countries are located in the fifth, sixth and seventh climates, ranging from cold to very cold to extreme cold.

80

Ibn Khurradadhbeh of mid-ninth century, whose interest in geography is inspired by the needs and informed by the files of the postal service of which he is a senior official,[190] introduces another interesting division into the discipline of geography, though neither he nor those who come after him follow up on it. In any case, he says that the earth is divided into four regions: 'Urufa' (Europe) comprising Andalusia, Byzantium, land of the 'Franj' (Franks), land of the Slavs, and the country from Tangier to the border of Egypt; Libia which includes Egypt, Abissinia, the Berbers; Ethiopia which contains Tahama, Yemen, land of Sind, India and China; finally Scythia with Armenia, Khurrasan, Turks, and Khazars as constituent parts. According to this classification, which originally derives from Greek sources, the European continent appears much clearer and more defined than others. Still, the concept of the seven climatic configurations dominates his world's picture.[191] We shall more occasions to review his work.

And of this concept, the fourth climate, again, where *Dar-al-Islam* is located, always gets the accolades from most geographers. However, at least in the case of one geographer, those accolades seem reinforced and enlarged by Abu Hanifa's binary division of the world. Al-Maqdissi (or perhaps al-Muqaddassi, first name Shams al-Dīn) of late tenth century prefaces his book with the following remarks, using the royal 'we': "We shall mention no other kingdom but that of *Dar al-Islam,* since it's the only one that concerns us in this work. In doing so, we won't, therefore, go to the trouble of describing those regions of *Dar al-Kufr* with which we're familiar. We, therefore, find it unprofitable to include them along with those of *Dar al-Islam.*"[192] But let's be cautious here. First, al-Maqdissi's statement doesn't become a jumping off point for later geographers.

---

[190] See Bernard Lewis, *The Muslim Discovery of Europe*, p. 138.

[191] Ibn Khurradadhbeh, *Kitāb al-Masālik wal- Mamālik*, ed. M.J. De Goeje (Leiden, 1883), pp. 155-156.

[192] See al-Maqdissi, *Ahsan al-Taqāsim fi Ma'rifat al-Aqālīm*, ed. De Goeje (Leiden, 1877), p. 15.

Secondly, Abu Hanīfa's concept, though at work in the text, should be carefully scrutinized as to its precise meaning.

Al-Maqdissi's remarks show a geographer holding up *Dar al-Islam* as a mirror to Arab-Muslims, first and foremost. A priority support opposing, I think, its construal as a sign of his limited knowledge of the world; on the contrary, his book is an encyclopedia of information and conceptions about Arab-Muslim world from which the West has been deliberately excluded.[193] The reason for this is that other geographers, as you saw, already have dealt with it, not that he hates it or deems it an enemy for being a part, as he puts it, of *Dar al-Kufr*. Besides, what he says hardly reflects the attitude of geographers preceding or coming after him. Actually, those preceding him, including historians, exert tremendous effort in gathering up information about global regions and countries, not just about those of *Dar al-Islam*. Yet within the scope of this knowledge, you can see its paucity compared with plenty of material on Arab-Muslim regions which are no longer framed in Abu Hanīfa's conceptual model. The ultimate conclusion to be drawn here is this: the concept of the binary division of the world is slowly disappearing from medieval scholarly concerns.

81

To return briefly to Ibn Khurradadhbeh, he may be the first half Arab-Muslim geographer to present a sort of rounded sketch of Europe. Though he himself never visits the continent, he obtains information in part from a certain Muslim Jarami (d. 845), onetime prisoner in Byzantium, and in part from government sources and archives. Jarami himself seems to have amassed a wealth of data about different peoples (Byzantines, Bergandians) and different countries (lands of the Slavs and Avars), all of which he passes on to Ibn Khurradadhbeh. The latter is also the principal source of knowledge of the Byzantine state. Most engaging are his reports on East-West trade relations, for example, between Arabia, East Africa, and China, containing such detailed and concrete descriptions that Arab-Muslim geographers as late as thirteenth century

---

[193] *Ibid*, pp. 7, 9-10, 19, 37, 138, 401, 408, 466; for further information see al-Khazen, *al-Hadāra al-'Abbāsiyya*, pp. 26, 35, 40-41, 67, 73-4, 81, 85, 89, 99, 126, 148-9, 156-7.

still use or elaborate on for their own purposes;[194] the same is true in the case of his colorful report on Slavs journeying over long distances to do business in Baghdad. He obtains this information from documents preserved in the archives of Baghdad. In doing so, he laces his encyclopedic book with an aura of historical objectivity.[195]

His most impressive contribution to Arab-Muslim knowledge of the world centers round the earth, its location, shape, circumference as well as its various climate zones. Its shape, he says in effect, is spherical, and it is lodged within the universe like the yolk inside the egg (what an image!). The breeze (atmosphere) surrounding it holds it in or draws it to space from all sides. And the bodies of living things on it are such that the breeze attracts to it whatever is light in them, while the earth's gravity pulls them down to its surface. This is because it is like the magnet that attracts iron to itself. Ibn Khurradadhbeh then presents what I consider his most interesting detail: the earth's circumference is 360 degrees; the degree is 25 leagues; the league is 12,000 cubits; the cubit is 24 fingers; and the finger is 6 barley grains set next to each other. He finishes by observing that humans are located in the earth's northern quadrant; the southern quadrant is almost lifeless due to severe heat, and each quadrant consists of seven climate zones, as Ptolemy says in his book.[196] You can easily surmise the importance of this information, also what has been added to it in later centuries, in the advancement of Western science in the late Middle Ages.

82

A few decades later, at the beginning of tenth century, Ibn Rusteh, another notable geographer, presents a lot of data whose source happens to be another prisoner named of Harūn Ben Yahya. Borrowing from this source, Ibn Rusteh, in his book *al-A'lāq al-Nafīsa*, details not only why, for instance, the people of Yemen prefer beef to mutton, but also presents extensive information about both

---

[194] See Ignatius Kratchovskii, *Tārikh al-Adab al-Jugrāphi al-'Arabi*, vol. I (Cairo: Lajnat al-Ta'lif wal-Tarjama, 1963), p. 135.

[195] See note 136 above.

[196] Ibn Khurradadhbeh, pp. 4-5.

Byzantium and Rome. Here he includes vivid descriptions of both the cathedral of St. Sophia and the great cathedral of Rome. In addition, he reports on the use of Arabian currency in Eastern Europe, particularly in Russia. And like Ibn Khurradadhbeh, from whom he might have derived information, he discusses the sphericity of the universe and that of the earth within it.[197]

Speaking of Western Europe, especially of Italy, he adds this rather interesting, perhaps intriguing detail: "From the city of Rome you sail for approximately three months before you reach the land of the king of Burgundy. From there you proceed through mountain and valleys for about a month till you end up in the land of 'Franj" (Franks). And if beyond that you travel for about fourth months, you eventually wind up in the city of Bartinia (Britain) which is a huge city situated on the cost of the western sea and which belongs to seven kings."[198] This interesting description wets the appetite of many later geographers and historians to explore Western Europe in more detail, to which they add the fruits of their own experiences and interpretations. Ibn Fadlan, for instance, in the wake of his embassy and travels in Russia and the land of the Slavs, Turks, and Khazars, paints a picture of Russia as a country steeped in decadence and barbarism. A picture that remains intact or unchanged until the end of the seventeenth century.[199]

83

I should like to pause here for a moment so as to dot the i's and cross the t's. I mean to sum up the foregoing paragraphs but also to look ahead with greater freedom from that bugaboo named prejudice, often shamelessly parading in the guise of a scientific character doling out knowledge about Arab-Muslims and Arab-Muslims view of the West and the world.

---

[197] Plagiarism is a respectable medieval Arab-Muslim tradition and practice. To this extent, it's not to be construed in modern terms. A writer at the time feels indebted to another without having to mention or acknowledge a name or source.

[198] Ibn Rusteh, *Kitāb al-A'laq al-Nafīsa*, ed. M.J. de Goeje (Leiden, 1892, pp. 119-130).

[199] Ibn Fadlān, *Risālat Ibn fadlān fi Wasf al-Rahla ila Bilād al-Turk wa-l al-Khazar wa-l Saqalibah wa-l Rūs* (Damascus, 1977), pp. 175-188.

As I sometime hinted at it, Arab-Muslims are no play-actors. That demands objectivity, reason, science to pull off. Which is the pride of the West, at least it likes to think so.[200] By contrast, Arab-Muslims are naïve, arrogant, but also endowed with goodness and integrity perhaps too subtle, not to say too natural, for the West to grasp. Above all, they meet the exigencies of life courageously, instinctively, which verges on the unconscious. For example, they're in Spain in the eighth century, face to face with the West: but they hardly register a threat or even evince the slightest trace of it. Or they're in regions quite distant from their home, those in northern France at the end of eleventh century. Such wars, or ditch battles as they're called at the time, certainly stir up the religious zealotry of Christians, but at no time do they produce rumblings of fear or danger in the corridors of Arab-Muslim world or mind.[201] Are Arab-Muslims insensitive or thick-skinned, you wonder?

84

Not at all. For their writings confirm the same natural, instinctive, simple disposition. The texts I cited (others in a moment) stand surety for this: you find nothing like a moral hyperbole about good and evil or picturesque effects relating to sin and damnation designed to influence your imagination. They say what they see instinctively, simply, unconsciously, almost like a child at play. They read cities, climates, topographies without interposing any prejudicial interpretation. This is because they encounter it as if for the first time, even though others before them have already written about it. What's more, nowhere in these texts do you discern in a word or voice expressions of relations of fear, threat, or danger. Nor any notions of hierarchy or of hubris, despite Arab-Muslim fantasy of moral

---

[200] On second thought, this is ironic. For no matter how much the West insists on the importance of facts, and of scientific facts at that, most people always reach decisions, pass judgments, or evaluate things based on their value systems, and the language and frames that invoke those values. The last presidential election proves the point. This is also true in the case of Arab-Muslims: their religious world, I called subjective fiction, ultimately makes them one with Westerners. In the final analysis, if both sides bring their little value systems to the table for discussion or sharing, things would probably fare better between them.

[201] Amīn Maalouf, *The Crusades Through Arab Eyes*. Here you find many anecdotes showing Arab-Muslim stamina and sure instinct that guide their resistance against the Franks.

sublimity. May I, then, say you better appreciate Arab-Muslims now that you see them in proper perspective?

Allow me to offer another perspective. Recall the binary division of the world into *Dar al-Islam* and *Dar al-Harb*. Certainly, Arab-Muslims perceive or treat peoples of the latter abode, and those (Arab unbelievers and non-Muslims) of the former as adversaries, perhaps even also as antagonists. But no word or deed shows they despise such antagonists or deem them hateful enemies. Is this trait endemic to Arab-Muslim ethos? Yes, it is. For example, historians and geographers come to form some unflattering opinion of, say, the 'Franj,' but it in no way implies hatred or enmity towards the latter. If it does, it would violate the ethic of equality or, if you like, that of respect for the enemy. Muhammad's statement about the enemy and Ibn Jubayr's remark about a Frankish bride are a case in point.[202] For Arab-Muslims really to view the other as a hateful enemy, Western (in this case Iberian) forces must become a reality to contend with, and this reality must pose imminent military danger to their existence. Neither condition materializes until the sixteenth century. That is, not until imperialism disguised as orientalism begins to manipulate its way into the Mid-East.

The upshot here is this: before the sixteenth century, I think Arab-Muslims evince a certain casual, care-free attitude about worlds other than their own. They ignore and have ignored the realities of European nations, particularly their sophisticated political apparatuses and military powers.[203] Could this be a state of false bliss, prompted by fantasies of moral superiority, and stemming from concepts like binary division of the world? I think so. But it's also psychologically rooted in what I'd call a state of mourning, a cumulative sense of defeat, failure, or emptiness that Westerners can't fully comprehend without actively listening to its voice behind language. All in all, superiority together with bankruptcy blinds Arab-Muslims to the real danger Western powers pose.

---

[202] See above page 91 and page 11 respectively.

[203] This explains why the Ottomans, for example, toward the end of the seventeenth century, begin to pay more heed to the West, in a serious effort to understand in particular the secret of its scientific and technological progress and to learn from it. But that's outside the purview of this work.

Truth to tell, it blinds them even today, though in a different way: culturally. Their incomprehension of Western complex history of science and epistemology not only distances them from the West; it alienates them from the West. They're then compelled either to seek refuge in religious fantasies, their staple in crisis, or, the fundamentalists among them, to commit atrocious acts.[204]

85

But many are the ways out of these deadly fantasies. Several of which I suggested before. Here's another, telepathized, as it were, by medieval savants to the ears of Arab-Muslims today. We teach practical lessons, they say. Action presupposes thought; to act well, you must think well. It's time you bethought yourself to reality—confronted the other's viewpoint, entered its frame of language, and began formation of self-hood by re-marking your difference. In short, it's time you saw yourself in the other's eye. Last but not least: give up all fascist tactics, for that impresses upon the world the feeling not to take you seriously. This is terrible. Not only it redounds to your discredit; worse, like a canker-worm, it blights your ability to shake off pessimism and insecurity which, in God's name, feed into more hatred of the other and yourself. Neither of which has any justifiable grounds in history.[205]

After this exhortation, a word about the ethic of *Jihad* would like to be heard. Like Muhammad, Arab-Muslims can convert anger and aggression into a *Jihad* against them. Which to reinforce, receives nourishment from *Ijtihad,* the

---

[204] Let me quickly add that Christian fundamentalism, leprous with sin since Adam's fall, encourages similar atrocities, though in non-physical, subtle ways: paradoxically or ironically, it supports Israel precisely by pulling the Old Testament from under the feet of the Jews with the assertion it contains nothing but Christian teaching and belongs to the Christians as the true people of Israel, the Jews being only usurpers. How, then, to get rid of the Jews? It's easy: by sacrifice. Its fantasy is to keep Israelis and Arabs apart and fighting, so that one day the former will vanish. This is how it sacrifices the Jews to atone for its sin. Question: have the Jews and Israel awakened to this fact? I wonder. My point is that if they have, they should hasten to make peace with Arab-Muslims right away before Christian fundamentalism, another form of orientalism, takes over Israel.

[205] The objection may be made here that the atrocities committed by orientalism-imperialism (including local autocrats as agents) constitute sufficient grounds for Arab-Muslims extremists to retaliate in like measure. My response is that, extremists or not, Arab-Muslim history contains many instances in which aggressive, belligerent, and angry feelings are converted into an ethic of Jihad as a means and tool of controlling them.

intellectual activity introduced in the eighth century. This etymological nexus— *Jihad-Ijtihad*—taps their potential for developing skill, technology, and diplomatic know-how as means to negotiating their political rights.[206] After all, what's needed today is this ethico-intellectual insight: convinced that the mind is a terrible thing to waste, both Muhammad and Abu Hanīfa, among others, set down a model for the value of enquiry, the ferment of doubt, the willingness to dialogue, the spirit of criticism, the moderation of judgment, the philological scruple, the sense of the complexity of things. In short, what both men fight for, what they uphold is the art of liberal discussion and personal initiative which, together with these pieces of insight, constitute the only and accessible native content of "democracy."

86

To resume my narrative, we now approach mid-tenth century to meet al-Mas'ūdi, a scholar of prodigious learning. His spirit and mind range far and wide across history, dipping into Greek and Syriac sources for knowledge of Greeks, Romans, and Byzantines. Then he wends his way into Europe, and Western Europe in particular. However, space here permits only a sliver or two concerning the latter. Though much of his writings derive from accounts of prior geographers and historians, his is by no means a copycat account. After all, there's nothing new under the sun, as the saying goes. Nonetheless al-Mas'ūdi's conscious attentiveness to small detail and control of material may earn him the worthy epithet of "scientific" investigator. In a word, not only he extends previous knowledge by shedding more light on the subject at hand; he elaborates on those accounts in the wake of his own extensive travels and sojourns throughout the world as well.

B. Lewis allots ample space to al-Mas'ūdi's work in his chapter on Muslim scholarship about the West. So I need not repeat the list he so atomistically piles up. One thing, however, he discounts either because he can't fit it into his mode of thought or because he deems it unimportant: namely al-Mas'ūdi's observations repeat Ibn Khurradadhbeh's. I think Lewis doesn't allow

---

[206] Muhammad Iqbal has been trying to do so precisely. See Boulares, p. 70.

for convention. You see, many medieval savants borrow or plagiarize information from each other; but none could off-handedly be said to make no contribution of his own. Now Lewis juxtaposes these two savants without underscoring each one's specific intellectual interest. Recall my saying of Arab-Muslim view of the West as being a plurality with one sense; that is, though the target remains the same, plurality concerns the different ways different individuals or societies view it. In other words, Arab-Muslims see and say the same object, the West, but not with same eyes and with the same language. Well, here we have a good example of that.

Ibn Khurradadhbah and al-Mas'ūdi, a century apart, see and say the same object: for them the world is portioned into four quadrants—North, South, East, and West. More specifically, for the former the West is a source of "eunuchs, slave girls and boys, brocade, beaver skins, glue, sables, and swords," no more, hardly more. Al-Mas'ūdi, however, sees the same West with different eyes and says what he sees in a different language. Being also a historian-geographer, he pays more heed to the variety climatic temperatures and qualities, with particular emphasis on their influences on body physiology as well as on formation of character traits, both of which he often describes simultaneously.

These influences occupy central position in his work. Not only does he describe Europeans, especially those inhabiting the North, as "dull in mind and heavy in speech, stupid, gross, and brutish" (certainly not a flattering description); he also explains the causes of this climatic influence without interposing moral or religious interpretations on it. The North, he says in effect, is the region known for its severe cold and high humidity because of its extreme distance from the sun. Constant snow and frost and rarity of heat take their toll on people's bodies and souls. Internally, the body, he says, inspissates and disposition desiccates, also discernment oscillates and manner coarsens, while behavior ruffles and language thickens. Externally, the complexion whitens so that it verges on pale blue, the skin becomes soft, the flesh dense, and the eyes blue as to match the skin color, while the hair bulks and becomes blond or reddish due to excessive moisture. He finishes by asserting that such inclement climate not only produces these spiritual and physiological effects, but they affect people's belief or value system in such a way that they grow lacking in firmness and stability.[207]

87

Once again, these observations come close to being scientific in perception and quality: al-Mas'udi offers them for his readers' benefit, without superimposing value judgment on them. Curious for details, he gathers them up with no intent to defame, praise, pigeonhole, love, or hate. That's why he receives the accolade of being a careful historian and observer from none other than Ibn Khaldūn himself.[208] If the latter knows of Ibn Khurradadhbeh's work, he would bestow a similar accolade upon him as well—think, for example, of his description of the earth and universe mentioned earlier. Each savant, then, grasps certain features of the West's topography and climates with no thought of bias for or against. But from curiosity for knowledge both historian-geographers share the same concern: to press into service information about the world and Western Europe for the education of Arab-Muslim public.

To sum up, all texts cited so far frame the truth in different ways: different words, different discourse, different eyes. All of which, though, amount to producing as much knowledge about the world as is possible for the edification of Arab-Muslim public. So when Lewis says with one breath that though Arab-Muslims know so much about the West, "we still cannot be but astonished at how little in fact they did know, even more at how little they cared," I find the remark quite amusing, as I do this one: "it is all the more remarkable that, despite the long confrontation of Islam and Christendom, there should have been such a complete lack of interest and curiosity among Muslim scholars about what went on beyond the Muslim frontiers in Europe."[209] Frankly, I'm quite unsure why he is "astonished..." or why he finds it "remarkable...." I do know, however, that Lewis depreciates what Arab-Muslim ethos is all about as much as he

---

[207] See al-Mas'udi, *al-Tanbih wal- Ishraf* (Dar Maktabat al-Hilal: Beirut, 1981), p. 47.

[208] Al-Muqaddimah, p. 29.

[209] *The Muslim Discovery of Europe*, pp. 139-42.

misunderstands the primary purpose these savants and the public interest they represent have in geography and history. I believe the reason is obvious. Lewis not only ignores Ibn Khurradadhbah's almost lyrical text on the earth's sphericity and circumference; he also disregards al-Ms'ūdi's description of both the world's four quadrants and the seven climatic zones.[210]

88

These omissions in themselves may be trifles, but they're symptomatic of larger omissions. Lewis never asks why Arab-Muslims, at least the majority, choose to inhabit the fantasy concept of *Dar al-Islam*. And to do so since the eighth century. He also never asks whether the medieval savants' work blazes the trail for Arab-Muslim community to dare to explore the world, in all the senses of the word. I'm really surprised at that, given his extensive scholarship. At any rate, I use Lewis as an example of a scholarship that can comprehend only what can be made calculable and constant just to lay a pre-judgment on it. No wonder he, and others like him (Maalouf, Ajami) are a product of Western epistemology of the orientalist type. Hence their lack of fine fingers for grasping the inner reality of Arab-Muslim ethos. However, their ability to write on East-West relations with an axe to grind needs no vouching for: it's quite impressive on the surface. But it's also a sort of what I'd call strategic initiative: describing an image or advancing an idea (Arab-Muslims lack interest, they don't welcome new ideas) that, being easy to repeat as powerful slogans are, automatically displaces other images and ideas of authentic mettle.

Arab-Muslims confine themselves within *Dar al-Islam* out of pride; they also follow their fateful fantasies which compel them to make this choice. For example, reflecting on Muhammad's wish to extend Islam to Christians, Jews, and Byzantines, they wrongly construe the gesture as an either/or affair; in other words, they manage to convince themselves and so create the impression that

---

[210] I understand and appreciate the selectivity all scholars have to exercise when considering a large volume of material. Even so, such selectivity shouldn't obscure the fact that they owe it to their common sense, decency, and integrity to look at the issues from as many sides as possible.

Islam shall somehow lord it over all other religions lock, stock, and barrel.[211] There's a name for this way of thinking: hypocognition: since their first conquests laced-up with concomitant divine presence, Islam becomes a transcendental experience of power, not just a brainchild. By the same token, they interpret Muhammad's exhortation to seek knowledge as something permitted only by *Sharī'a,* in so far as it reinforces performance of religious duties. That's why they reject even astronomy. A science which easily integrates in religious ritual and daily life, say, in determining times of prayer or direction of *Qiblah,* and so on, is unacceptable because it's foreign; it derives from the Greeks who are chock-full of godlessness.[212] If anything, this hyper-moralism mixed in with hypocognition indicates that Arab-Muslims feel threatened, lost, or rootless the moment they turn away from Allah and Islam.

What kind of threat? Well, that of alienation or perhaps extinction. Consider this: The Abbasid dynasty, claiming to be the true defender of Islam, ousts the Umayyad dynasty in 750 A.D. precisely for its unIslamic behavior and impiety. Well and good. Half a century later, however, this dynasty opens the gates to Greek philosophy only to slam them again, declaring it to be adverse to the spirit and principles of religion.

What has happened? Perhaps the Abbasids, initially, have no knowledge of the actual content of that philosophy. But when translators and commentators disseminate its ideas, the Abbasids excise it from the collective body for fear of alienating the latter and themselves from Islam. The act, obviously, reveals yet another facet of Arab-Muslim ethos, namely self-preservation, which an anecdote I mentioned earlier seems to confirm. The tenth-century al-Tabarī reports how Caliph Harūn al-Rashīd rebukes his jester for joking while at prayer, "Beware of the Qur'ān and Islam," he says. "Apart from that, you may do and say whatever

---

[211] Quite frankly, Americans understand well Muhammad's gesture, for they too, at least whoever is in power at the White House, would like to see their values and policies promoted and extended to the rest of world. See also note 172 below.

[212] See Abdul Rahman Badawi, p. 123; also p. 145.

you wish."[213] Though this anecdote may be a fiction, it nevertheless betrays an anguished dilemma: could Greek learning coexist with Islam? Yes, but only if it's filtered through *Sharī'a*. Why? Not because, says Ibn Qutayba, Greek philosophy contradicts *Sharī'a* or leads to apostasy; rather, because it's foreign to the more useful Qur'anic learning whose aim is man's deliverance from evil.[214] No wonder that Arab-Muslim philosophers who think in terms of strategic initiative feel not welcomed. [215]

89

Lewis, and other scholars, rarely hits the nail on the head when it comes to the complexity of Arab-Muslim ethos. He also misjudges the value of binary division of the world for Arab-Muslims in general when he makes it out to be a matter of war and peace. For them, you see, to think binary is to think noumenally, first and foremost, a sort of theoretical state of mind, if you like, not a phenomenal one, in a word, not a reality. It's similar to Kant's concept of the thing-in-itself. The plinth supporting this noumenon is instinctive self-interest, pure and simple. Yet it has an ethico-religious function, similar in another sense to that of pre-church Christian moralim of benevolence and decency of disposition. For Arab-Muslims it works through Greater *Jihad,* the struggle never to cease to become what they are—good, decent Arab-Muslims until benevolence and decency prevails in the whole universe. To this extent, binary thought has a

---

[213] See Muhammad Ibn Jarir al-Tabarī,,*Tārikh al-Tabari*, vol 8 (Cairo: Dar al-Maarif fi Masr, 1966-69), p. 349. The jester utters the joke while the Caliph prays: "How is it that I shouldn't worship Allah who created me"? And the jester answers: "Yes, I don't know why." This is the same anecdote I quoted above page 91. In that context it serves a different purpose than it does here.

[214] See William el-Khazen, p. 115.

[215] John Bowker's book *What Muslims Believe* portrays Islam at a cross road today: the *Sharī'a* is still the way to go in all endeavors of life; but even then certain ideas, feelings, concepts require change to bring the faith up within the frame of the current world. Most of Muslims (though not Arab-Muslims) who speak in the book are advocates of this necessary need for change.

double aim: to find stability in a troubled and troubling world;[216] to assimilate this world to Islam without coercion; if not, at least to utilize what's good in it.

Unless I'm wrong, medieval savants, though not explicitly saying so, have this aim in mind. But somewhat transposed to a different key. Surely, they sing the hymn of the fatherland, but at the same time show by example that humans, Arab-Muslims included, need the local as much as the universal, a sense of belonging as much as the experience of mobility. To put it in another way, the majority of Arab-Muslims, these savants intimate, dwell in a closed, self-regarding, perhaps also morally smug mode of life as a means of protecting themselves from the troubled and troubling world. That, of course, gives them the sense of being of their own kind, unique, or peculiar just as any other people in the world who live in a similar fantasy. But this isn't a choice they've willingly made. Rather, it's been formed in the heads of those around them (Sunni leaders) and has been communicated to them.[217] As a consequence, they all dwell in a fantasy of impersonal, semi-personal opinions and evaluations. What medieval savants attempt to do indirectly is to break through that fantasy by setting themselves up as models of daring and intellectual curiosity grounded in the world as it is.[218]

The upshot here is this: medieval savants, if I read them correctly, and later modern cultural theorists in their own more articulate style—these savants really want all Arab-Muslims to know that the fantasy world in which they've

---

[216] You can imagine the troubled and troubling world of that period. Arab-Muslim world witnesses two dynasties whose existence is threatened by hostile forces from all sides almost every day of their long rules. Today they still feel threatened.

[217] I discuss this matter in more detail concerning myself and my relation to East-West relations in Part Two of "Instead of an Introduction." By sheer coincidence or by fate, it seems medieval savants and after them modern cultural theorists and I are two peas in the pod.

[218] I think most Americans, if I may restrict my reference to them, can appreciate Arab-Muslim choice. After all, they, too, live by, celebrate, and even vote their identity—I mean on the basis of who they are, what values they have, and who and what they admire, not to speak of their ethnicity, their values, their cultural stereotypes, and cultural heroes. They are also the people who live by metaphors, not as something they think about, but as a way of structuring their understanding of the enormous hard-to-conceptualize nation. It's something they do automatically, usually without consciously thinking about it. In short, like Arab-Muslims, Americans behave and think hypocognitively, though they're slowly awakening from it.

lived long, along with concomitant habits and opinions, has actually grown independently of them. That means they aren't the authors of that fantasy or those opinions and habits, but rather the moral disposition that has been imposed on them. Such recognition will in time raise their consciousness to a struggle going on inwardly between adherence to this morality and desire to be free of it. Should that happens, there's no need to take sides: morality or freedom. Arab-Muslims can be the noble, decent, God-fearing believers they are, but also egoists. For the latter they've done nothing so far. Now they're going to let reason take as clear and cold view of things as possible. And to do so without worrying if their act of reason poses danger to authoritative morality or diminishes its power and influence if they themselves gain power and influence. After all, they've lived too long under the canopy of this morality. Now it's time to set up next to it a real ego, accessible to them and fathomed by them.

90

Following al-Mas'ūdi in the same century, Ibn Hawqal and al-Istakhrī hardly add anything substantially new.[219] However, al-Maqdissī, whom we met a few paragraphs earlier, whose book (translated *The Best of Divisions*, recalling binary division and reflecting his attitude), deliberately refuses to mention any other climate except the fourth in which Arab-Muslim world is situated. If anything, this is a classic example of the dilemma typifying Arab-Muslim position with respect to foreign learning: do we want it or not, they ask? The answer is both yes and no, which is different from Ibn Qutaybah's categorical decision in favor of the latter.[220] The way out of this dilemma is to forge ahead as at once Muslims and believers. And that's what al-Bayrūni, a devout, curious Arab-Muslim, does at the beginning of the eleventh century. He takes more to the East, India in particular, than to the West. Even so, he can't resist including some interesting details about the location and climate of the Baltic Sea and North Sea as well as about the inhabitants of northern Europe, especially the Normans and

---

[219] See Ibn Hawqal, *Kitāb Surat al-Ard*, ed. J.H. Kraemer (Leiden, 1938); see also al-Istakhri, Abu Qasim Ibrahim, *Masālik al-Mamālik* (Leiden, 1873).

[220] See above note 215.

Scandinavians. Finally he reports his fascination with a detail concerning the far northern regions where the sun never sets in summer.[221]

In Arab-Muslim Spain, some geographers develop further received information of Europe, without altering its basic lineaments. Abu 'Ubayd al-Bakrī presents data deriving from the personal reports of Ibrahim Ibn Ya'qūb al-Isra'īli, an Andalusian merchant, who reports his observations of European cities and countries (Bohemia, Ireland, the city of Prague, Frankland) he himself visits in the later part of the tenth century. Of specific interest are his travels in southern Germany where he meets with the emperor Otto; he also describes Bulgaria, today's Poland, and Czechoslovakia, and gives detailed and concrete descriptions of costal cities in France, Holland, and Germany. Likewise al-Bakrī, following Ibn Ya'qūb, gives the account of the Slav peoples in Poland, Czechoslovakia, and East Germany, which is an important source of the early history of these countries.[222] Arab-Muslims, you see, continue insatiably to learn more about the world.

91

Among the twelfth-century Arab-Muslim geographer-historians pride of place goes perhaps to al-Idrīsī. He represents the high water mark of knowledge of both Europe and the world. Long story short, of this knowledge the larger portion derives from personal observations and extensive travels, though here and there he includes bits of information from Arab-Muslim merchants, Jews, and Europeans (Ptolemy and the Iberian historian Orosius). It also contains a plethora of data on Italy where he eventually settles in Palermo, no less than detailed descriptions of most of Western Europe: England, France, Germany, Scotland, North Sea cost, including Romania and the Balkans. In a word, this mass of knowledge outstrips the bulk of accounts of most other travelers in Europe who precede him.[223] As for the Persian al-Qazwīnī of late thirteenth century, who

---

[221] See Kratchovskii, p. 240.

[222] See al-Bakri, *Jughrafiya al-Andalus wa-Urûba*, ed. A.A. el-Hajj (Beirut, 1968).

[223] See Cratchovskii, vol. 1, pp. 279-285.

depends for his knowledge on Arab-Muslim information, B. Lewis devotes to him at least three pages in his book.[224] The same is truer for Ibrahīm Ibn Ya'qūb to whom Lewis also devotes several pages. Therefore, both geographers don't belong in my study here. Nor do such geographers as al-Gharnātī, Ibn Saīd, and others, since Carole Hillenbrand deals with them, among others, in her book.[225]

In the same century we encounter the Arab-Muslim Syrian Usāma ibn Munqidh and Ibn Jubayr, a native of Valencia, Spain, and whom we met early on in A. Maalouf's book.[226] Both live through the Crusades era and report about their closer relations with the Franks.

92

B. Lewis, of course, includes the former among his catalogue of Muslim discoverers of Europe. He reports an interesting detail but fails to evaluate its import properly. Apparently, Ibn Munqidh and a Frankish knight establish a sort of "bonds of amity and friendship between them." One day, about to leave Syria, the knight suggests that Ibn Munqidh's son should accompany him to his own country "to live among the knights and learn wisdom and chivalry." Now the knight's is surely a gesture of good will. But it doesn't occur to Lewis that for Ibn Munqidh the knight can't be more than a pied piper and basher of what may be called Arab-Muslim framing—the values and the language that invokes those values. He belittles those values precisely by getting, or better, by forcing them to fit his worldview. That's why Usāma is struck speechless, but silently thinks the knight is monstrously absurd, if not off his rocker. Usāma then fabricates a story to the effect that the boy's grandmother loves him and won't let him out of her sight. "Is your grandmother still living?" "Yes." And he said: "Then do not disobey her."[227]

---

[224] See Lewis, p. 187; also 147-48.

[225] See above note 27.

[226] See above pages 9-10.

[227] See B. Lewis, p. 92.

Ibn Jubayr, who writes on European lack of personal hygiene compared with Arab-Muslim higher standards, also reports the troubling situation of Muslim peasants under Arab-Muslim rule compared with the humane treatment they receive at the hands of Frankish masters. He himself is troubled by the difference: "the way they are treated is the reverse of the kindliness and forebearance of their Frankish masters." He's even more perturbed by the fact that it's one of the misfortunes befalling the Muslims "that the Islamic common people complain of the oppression of their own rulers, and praise the conduct of their opponents, the Franks, who have conquered them and who tamed them with their justice." He finishes by urging them to complain instead to God about these things because, and he quotes the Qur'ān, God "leads into error whom he pleases, and guides whom he pleases into the right path." At this point Lewis's ready with his usual dismissive comment: this is another instance of Arab-Muslim "lack on interest" as well as "horror of venturing among infidels."[228] He says this without batting an eyelid as to any doubt he might have.

Anyhow, for me these two portraits or stories illustrate the two points I've been trying to make here. First, no two savants ever see and say the same thing about the West; or rather they do, but not with same eyes and the same language. Secondly, like Maalouf, Lewis barely discerns these portraits' import for today's Arab-Muslims. Ibn Jubayr criticizes oppressive Arab-Muslim rulers, not because he finds the Franks more humane or just, but because he's ashamed that the former, instead of acting as models of ethical conduct to be emulated, behave in an unethical manner toward the people. On the other hand, through such criticism he underscores, perhaps unwittingly, the significance of "democratic" confrontation. As if he thinks, to say it with Foucault, that democracy begins with the common people talking to, informing, and confronting their masters.[229] A fact which I think he points to (covers up?) by citing the Qur'ān.

---

[228] Ibid., p. 98.

[229] See M Faoucault, *Power: Essential Works of Michel Foucault: 1954-1984*, Volume Three, ed. James D. Faubion (New York: The New Press, 1994), pp. 32-35.

But neither Lewis nor Maalouf in particular, who accuses Arabs of close-mindedness, picks up on it. You know why? Well, because both writers get sidetracked by their own penchant for dismissive formulas. After all, it's the degree of oppression that Ibn Jubayr fulminates against, not his preference for Frankish or Western ideas. Ibn Munqidh, of course, makes a similar point from a different perspective: if he criticizes the Frankish knight's presumptuous attitude, it's because he respects Arab-Muslim framing (beliefs and moral values), and wants Arab-Muslims (rulers or not) to observe and uphold the same. In a word, both savants, though without having read or known of Plato, nonetheless, think within a Platonic-like perspective: their portraits present the West, the other, as indeed the eye-mirror in which Arab-Muslims may contemplate their soul and recognize their ethical element.

93

As I mentioned a moment ago, thirteenth-century savants are mostly Persian and Turkish whom Lewis discusses quite generously. By the same token, Maalouf and Hillenbrand present the works of Arab-Muslim savants of the Crusades period. So it would be redundant of me here to repeat in brief what could redound with greater profitable by reading the entire works.

Now we approach the fourteenth century and meet the outstanding savant Abu-l Fida, a scion of the Ayyūbi dynasty. He's both historian and geographer, also a witness of the last years of the Crusades in the Mid-East.[230] As historian, he offers disparate data on European kings; but as geographer, he's a genius for systematizing all information he can lay hands on in previous sources, lacing it, now and then, with political and economic details that are quite refreshing and relatively new. For instance, he notes, as a peculiarity of England, that because of all-year round rain people grow their crops by it. More than that, they have mines of gold and silver and copper and tin. The island has no vineyards because of the severe cold. People transport the metals to the land of France and trade them for wine. Hence the ruler of France owns much gold and silver. There, too, they

---

[230] See Amīn Maalouf, pp. 254-59.

make *ishkarlat* (a particular fine quality of cloth) from sheep's wool as soft as silk. They cover their sheep with cloths to protect them from rain, sun, and dust.[231] In addition, he presents information on Mediterranean islands, Italy, France, England and Ireland, which he elaborates on extensively, noting their rivers and their trade, and distribution of population. In short, Abu-l Fida's work, to say it again, reflects Arab-Muslim increasing interest in what transpires beyond the confines of *Dar al-Islam*.

94

Such an interest is further manifest in Ibn Fadl al-ʿAmrī, a contemporary of Abu-l Fida and a first-rate classifier of data. In his encyclopedic work he classifies almost every bit of data penned by previous compilers, particularly those of Abu-l Fida and al-Idrīsī. But he also includes new information whose source is a citizen of Genoa, Labān al-Janawī, a one-time prisoner in Egypt. This fellow appears, at least in al-ʿAmrī's eyes, to be a mine of knowledge, and so al-ʿAmrī develops a pretty good idea regarding several European countries and peoples. For example, he gathers up bits of political low-down about France, observing perhaps with special interest to him, that the principal political role in Europe at the time seems to be arrogated by France, and that the king of Spain is no more than a deputy of the king of France. If anything, this observation indicates that Arab-Muslims seem to be gradually awakening to what transpires or has transpired politically in Europe.[232] Ottoman-Muslims will be similarly awakened to the same beginning in the sixteenth century. In any case, he also reports that the Germans are stronger than all other Europeans nations on land only. And he doesn't forget to include data on Provencal, Lombardia, Cicily, Venice, Pisa, Florence and Caltalina.[233]

---

[231] See Abu-l Fida, *Taqwīm al-Buldān*, ed. J.S. Reinaud and M. de Slane (Paris, 1840), pp. 187-88.

[232] See Khaled Ziyada, *Iktishaf al-Taqadum al-Oropi: Dirasa fi-l Muʾtharat al-Oropiyya ʿala al-"Othmaniyyin fi-l Qarn al-Thamin* ʿAshar (Beirut, 1981). Possible translation of this book: "The Discovery of European Progress: a Study in European Influences on Ottomans in the Eighteenth Century."

[233] See Kratchovskii, vol. 1, pp. 412-20.

Abu 'Abbās al-Qalqashandī, who survives into the fifteenth century, is another Arab-Muslim luminary. Like al-'Amrī, he composes his work of encyclopedic dimensions deriving, among others, from earlier accounts of Ibn Saīd, al-Idrīsī, and Abu-l Fida. In that sense he's equally a great synthesizer of information. But he also adds a lot of data pertaining to the kingdoms of Portugal and Barcelona, Cyprus, Rhodes, Crete and other islands of the Mediterranean. About England in particular, his work gives you the impression of his being a link in a long chain going back to Ibn Khurradathbeh of mid-ninth century. He reports with some fascination about Byzantine kings who usually dwell in the southern and northern parts of Constantinople. Interestingly enough, he observes that the German kingdom is the largest Christian nation. With respect to Rome, he repeats almost verbatim the anecdote Ibn Khurradadhbeh records six centuries earlier. Finally, he mentions the countries of Bulgaria, Serbia, and Czekoslovakia which are so severely cold that snow lasts more than six months and which have very little of impressive buildings.[234]

95

Ibn Khaldūn is a contemporary of al-Qashqandī. He, too, adopts and adapts the theory of the seven climates for his own interests and purposes—for example, the influence of a particular climate on the development of human character, or that of the quality of air upon human complexion and physiology of the body in general. But he feels no need to elaborate further as such climatic influences have been discussed by al-Idrīsī, al-Bakrī, al-Mas'ūdī as well as Orosius before him. Writers for whose keen observation and insight he has utmost respect. The only distinctive body of information he presents is the genesis of science among Greeks and Persians and other peoples of antiquity, including its development under Arab-Muslims and its spread westward across North Africa into Spain.

There's a curious little remark he appends to the end of his review: "But God knows best what goes on in those parts (West)," and then finishes by quoting

---

[234] See Abu 'Abbas Ahmad al-Qalqshandi, *Subh al-a'sha fi Sina'at al-Insha'* (Cairo, 1913ff), 5, pp. 403-418.

from the Qur'ān: 'God creates what He wishes and chooses.' As you saw earlier, he, like Ibn Jubayr, quotes a Qur'anic verse as a cover-up. For what? Let's first hear what B. Lewis has to say. He reads this little curiosity as follows: "even something as extraordinary as the birth of learning among the Franks is not beyond the scope of God's omnipotence."[235]

Well and good. But as usual, Lewis disregards or discounts what's pertinent. Now the passage just preceding Ibn Khalūn's remark reads, among Arab-Muslims "the sciences decreased with the decrease of civilization. As a consequence, scientific activity disappeared."[236] If you juxtapose this statement with the Qur'anic verse, Mightn't he be saying this, though without saying it: since Arab-Muslim scientists have already "assiduously studied the Greek sciences...and enjoyed especial fame and prestige," and since medieval historians and geographers have shown great appetite for knowledge of the world, Arab-Muslims should have allowed all sciences to prosper? As it is, "the intellectual sciences," he concludes, "succeeded to some degree in penetrating Islam. They seduced many people who were eager to study those sciences and accept the opinions expressed in them. In this respect, the sin falls upon the person who commits it."[237] If I read all this correctly, Ibn Khaldūn, if he's alive today, would have advised Arab-Muslims: let's develop our potential and the sciences, and be as strong as the West; but let's be ethical, above all. We've got the makings of it all in our community's historical backyard.[238]

---

[235] Lewis, p. 149.

[236] *The Muqaddimah*, p. 375.

[237] *The Muqaddimah*, p. 374.

[238] I think Ibn Khaldūn, hearing the rumblings of Europe's military machinery, is quite aware of the dire necessity for Arab-Muslims to be both materially and spiritually as strong as Westerners are. If I read his text correctly, the reason has to do with international balance of power or simply power-relations among nations. You see, when a strong nation views or realizes another as weak, it might interfere to raise the latter to its level, and make it its equal in order to do business with it; but if it can't do that, because the latter's power is deeply shaken and broken, then it begins to hold certain rights over it and, worse, denies its rights. Indeed, where rights prevail, a condition and degree of power is being maintained; and should the weak nation's power continue to decrease, it certainly opens itself up for domination. In short, when nations are balanced as far as power is concerned, then no nation would dare to lord it over another. Ibn Khaldūn's foresight is quite amazing, to say the least. It deserves just a whole study by itself.

After Ibn Khaldūn, Ibn Iyās of the sixteenth century utilizes and exploits much previous knowledge in order to present in depth and systematically his views of Russians and Bulgarians. About Europeans, however, he seems less enthused, and so relies for his information on the twelfth-century historian Abu Hāmid al-Gharnātī. Most interesting in this connection, which may reveal his lack of enthusiasm, is the detail concerning the Atlantic Ocean: no one, he says, has as yet dared to sail it or across it, despite the fact that the Spanish navy has already crossed it and made the discovery of the new continent. Well, America has already been discovered. In any event, by the end of the sixteenth century, then through the seventeenth, and even into the eighteenth, you find geographers and historians alike repeating, with slight augmentation, former information about the seven climates and earth's divisions. Of which Ahmnad Sādiq al-Isphahānī who dies in 1680 still speaks with a lot of interest, although, unlike Ibn Iyās, he knows about the discovery of America. On the other hand, like al-Qashqandī, he forms a link in a chain of information deriving from Abu-l Fida two centuries earlier. In Arab-Muslim Spain, finally, Qāsim al-Ziyyāni (1734-1833) hardly advances anything new, but mainly repeats the theory of the seven climates, to which he adds the map that al-Idrīsī includes in his geography, and so on.[239] In sum, the main interest in those centuries, you see, centers on fascination with the earth's climates and topography.

97

The foregoing exposition draws up, I hope, a relatively clear, though not a complete, picture of Arab-Muslim traditional view of the West. I mean it still lacks the lineament of politics. In point of fact, it hardly involves data connected to the political and military situations of the various countries comprising it, especially those of Western Europe. Does this lack follow from a decision or purpose to emphasize certain points and not? But then I think the word decision or purpose is inappropriate here. After all, every time anything is said or done

---

[239] This information is condensed from Kratchovskii, vol 2, pp. 492-541.

with a purpose in view, something fundamentally different and other occurs. Consequently, it would be irrelevant to speak of purpose when something else like ethos assumes greater role in life.

The non-political picture itself, as you saw, acquires its proper lineaments between ninth and fourteenth centuries. A bevy of geographers, historians, historian-geographers, explorers, and travelers in a long series of changing views converge spatially in a text that seems to be aimed at a single target: to seek knowledge of Arab-Muslim world first of all, its climate, topography, faith and ethical stance. In a word, it's the Platonic idea of the other in whose eye-mirror they wish to contemplate themselves in order to increase their selective and self-nourishing forces. Something they wholeheartedly wish all Arab-Muslims pursue as well.

You could, therefore, say this bevy of savants hold the eye-mirror up to Arab-Muslim nature so as to sees itself and its world (its physical, ethical, and religious ideals) from another perspective—and pay homage to it. But then it may happen that the other may well shift the angle of the mirror wherein our savants seek their image, in which case the mirror reflects unexpected, albeit unpleasant likenesses of themselves. That, too, is in the nature of things. For example, some savants aren't all perfect stylists or flawless synthesizers of information; others contradict themselves.[240] Or, finally, Arab-Muslim nature may appear in this angle of mirror as somewhat too fanatic about faith and all the rest of it. Nevertheless, our savants' interest in geography and history goes hand in hand with their desire and will to know, to discover, to explore. Qualities they inherit, no doubt, from the first half of ninth century's intellectual ebullition (*Ijtihad, Qiyas, Ijma'*), which, as you recall, symbolizes personal initiative and inventiveness. Even if they have no direct knowledge of this period's intellectual

---

[240] For example, at one point al-Mas'ūdi reports that the Franks are courageous and strong and that they and all other (Christian?) peoples are united in their fight against Arab-Muslims in Spain (which is the case historically); yet, at another point, when speaking of climate, he adopts an opposite view, namely these peoples are ignorant and barbaric. On second thought, this is no contradiction at all if you realize that the qualities of courage and strength can also include those of barbarism and ignorance: it all depends on the circumstance at hand and the construing point of view of those qualities attending upon it.

activity in all its aspects, they nevertheless breathe the same air of curiosity and initiative.

So the second half of ninth century opens wide its gates to let Greek sciences and philosophy flow into its midst.[241] Soon enough, certain thirsty Arab-Muslims who also possess the making of scientists come to imbibe its goodness and to spread it around. They even attempt to reconcile philosophy with Arab-Muslim faith.[242] But then jealous orthodoxy, and that's the unfortunate thing, fears the outcome; and so it instantly clamps down on them all—mind, spirit, philosophy, logic, initiative, inventiveness, everything. You could say it short-changes Arab-Muslims of their right to think. Finally, the gates close shut while and Arab-Muslim spiritual world, after a century of brilliance, plunges into tenebrous dungeons. Social and political conditions follow—the kind that leads to despair that's still with the Mid-East today.

98

All isn't lost, however. The proof is our savants. You see, they may have deferred to the disdainful mode or mood in which orthodoxy stamps Arab-Muslim world—as one stronger, purer in faith, more theologically sound than any other near or far. They certainly reverently subscribe to this hubristic world. At the same time, though, they try to work from within it. In other words, inwardly they refuse to submit to mental coercion, or they don't see why they have to submit to it lock, stock, and barrel. At that, they begin to seek avenues of self-expression without undermining orthodoxy's position. In a word, they work with orthodoxy without opposing its will. Well, if no more Greek sciences and philosophy, they seem to think, then let it be geography, at least, and a Greek one at that, something the orthodox community might be willing to accept. Which apparently it does since it makes no effort to stifle it.

And so Ptolemy's Geography assumes the significant role it has for nearly all Arab-Muslim savants. At least, this branch of Greek learning keeps open a small aperture: I mean the whole interplay of geography, history, explorers' and

---

[241] In addition to Badawi's book, see F.E. Peters as well.

[242] *Ibid.*

travelers' accounts appears as a beam of light through the gloom that settles upon the Arab-Muslim world as a whole. Even in its narrow luminance in darkness, it promises continuity of individual initiative and inventiveness, and, as an additive, sheer joy, almost child-like, in encountering the world. In point of fact, the repetition of some of the same information reported by one geographer or historian after another is symptomatic of this joy. It also becomes a way of insisting, politically and socially, albeit at the level of being child-like, that Arab-Muslims, like it or not, can't do without the world. They're a part of it, pure and simple. An undeniable earthly truth that should strike a sensitive chord, perhaps even also incite today's Arab-Muslims to further initiatives and inventive turns.

At least one encouraging truth inheres in this question: what do Arab-Muslim historians and geographers see in Europe? Or perhaps a better question would be this: granted they don't, as you just learned, report about political and military situations, why is it that they don't record much information about Europeans, say, their ways of living, thinking, doing things, or, as a continental peoples, of having a common characteristic, but limit their writing to analyses and descriptions of climate and its effects on behavior and physiology of the body? The answer is simple: because a common characteristic is still in process of crystallization at the time, and also because European consciousness won't distinguish itself as such until the seventeenth century. (Of course, our savants wouldn't have known that.) And when it does, Europeans, who formerly lag at least six centuries behind Arab-Muslims in the sciences and philosophy, now outstrip them. More than that, they get to be in the first stage of developing science and technology that would be the glory of their civilization and the edged weapon of their imperialistic expansion. But that's another story.[243]

99

What's important here is the fact that Europe or Western Europe, at least from fifth to twelfth or thirteenth centuries, isn't yet a united world, but rather a divided world: a Roman-Byzantine world and a multi-Viking turbulent world.

---

[243] See Alfred W. Cosby, *The Measure of Reality: Quantification and Western Society: 1250-1600* (Cambridge: Cambridge University Press, 1997).

Consequently, most Arab-Muslim savants who are contemporary with this world can't identify or observe a common characteristic. Then you may ask, why European consciousness dawdles behind a bit? The answer, to cut corners, should explain why Arab-Muslims, from their ethico-cultural frame, have hard time recognizing it. So when a tenth-century Arab-Muslim geographer or historian speaks of Byzantines and of northern barbarians, his information, or at least a portion of it, derives from Europeans sources that also speak of a divided world. While the stories he hears from the mouths of merchants, travelers, and prisoners about the decline and barbarism of those northern peoples, confirm the accumulated lore gathered from Byzantine sources.

Needless to say, the idea that these peoples are barbaric, belligerent, also steeped in ignorance isn't a fabrication of the Arab-Muslim imagination. If anything, Arab-Muslim imagination, its ethico-cultural frame of reference, is already saturated with thoughts of equality and justice for all peoples of the earth.[244] And this is exactly what in his mind precedes any thought of distinguishing all people into one distinct ethnic type or another, something which he otherwise obtains from those Byzantine and Greek sources. What's more, whether this redounds upon his naiveté, he endows barbarism itself with a religious and cultural signification than he does with a racial one. This is the very frame from which he, as symbol of all Arab-Muslims, sees the world.

In any event, an Arab-Muslim historian or geographer or explorer comes to view Europe and its peoples not as a unit but differentially. The Byzantines differ from the Slavs, and the latter from the Romans, and from the Franks, and so on. It's actually something imposed upon or communicated to him historically, that is, a child of habit and discipline. He knows difference, so he sees difference. One final little curious thing, though: you always find him awarding the cities of Rome and Constantine the place of honor or highest distinction. But soon he, or say, a twelfth- or thirteenth-century savant, gives more attention to the Franks, that is, the peoples of Western Europe who invade his land. Still, the greatest

---

[244] See "Umar Farroukh, pp. 74-85.

portion of this attention, as you saw, goes to Eastern Europe.   In any case, this is another interesting matter that required a separate study.

Chapter Two
Traditional View Modified

100

Early in the second half of the fifteenth century the Byzantine Christian Empire falls to the Ottoman-Muslims. At the end of same century the Arab-Muslim Empire's last bastion in Spain falls to the Christians.[245] What reversal of fortune! What coincidence also! I mean Muslims and Christians (East and West) at once win and lose in almost equal terms. As if they're ordained for it by destiny or chance itself. Chance, I think, has the lion's share here, and more often than not, has it in its infinite wisdom to steer things for the better (or worse) unconditionally. So from that reversal of fortune chance, as I read the handwriting on its own nature, brings the two sides together, and wills them at last to begin a new era of salutary relations. This event is still on its way and will soon convert their fall, so to speak, to a rise again. What's more, it will go far enough to modify Ottoman-Muslim view of the West.

These aleatory operations and their epiphenomena almost magically, as it were, send ripple effects into my theme. For Arab-Muslims, too, in the wake of Ottoman-Muslims' experience with the West, eventually come to modify their old traditional view of the West as well. In both cases, the modification has to do with Ottoman-Muslims' and Arab-Muslims' roused interests in the two elements that are missing from the older view: politics and militarism, or governmentality (art of government) and technology. You see, to the older view, it's been a matter of selective intellectual profit attending unexpected and permitted liberation from one-dimensional piety and monochromatic duties. Now it's a matter of explicit,

---

[245] In the East, Arab-Muslim Empire has already come to an end roughly four centuries earlier.

necessary structure of power-relations of which maintaining a strong nation is of paramount importance.

The new elements, inevitably, come to assume greater significance than ever. Inevitably, because, first, they serve the ruling elites' immediate needs for power and prestige; and do so despite the nearly unshakeable grip those religious sentiments still have on other individuals and groups.[246] And because, secondly, they generate the feeling that Ottoman-Muslim civilization, also Arab-Muslim civilization, is no longer one in a state of clash with Christian Western civilization; it's now one state or nation in relation to others, among whom there might allies and enemies, and in which one state, in promises certain things, binds itself to perform them.[247] This is called rights. Ultimately, prudence, caution, and the drive of curiosity to learn about the other, its attitude, its nature, its bad or good will coalesce as material for reformation of rights between nations.

101

But in so far as my theme goes, all these are external factors. The question is whether there are some internal factors working in tandem with them. Some impetus, some interior, vehecular force that, in addition to chance or perhaps as an aid to it, has contributed to the upcoming of the new era of relations. Well, the answer is quite simple: history and geography (the latter more than the former). You see, medieval Arab-Muslim savants, having developed these sciences in the best way they know how, hand them down to the Ottomans. And the latter are, of course, more than grateful for it. In point of fact, their abiding loyalty to Arab-Muslim classical tradition, its many domains of learning—medicine, philosophy, science, Sunnah, Qur'ān, theology, and now geography and history—confirms that feeling of gratitude.[248] Even their politico-

---

[246] See M. Rodinson, "The Western Image and Western Studies of Islam": *The Legacy of Islam*, p. 8; see also S. J. Shaw, *Between Old and New: The Ottoman Empire Under Sultan Selim III* (Boston: Harvard University Press, 1971).

[247] Here we have a historical piece of knowledge or evidence to scuttle the theory that would have us believe that Islam and Christianity are locked into what's called "Clash of Civilizations."

[248] See Gustave E. Von Grunebaum, *Medieval Islam*, pp. 62-63.

religious hegemony over the entire Mid-East region for almost four centuries alters nothing of their feeling.

Nor do they stop at that either. All things being equal, and given the two new elements, Ottoman-Muslims prove to be innovative in their own way. In time they introduce further diversity into these sciences: for one thing, they include human geography; for another, they replace the concept of the seven climates with the concept of continents; and for a third still, they amass extensive knowledge of the world, Europe, and Western Europe in particular. The outcome can be seen in the new book appearing in Istanbul in the middle of the sixteenth century—*History of Western India*, a compendium of history and geography containing in particular ample information about the importance of the discovery of America at the time.[249] If anything, the Ottoman-Muslim learned circles, and the Arab-Muslim ones after them, double up their knowledge of this discovery, among others, which rightly gives the era its distinct mark—the age of discovery in all the senses of the word.

102

However, I can't in good conscience pursue this aspect of the subject any further. I mean the Ottoman-Muslim view of the West. Otherwise, I'd merely be duplicating what has already been vastly studied and documented. In fact, B. Lewis, among others, both Arab-Muslim and Western scholars, examine and have examined many significant features of European life of the sixteenth, seventeenth, eighteenth, and nineteenth centuries—political, cultural, artistic, economic, scholarly, administrative, and technological—pertaining to that view.[250] So,

---

[249] See Ktratchovski, *Tārikh al-Adab al-Jugrāphi al-'Arabī*, Vol. II, p. 570.

[250] Here are a select few: Kratchovskii, two volumes; in addition to the other two books cited previously in chapter one (p. 6, note 9 above) see B. Lewis, *The Emergence of Modern Turkey* (London, 1961), also "The Impact of the French Revolution on Turkey," *Journal of World History*, vol. 1 (1953), pp. 105-125; S.J. Shaw, *Between Old and New: The Ottoman Empire Under Sultan Selim III*; Niyazi Berkes, The Development of Secularism in Turkey; Husayn Muīb al-Masri, *fī-l Adab al-Turki* (Cairo, 1965); Muhammad bin 'Uthmān al-Miknāsi, *al-Ikseer fī Fikak al-Aseer* (Manshurat al-Markaz al-Jami'I li-l-Bahth al-'Ilmi (Ribat, 1965); and Khalid Ziyāda, *Iktishāf al-Taqadum al-Oropi: Dirasa fi-l Mu'atharāt al-Oropiyya ala al-'Uthmaniyeen fi-l Qarn al-Thamin 'Ashar* (Beirut, 1981)—approximate translation: "The Discovery of European Progress: A Study in the Influences of Europe on The Ottomans in the Eighteenth Century."

again, it would be redundant if I'm to repeat or even summarize their work. Nevertheless, there are three points that I'd like to mark off as having crucial importance for my theme.

First point: thanks to Arab-Muslim savants, Ottoman-Muslims inherit and develop further the sciences of geography and history (some Ottoman-Muslims are both historians and geographers[251]). And this development, in turn, as their knowledge of Europe broadens during the course of eighteenth century, acts like a booster giving initial acceleration to new tactic in political and cultural relations: diplomatic representation, among others. Geography, in effect (unfortunately or not), takes the back seat, so that European life can be personally observed closely. Even such observation soon mutates and evolves into exchange of diverse, expert personnel between the two sides. Well, you've guessed it, Ottoman-Muslim view of the West is no longer what it's been in the sixteenth and seventeenth centuries. At that time Europeans, particularly the French, are thought of as being no more than benighted infidels, contemptuous, ignorant, and barbaric fit to be conquered and converted to Islam; now, however, they're seen as powerful rivals, also helpful, useful, and whose technical ways and even styles of living are worthy of imitation. What's more, the public acquires wider knowledge through the many reports by travelers and merchants. The seventeenth-century Olia Jalabi, for example, like Ibn Battūta, travels through many European countries and makes his cogent, positive observations available to the public.[252]

In the final analysis, Arab-Muslim sciences prepare the grounds for what may be called Ottoman-Western or Christian-Muslim détente, perhaps even also coexistence, in many domains of life. It's on the verge of happening, actually— and not a mere tacit wish-fulfillment on the part of both sides. Perhaps it's a case what's impossible becoming possible. Anyway, these sciences generate interest in diplomatic exchange and student exchange, act as vehicles for encouraging the growth of economic and technological know-how, and other vehicular access and innovation for social enhancement—in short, you could say that by the middle of

---

[251] See B. Lewis, *Muslim Discovery of Europe*, pp. 162-70.

[252] See Ktratchovskii, vol 2, p. 638.

the eighteenth century a drastic modification occurs in the old traditional view. Not only this view becomes on the whole a positive one; as well Abu Hanīfa's binary structure of the world into *Dar al-Islam* and *Dar al-Harb* gives way to the realization that a weak world now confronts a strong one: the Ottoman world and the Western world. The Ottomans now see their own image in the West's eye-mirror. In contemplating their soul therein, they see an unpleasant image of themselves, the image of weakness. And the image produces, not resentful or envious feelings, but rather proactive impulses to do something about it, consciously. And they do. From now on their experience with the West assumes the form of constant alertness (though punctuated by setbacks now and then) to enhance and strengthen their world. In the nineteenth and twentieth centuries Arab-Muslims will follow suit.[253]

103

Allow me to elaborate here a bit more, which brings me to the second point I want to make. Recall Ottoman-Muslim and Arab-Muslim learned circles, also the manner in which the ruling elite and the public in general acquire in-depth look at the sundry dimensions of European-Christian life as being worthy both of admiration and emulation. However, such positive feelings are not without tension or complication. Indeed, a large minority, including a few members of the ruling elites (as will be the case with Arab-Muslims in general) remain profound believers in the supremacy of Islam as a religion and a way of life for all time—in a word, a state sufficient unto itself having all the necessary means to ensure socio-economic justice among the believers whoever they may be. Add to this the fact that since the fifteenth century, Ottoman-Muslim military is still a force with which European kingdoms and princedoms have to contend. These instances, you see, reinforce each other, and at the same time underscore the conviction that Ottoman-Muslim civilization enjoys immeasurable and immutable supremacy over all others.

(An example of this built-in tension among Ottoman-Muslims is given by B. Lewis. Ahmed Asim Efendi, the imperial historiographer, represents both the

---

[253] See my comments on Ibn Khaldū n, above note 238.

sentiment of certain ruling elites and the sentiment of the public. He writes a chronicle of the years 1791-1808 which conveys some impression of the reform movement in general and of the effect of French influence in particular. In effect, Asim Efendi is in favor of reforms, which he hopes would restore the failing military strength of the empire and enables it to confront its enemies. In fact, he adduces Russia as an example to show how it emerges from weakness and barbarism and becomes a great power precisely by adopting Western sciences and techniques. If so, then why not the Ottoman Empire, he asks? But he's a Janus-faced scholar, actually. Tension marks him when he thinks the West is both necessary and undesirable. So that he accepts Western aid but refuses to deal with Christians because they're enemies of Islam. In his view, nothing but evil could arise from agreements with those Christian powers. He's particularly hostile to the French and derides the pro-French element in Turkey as deluded fools. He has little to say about the internal affairs of France, and even that little is negative, too. The French republic, he says, is ""like the rumblings and crepitations of a queasy stomach." Its principles consist of "the abandonment of religion and the equality of rich and poor".)[254]

This whole unthoughtful retort is but theory. In practice, however, things are quite different. As if to show that religious one-up-ness (Christian or Muslim) is a blasted notion and should allow time for reason to intervene for a change. After all, Ottoman-Muslims in general have national interest at stake. Their eyes and noses tell them there's systemic weakness in the political machinery damming up the course of national progress. And so they set about analyzing it thoroughly and find it's located in the areas of economics and administration where corruption, the subsumption of all causes, lurks. They also find with hindsight that this systemic corruption is behind the greatest disaster the empire has experienced so far—the defeat in 1699 and the negotiation of the Peace of

---

[254] See *The Muslim Discovery of Europe*, pp. 214-215. The implication, especially in the last quoted phrase, is that Islamic ethic of equality and social justice is real and for ever; something the Western world could study with profit, along side with Greko-Roman ethics, since it resonates with possibilities of bridging differences between East and West.

Carlowitz. [255] Right off, Sultan Ahmed III embarks upon drastic and direly needed reforms, which, consequently and ultimately smooth the way for better, more cooperative relations with Europe. But that, again, falls outside my purview here. All that I wish to stress is the Platonic ontology of the eye-mirror, a very practical approach to putting reason to practice, as Kant would say.

104

My third and last point concerns the concept of freedom. It actually proves of foremost importance to Ottoman-Muslims at this time and more so to Arab-Muslims later. Once more, I hesitate to rehash what scholarship has already so impressively set down in scores of books. So let me say briefly that Ottoman-Muslims embrace the cause of freedom like their newly beloved, for which they thank Sultan Selim III, whose accession to power, interestingly enough, coincides with the French Revolution. Telepathy, aided by practical reason, may be at work here: for he makes it known that he's bent on continuing the technological, economic, and political reforms initiated by other Sultans before him. In so doing, he's, of course, encouraged by the long-standing friendship between the Ottoman Empire and France.

Now the revolution, he maintains, isn't of immediate interest to the Ottoman state. Its interest lies in the French willingness to supply the means needed for his urgent reforms. He finds they are and do. Which, in turn, perhaps with a sigh of relief, abrogates the necessity of analyzing the historical reasons leading to the revolution and the latter's significance for the French people and the world beyond, regardless of lack of sympathy it meets with at the time. But history shows that he and the Ottoman state should have done both: to gain experience in global politics and so deepen the national insight (if I may say so) into the empire's status as a partner in the world. Still, despite these omissions, the empire's coming closer and closer to the verge of actualizing that political insight and role. At any rate, the point here is that, with or without the omissions, the Platonic idea—only through the other (in all its aspects) a person, a people, a nation comes to know itself—is at work. Incidentally, if I'm right, mustn't

---

[255] See S.J. Shaw, *History of Ottoman Empire*, vol. 1, pp. 223-5

today's Arab-Muslims do so, too, as their not-long-ago ancestors, medieval savants and Ottomans, have done before them?

105

Still, you find some negative reactions here and there, especially among certain members of the Sultan's administration. These members feel that the French may be playing a dangerous political game. For example, right after the revolution, the government declares that reason, not emotion, is now its guide and, therefore, no longer views Ottoman-Muslims or Islam as a whole as being enemies. But removal of Christianity from French-Ottoman relations, these members feel, at least on politico-moral grounds, barely isolates the danger. In fact, it compounds the danger: the French government masks its operations in subtle ways: now it appears as a true Muslim to elicit sympathy from the naïve Ottoman-Muslim public; now it fakes subversion of church and its influence in people's moral decisions. So it publishes books by Voltaire precisely to corroborate its position; but since the public can't read French, it has them translated into Turkish, Greek, and Armenian. All in all, this is just calculated to show how much the French government has its egoistic interests at heart.[256]

However, the question remains: if the French government plays games, if it tries to hoodwink people, are the members' feelings justified? Perhaps. Yet they change nothing respecting the demand for freedom; after all, the Sultan and public daily wax enthusiastic about their openness to Europe, and to France in particular. Openness without backing down, as it's been termed.[257] In fact, in the first half of nineteenth century progress becomes the catchword for a general liberalization of Ottomans. To which is added the discovery of the significance of rationalism and critical scrutiny, one of the Enlightenment's legacies, including utility of institutions—for example, systems of taxation and legislature guaranteeing people's rights and liberties. So long as such rights are institutionally guaranteed, no king, president, or otherwise dares to interfere in

---

[256] Much more is discussed in S.J. Shaw, *Between Old and New*, as well as B. Lewis, "The Impact of French Revolution on Turkey."

[257] N. Berkes, *The Development of Secularism*, pp. 47-48.

people's daily affairs and desires. The individual says, thinks, and does what he or she wishes without restrictions. In other words, government's excessive regulations, if any, diminish before the people's will to freedom which extends even to matters of marriage and inheritance. Seen from this vantage point, Western Europe can no more be subsumed into the general category of *Dar al-Harb* or even that of "People of the Book." [258] It's now viewed as an experience on the basis of which Ottoman-Muslims can invent and fend for themselves.

106

The upshot here is this: obviously we have two opposite views of France, perhaps of the West, too. Call them negative and positive if you will. The negative being, of course, the minority view. Albeit, the majority respect the French Revolution's secular and democratic ideals, though are critical of the officials entrusted to enforce these ideals. These officials are like paper tigers, weak and indecisive, yet manipulate the French public with whom Ottoman-Muslims empathize most sympathetically. Indeed, they know these officials have rallied the worst and lowest orders of society as their henchmen by falsely promising them liberty and equality with everyone else. They are also wary of the latter, ragtag and bobtail in power as they are, since they hardly let on that they have Ottomans' best interest in mind, especially after the Ottomans have demonstrated genuine friendship and concern by both word and deed for the safety of the French government against, for example, the Hungarians.

Ottoman-Muslims, you see, are gradually becoming pragmatists, and politically savvy no less. To express profound admiration of the Revolution's idea apart from the men behind it is a critical masterstroke. I mean the ability to separate its generals from their work—the work being the Revolution itself. As if to say quite astutely: this work's like a work of art; you must think of it as separate from the artist if you wish to enjoy it and its wholesome benefits at all. They think so because they feel the putting in place of a mechanism to serve human progress both and internationally, is a force of nature not to be equated with its creators or their behavior. A creator may be good or bad, admirable or

---

[258] S.J. Shaw, *Between Old and New*, pp. 92-96.

despicable, but that changes nothing of the creation's or created's value. After all, the creator-artist is merely a preliminary stage, a jumping-off point no more. And so Ottoman-Muslims can look at the Revolution's body, its organization, its principles of ethico-political order and freedom, and see in them models to be emulated by peoples everywhere in the world.

107

To resume my narrative, for roughly five centuries Arab-Muslim culture, not to speak of community, is all but extinct. Still more, Egypt itself, an Ottoman province until well into late nineteenth century, boasts of no government independent enough to be called Arab-Muslim. And so like other North-African provinces, Egypt lies shrouded in its own world, cut off from Europe, though not from its Mid-Eastern sister-provinces, also under Ottoman rule, with which it maintains relations. But Napoleon's expedition changes many things. The eye of heaven becomes a beneficent eye when most Egyptians interpose themselves between it and the country it looks upon to bless.

What is it that the French bring to Egypt? Well, it's easy: as you saw, science and technology, the achievements of Western civilization. Napoleon, symbol of France, dangles these brilliant achievements before the Egyptians who, according to Jabarti's eyewitness account, gaze upon them with almost idolatrous eyes. For example, in Tal al-'Aqāreb, a region in the borough of Nāsiriyya, their crankshafts construct warehouses, arsenals, towers, and, of course, garrisons. With other stupefying machinery, the French demolish many ramshackle old houses and use the wreckage and marble (of which some are made) to build their homes. As for scientists and technicians—planners, astrophysicists, sculptors, astronomers, landscapers, mathematicians, geometricians, photographers, writers, editors—the entire borough of Nāsiriyya is set aside as residential area. Here, too, more wondrous, intricately made machinery is drafted for the purpose: Brass-plated machinery, elevating machinery (pulleys?), each of which consisting of several pieces fitted together with bolts and cords twirling and twisting beautifully, so that when all is in place, the finished machine looms so large as to occupy a huge space.[259]

Jabarti's isn't the only favorable view of European technology; it's shared by many Sheikhs of the College of al-Azhar (tenth-century most important Islamic university in the world) share the feeling with him—for example, Sheikh Hasan al-'Attār and Sheikh al-Khashshāb. And this view seems unaffected by a distasteful or perhaps shocking behavior of Frenchmen; even if it is, shock or distaste never grows into hostile feelings against them. After all, they have fabulous construction skills and expertise; they are also adept at organization; and they never exploit any of their workers. "What they create and what they build— towers, fortresses, and garrisons—in the direction of the bay of al-Iskandariyya, Rashīd, Dumyāt, and the land of Saīd are so abundant and so amazing that they are able to complete them in such a short period of time."[260]

108

Such, at least in its initial lineaments, is the portrait the Egyptian eye, brush, and color paint of the French. Though not without a modicum of chariness stamped upon it; and this perhaps for lack of experience as yet to fathom who the French really are and what they're doing in Egypt. They will in due course.[261] At any rate, when the French leave the country after three years sojourn, that chariness, paradoxically, dissipates or gets displaced. Only the memory remains: inscription of Western science and technology's dazzling accomplishments all wrapped up in feelings of admiration and amazement. This is precisely what Muhammad Bek al-Ilfi's memory reflects. Al-Ilfi is a Mamlūk prince whose ancestors, the Mamlūks, build an empire comprised of Syria and Egypt but whose glory comes to an end by the beginning of the fifteenth century. In any case, al-

---

[259] Abdul Rahman Jabarti, *Tārikh 'Ajā'ib al-Athār fi al-Tarājim wal-Akhbār* (Beirut: Dār al-Jīl, 1978), vol. 2, pp. 232-234.

[260] *Ibid*, p. 213.

[261] That is, when Egyptians, and afterwards Arab-Muslims in general, begin to review their view of the West: then they learn to view their own experiences with the eyes with which they are accustomed to view them when they are the experiences of others or, in this case, Westerners.

Ilfi's experience, especially in England where he stays for six months during the French presence in Egypt, is a unique one.

Al-Ilfi himself never writes about his experience in England or his observations of the English people. He must have communicated his thoughts verbally to Jabarti who then sets them down or inserts them in his historical account. Al-Ilfi's observations of the English, Jabarti says in effect, are similar to other Egyptians' observations of the French. During his stay, he cultivates his mind by taking note of the country's art of architecture, its government's excellent rule of law, its wealth, well-being, and craftsmanship no less than its fair treatment of the citizens among whom, given their unbelief, there's none who's either destitute, needy, or indigent.[262] What's more, before he leaves the country, he receives all kinds of presents: jewelry, astronomical tools, geometrical designs, astrolabes, globes, and binoculars (one of which enables anyone to identify at night certain constellations, because of the greater magnitude afforded by it, and other constellations surrounding them not possible for to the naked eye to see). He's also enthralled to sees all kinds of weapons, the awesome polyphonous brainchild of English science and technology. One memento he accepts from the English is a musical instrument inside of which there are little mechanisms that all automatically rotate or work together to produce music.[263]

Al-Ilfi's six-month visit in England is a pioneering adventure that paves the way for many more individuals to make similar visits or to be sent on similar educational expeditions to Europeans countries—for example, al-Tahtāwi's visit to Paris a quarter of a century later, in 1826. In between, though, that is, between the end of the eighteenth century and the first quarter of the nineteenth century, Egypt gets to take large strides in assimilating and adapting European science and technology in such domains as the military and industry. Muhammad Ali, chief modernist governor (or Pasha) makes the country virtually independent of

---

[262] It's almost irresistible urge on the part of a lot of Arab-Muslims to interpose with expressions of this kind: unbelief, infidel, etc., even in the midst of the most favorable encomia of Westerners. This is a significant aspect of their ethos which the West can't ignore.

[263] *'Ajā'b al-Athār*, vol. 3, p. 171.

Istanbul.   More than that, he creates a modern army and navy trained by French officers, and a relatively centralized system of administration and taxation.[264]   He also he initiates the first educational mission of Egyptian students to European cities to study at their institutions in 1826.[265]

109

Among the first bevy of exchange students is one Rifa'a al-Tahtāwi, a student-sheikh at al-Azhar university and protégé of his professor Sheikh Hasan al-'Attar. The latter enjoins al-Tahtāwi to write down, upon returning from Paris, his observations and what he's learned. Which al-Tahtāwi does most willingly in 1832. Like many savants before him, he records how enthralled he is by the new ideas and achievements of the European Science and technology, no less than of European enlightenment which reminds him of Arab-Muslim philosophy. He has visions that such enlightenment can stimulate Arab-Muslims to reconnect with the rational sciences they already have in their backyard.   As to Paris itself at the time, it certainly isn't the same city as that a century earlier when Ottoman-Muslims visit it.

The change isn't alien to the Egyptians in general. In point of fact, before al-Tihtāwi's visit, news or knowledge of European achievements in science and technology, including those in philosophy, are quite familiar to the Egyptians. So that, on his way to Paris, for example, where he'd be at the source of all such endowment and progress, he has another vision before he actually sees the French cities. The idea occurs to him that al-Iskandariyya (Alexandria) and any big city in France are comparable; after all, it's very close in its present circumstance and status to such cities. "But I can see in imagination what I've seen in it, excluding other Egyptian cities, especially since there are so many Europeans already living in it."[266]   All of which eventually gets corroborated when he arrives in the city of Marceille and learns about the French character.

---

[264] See Horani, pp. 50-54.

[265] See Khaled Ziyada, *Iktishāf al-Taqadum* al-Ōrōpi, pp. 25-75.

[266] Rifā'a Rāfi' al-Tahtāwi, *al-Mu'lafāt al-Kāmila* (Beirut: al-Mu'asasa al-'Arabiyya lil-Nashr wa-l Dirāsāt, 1973), vol. 2, p. 39.

The uniqueness of al-Tahtāwi's visit resides in the fact that it's a scientific mission, not a diplomatic one. This implies, of course, his acknowledgement of European advance over and above Egyptian science and technology. Put otherwise, the goal of the visit is the acquisition of learning and nothing else besides. At the outset of his book he names all sciences and arts that are the specialty of one European country or another: economics, military training, seamanship and naval operations, diplomacy, arcade, mechanics, military engineering, artillery, metallurgy, chemistry, medicine, agriculture, physics, printing, and translation. These arts and sciences, which as resources are quite meager in Egypt, can be used to educate and train Egyptian youths. These youths, to quote Horani, "should enter the main stream of modern civilization by adopting the European sciences and their fruits."[267]

A bit later in the preface al-Tahtāwi pauses awhile to consider the geographical location of Europe. In doing so, he hardly means to suggest that the Egyptians are ignorant of Europe or that it's unknown to them. Rather his idea is to put an end to some confusion: to replace the old, floating, obscure terminology with more modern, clearer, more identifiable demarcation which would designate the exact location of Europe. (Incidentally, I think al-Tahtāwi here, though he doesn't say so, wishes to pay tribute to medieval Arab-Muslims who inaugurate the science of geography; after all, it remains alive and well, operative, and serviceable.) For example, he notes that some interpreters of geography Arab-Muslims as well as Ottoman-Muslims, subsume Europe and the land of "Franj" into one concept or name. But that's a fantasy, pure and simple—"unless, of course, they generalize the term to include Byzantium, the land of Rūm, the Balkans, and Greece under the rule of Ottoman Empire, and so call their empire by the general name the Empire of Rūm or the Empire of Rome." [268]

---

[267] See Horani, p. 83.

[268] *Ibid*, p. 26.

145

But that's untenable, al-Tahtāwi argues. You can't simply apply a vague generalization or use a word-rubric to designate the whole of Europe. On the contrary, this Western continent's neither inscrutable nor inaccessible; rather it's a well-known reality even outside its borders, as in the case of Iskandariyya where you can easily recognize who's who among the citizens. Besides, each country's character and laws differ from another's. When, for example, he arrives in Marseilles, and has his first hands-on experience, as it were, of Western civilization, he's required to be quarantined before being allowed free movement. At this point al-Tahtāwi has a chance to comment on the moral suitability of the quarantine or lack thereof among Arab-Muslims, particularly in Egypt. He knows or recalls the controversial divide that the subject of quarantine has caused among Arab-Muslim *'Ulama*. "Sheikh al-Mana'ī al-Tūnisi," he says, "forbids any Arab-Muslim to submit to it; while Sheikh Muhammad Birm allows it." Al-Tahtāwi thinks, perhaps with a happy turn of humor, that the latter's liberal attitude must be influenced by his unshakeable belief in the sphericity of the globe.[269]

111

The question now comes up: Who are those French people? And he answers it quite directly. They are, he says in effect, realistic and honest, also submissive before any kind of reality, strong-willed, energetic, passionate, and voluptuous. They deny that social or moral customs and rituals abide in social intercourse for ever; above all, they despise narrow-mindedness, believing nature combined with reason to be the source of justice. Hence religion comes to guide people to performing the good and eschewing the evil, no more. But in matters of beauty, originality, inventiveness, reason, and progress in arts and sciences no religion can be an adequate substitute at all. Finally, they think that prosperous countries develop the art of politics or political procedures as their living sharī'a. In this connection, a philosophical dogmatism of theirs has it that the minds of

---

[269] *Ibid*, p. 70.

their wise men and naturalists are by comparison greater than those of the prophets.[270]

Such views permit him next to delve into certain differences he recognizes between the French and Arab-Muslims. He also states his remarks gently, thoughtfully, with as much neutrality as he can command, even if they contradict his own personal opinions. Briefly, these differences concern moral issues in particular. For example, the French believe in human reason. What's more, their constitution does embody a certain principle of justice, but it's far from the precepts of the divine law. Finally, they deny that miracles can occur and believe, too, that no one is like to break the laws of nature.[271]

But such differences are endemic to different cultures, and so he, prudently, leaves them aside. When he brings up the subject of French politics and law, as inscribed in the text of the constitution, he interprets its provisions in the most objective fashion he knows how—which, he says, "is accompanied by observation bearing deep significance." Reviewing the first provision, for instance, he carefully marks its astonishing matter: it equates all individuals before the law. That's to say, all persons, socio-economically high-ranking or low-ranking, differ from each other not a bit in any sense or procedure named or cited in the law. Even the king himself is subject to the same legal procedure. In a word, this constitutional provision bears great authority, al-Tahtāwi thinks, for establishing justice, succoring the oppressed, and satisfying the needs and desires of the poor. Anticipating objection, he says: "you might think this is all mere aggregate of words. Not at all. It denotes clearly that justice among the French has reached a high degree."[272] Even if, he later adds, it's still far from the precepts of the divine law.

112

These remarks suggest deep import, no doubt, especially because he grounds them in the text of the constitution itself. He speaks of justice,

---

[270] *Ibid*, p. 79.

[271] Ibid, vol. 1, p. 81.

[272] *Ibid*, p. 102.

oppression, and fairness which he actually reads in the text. While doing so, you get the impression, and a solid one at that, his mind inches along the path of reconciliation between European and the precepts of Islam. Indeed, he stresses his belief that what the French constitution contains by way of justice and equity among people is also already contained in the Qur'ān as well, which in a different sense is the constitution of the Arab-Muslims. Though his exposition might not have elicited the desired responses from his Egyptian readers at the time, it hardly means they've continued without proper influence. In point of fact, half a century later, Egypt experiences two simultaneous movements: a political movement and a movement of exciting argumentative debate whose subjects are precisely those pertaining to fairness, justice and oppression.

Al-Tahtāwi isn't, of course, satisfied with just this range of the exposition. He returns to the question of the constitution again when he takes up the French revolution which has amended all provisions, if not make them more radical than before. He now sums up the rights of citizens after the year 1830 and after the amendment as follows: the French people, despite differences of social status, class, rank, wealth, are nevertheless equal in judicial proceedings. These differences, while meaningful only within the limits of society or civilization, have nothing to do with the law. Therefore, majority of people either serve in the army or work for civil service. And if a person can, (s)he supports the government financially when necessary. What's more, the law guarantees personal freedom, so that no one gets arrested except according to the form of the law. Finally, among the inalienable rights is a person's freedom of worship, a measure protected by the state. Once more, al-Tahtāwi can't resist comparing Arab-Muslims: "What the French call freedom (in all the senses of the word) is exactly the same as our equity—though with a different name."[273]

Over and above these discursive comments on politics and the law al-Tahtāwi never forgets he's a member of Egyptian expedition to France: a student seeking knowledge in France. As such, he elaborates on the various facets of French progress which his professor enjoins him to set down in a book. The

---

[273] *Ibid*, pp. 104-105

upshot is this: Paris is the greatest of all French cities, to which many people come from the world's four corners seeking knowledge of the arts and sciences. Fascinated by the philosophy of European Enlightenment which reminds him of Arab-Muslim philosophy, he loves the way everything works properly in Paris; he's impressed by the rational precision of French culture, the ease of its language, the literacy of even the common people, and he's intrigued by the passion for innovation. He longs to help Egypt enter this brave new world.

Not, however, by copycatting everything French to the letter, for no one could do that for sure. Rather, he means European Enlightenment contains a treasury of ideas, techniques, devices, procedures that can't exactly be imitated or even reactivated, but that at least constitutes, or helps to constitute, a certain point of view which can be very useful as a tool for analyzing what's going on in Egypt now—and to change it. Change it by means of *Ijtihad*.

Al-Tahtāwi profoundly believes that Arab-Muslim *Sharī'a* doesn't object to this form of change. In fact, not only is it necessary to adapt the latter to new circumstances; it's also legitimate to do so. The door of *Ijtihad,* though it has been closed for some time now, can be pushed open again. And he takes the first step in that direction. After all, there's every opportunity, now more than ever, to start bridge-building between France and Egypt, between Islam and West. So that Arab-Muslims can amalgamate into a new, balanced order what's beneficent in both cultures: Arab-Muslims offer faith, honesty, ethics of social justice, despite the state of turmoil or decline they find themselves in; the Westerners offer Enlightenment, despite their straying from the right path.

113

Ijtihad through which Islam and Europe may be harmonized, or the gulf between East and West bridged over is carried on further by al-Tahtāwi's contemporary Ali Mubārak. Mubārak, of course, never mentions the word, but its presence is ineluctably felt at every step of the way. But first, let me say this: he lives through most of the same circumstances and developments experienced by his country in the nineteenth century. He later writes a book bearing the expressive title "'Alām al-Dīn" (The Banner of Religion). Mubārak's formative years start at one of the schools inaugurated by the progressive Muhammad Ali, to which he adds a four-year experience as a student in France. Upon his return, he takes on the tremendous responsibility of minister of state in the second half of the nineteenth century, that is, during the reign of Isma'īl Pasha. At least two innovative and prominent modernizing efforts bear the imprint of his name: the organization of the country's capital so that "its public utilities resemble those of a European city"; and the establishment of the famous institute known as Dār al-'Ulūm (The Institute of Arts and Sciences). Both feats are commissioned by Isma'īl.[274]

Mubārak composes his book thirty years after al-Tahtāwi's. The two books, interestingly enough, perhaps even also significantly, differ in terms of the manner or style of presentation. While al-Tahtawi's features the discursive style throughout, Mubārak's employs the technique of narrative cast in the form of a two-level dialogue between four speakers, one of whom is a Sheikh from al-Azhar University. These dialogues, between an Englishman and a Frenchman, on the one hand, and between an Egyptian immigrant to France and the Sheikh, on the other, have the virtue of placing two worlds face-to-face with each other— East and West.[275] Which, if I'm right, is an unprecedented example of a textual *Ijtihad.* Besides, given this interfacing technique, you couldn't have dreamed of a better, more appropriate symbol for Plato's ontological idea in which one side contemplates its soul in the other's eye as in a mirror. The entire work, you see, reflects Mubārak's vision of the European and Arab-Muslim worlds sounding a note of agreement or entente.

114

The book's an encyclopedia of his wide ranging knowledge of European scientific achievements. You observe him leisurely zigzagging between several topics in the most neutral fashion he can muster. For instance, he devotes over fifteen pages to an analysis of steam; in others he discusses European arts: theatre,

---

[274] 'Ali Mubārak, *The Complete Works*, Two Volumes (Beirut: al-Mu'assassa al-'Arabiyya lil-Dirāsat wal-Nashr, 1979-80), vol. 1, p. 69.

[275] We shall see a replication of this technique, though from a critical perspective, toward the end of twentieth century.

pedagogy, geography, agriculture, and so on.[276] And he wends his way on to the French, he thinks the world of them. They devote mind and soul to perfecting the workmanship of things, and he thinks this is the key that unlocks the secret of their progress. He also admires, though cautiously, their belief in human reason, which can take the place of religion. In France, all begins with little things. For example, when navigation and commerce are in place, they improve the socio-economic quality of life in France. When money is poured into agriculture, it doubles up that quality of life. That's not all. Having navigated lakes and rivers nearby, the French, always resourceful, now navigate the oceans, gulping down islands and countries in the process; then they dominate and exploit the lands' wealth, thereby waxing richer, stronger by the day. Meanwhile the conquered peoples have no choice but to adopt the ways of their conquerors.

As you can see, Mubārak echoes Jabarti; or better, they complement each other, the one describes imperialism, the other the advent of orientalism at the time of Napoloeon's expedition into Egypt. And the two systems, as each unveils its works, are like two peas in the pod. Mubārak, in particular, underscores imperialism's role in enabling Europeans, technical, to dominate the Americas, African costs, and other areas in Asia, including so many island of the Atlantic and Indian oceans. The result is obvious: Europe becomes the richest and strongest continent in the world.[277] And all on the backs of the poor and weak.

Mubārak, however, hardly condones such behavior. Which is why he raises a telling question, the point he's been driving at: could Europe, ultimately, have accomplished these things without Arab-Muslim philosophy and sciences? If Hunayn ibn Ishāq, a ninth-century translator, hasn't made the Greek science of astronomy available, could the astronomer James Edward Keeler have ever dreamed of developing further the principles of this science by means of the arts of addition and deduction, which already exist in their fundamentals among the

---

[276] *Ibid*, p. 452.

[277] *Ibid*, p. 487.

Arab-Muslim astronmers?[278]   And here Mubārak concurs with al-Tahtāwi—
Islam has always exhorted the pursuit of science, also economics and
administration. And if before the sixteenth century Europeans lag behind Arab-
Mulsims, it's because Christian theologians forbid it. The opposite is the case in
Islam. No theological text or procedure denies a person the wholesome pursuits
of learning and knowledge. In point of fact, the Qur'ān, the Sunnah, and
Muhammad himself—all enjoin such pursuits.[279]   So saying, you can realize
what Mubārak is after: to humble European arrogance, at the same time to hold
Europe's progress as a model.

115

The latter point is the upshot of Ali Mubarak's entire dialogical book. It
comes at the point at which the Sheikh from al-Azhar University addresses his
own son whom he has brought along to Paris. This is what he says in his florid
way: what do we care about the morals and customs of the French people, good or
bad? After all, this is what they value and live by. So be it. What we care for,
what's significant to us amounts to this: if we discover something in their
inventions, arts, constitutions, legal procedures, architecture, and so on, that can
be advantageous to us here in our country, we do well to acquire it, so that we
may najtahid (plural verb from Ijtihad), that is to say, struggle to perfect it, built it
up, and adapt it our own ways of life. We will then commend it to our
community by describing in detail its merits and analyzing its usefulness and
rewards. Perhaps, then, we can persuade our people to desire it as their own,
since it isn't contrary to the Sharī'a.[280]

Everything having to do with technical, educational, and military fields the
Sheikh speaks of to his son has been actualized in Egypt. Mubārak, of course,
can't but look upon all that with a favorable eye. Ultimately, it has been made
possible by dint of the country's fruitful communications with Western Europe.

---

[278] *Ibid*, p. 457.

[279] Let's remember that Mubārak may not have known about Ibn Qutayba who represents the
voice of Arab-Muslim orthodoxy and what he says. See above page 114.

[280] *Ibid*, p. 623.

But he also doesn't forget to pay tribute Muhammad Ali and his grandson's daring efforts in speeding up the process of change. Today the country, Mubārak further observes, isn't the same as it has been fifty years earlier. "Yesterday, you saw it there slumping in the corner of oblivion, its lands haunted and desert-like; today, the garb of civilization sits upon it with great pride."[281] Mubārak believes this is the right way to do things: to keep open the channels of communication with Europe and the world on all levels, for Islam denies no learning that can drive the clouds of ignorance far away.

116

The same holds true in the case of Khayr al-Dīn al-Tūnisi of Tunīsia, North Africa. He's one of those pre-visional heroes of a limited reform movement in the second half of nineteenth century. Pre-visional, since he anticipates 1881, the year Tunīsia becomes a French protectorate, and says so. The reform movement itself isn't simply a matter of free choice; it's also prompted by socio-economic and political pressures France brings to bear on the country. Perhaps the centerpiece of al-Tūnisi's thought concerns this very situation which is initially fraught with tension, and which eventually ends with French hegemony over Tunīsia. He himself originally endeavors to circumvent this end-result through reforms both genuine and without strings attached. Apparently he fails in praxis, however. Though not in theory: to use Horani's words, in his "one literary work which is a political study," he attempts to transcend that disquieting situation, and above all, to explain the necessary and important reasons for reforms after European models.[282]

In the introduction, he first clears the grounds with respect to the unpolitical reason for which he writes the book, namely to ensure that his fellow countrymen and women can read his mind unambiguously. Then he tries to square away his thought with the demands of *Sharī'a*. *Sharī'a*, he argues in effect, stands in no one's way to appropriate from Europe what redounds to the benefit of Tunīsian Arab-Muslims as a whole. To corroborate, he cites the

---

[281] *Ibid*, p. 455.

[282] See Horani, p. 87.

considered opinions of several Sheikhs who, in fact, spur on such appropriation. For instance, Sheikh Mawāq says, *"Sharī'a* doesn't prohibit our likeness to or comparison with those who do what Allah permits." Also Sheikh Muhammad Ibn 'Ābidīn: "the image of likeness or comparison pertaining to the prosperity and propriety of human being is certainly harmless."[283] After which al-Tūnisi adds a statement that's either unlike anything al-Tahtāwi and Mubārak have written or not possible for them. Emboldened by the Sheikhs, he cautions careless, unthoughtful Arab-Muslims to avoid extreme statements "denouncing an other's praiseworthy deportment that tallies with *Sharī'a* simply because everything pertaining to a non-Arab-Muslim's conduct and disposition must in their mind be discarded as worthless."[284] What's remarkable here is the use of term "other," I'm assuming for the first time, in an Arab-Muslim text.

117

At any rate, al-Tūnisi's insistence on the necessity for his country to adopt what would accrue to its well-being and prosperity is undoubtedly justified. After all, a man of his intellectual caliber perceives the danger posed to all Muslims everywhere by European powers waiting, as they are, like tigers to leap at their helpless prey any minute. So when he completes his book in 1867, not only some Arab-Muslim regions are already under European rule (Algiers, for example); Tūnis itself is threatened by the same wakeful trump of doom if it doesn't rise and fend for itself.[285] He also realizes that no Arab-Muslim country, now or in the future, can resist European military, political, or economic powers when they rage and foam at the mouth.

Reason enough that Arab-Muslims utilize Europe's achievements in the arts and sciences in order to forestall its overtaking their lands. European progress, he says in effect, is like a strong current sweeping over the entire globe,

---

[283] Khayr al-Dīn al-Tūnisi, *Aqwām al-Masālek fi Ma'rifat Ahwāl al-Mamālek*, ed. Ma'n Ziyada (Beirut, Dār al-Talī'a), 1979, p. 112.

[284] *Ibid,* p. 110.

[285] Particularly so when The Ottoman-Mulsim Empire of which al-Tūnisi becomes minister of state for a brief period is in decline financially and militarily. So there's no hope of rescue or aid from that corner. See Karen Armstrong, *Islam: A Short History*, pp. 110-116.

so that anything standing in its way gets uprooted and carried along. I fear the kingdoms or republics adjacent to Europe, he says, may be subject to the same uprooting and imperialist deluge. A fate Arab-Muslims can shun, however, if they pursue European examples of secular planning so as not to drown.[286] These words, again, ring with gospel-like news, not with threats or finality of doom.

Good news actually fills his book as gentle breeze fills the sail. He discusses the becoming-enlightened of Tūnis, and beyond that, of all Muslim and Arab-Muslim states. At the end, he writes this upbeat statement: "Freedom is the magnitude of a culture's domain of knowledge that European nations themselves have attained."[287] Freedom, he elaborates, is two-fold: personal freedom, the choice of one's own course of action to secure honor, wealth, and equality with one's compatriots; and political freedom, the practice of debating in freedom what's best for the country. Europeans possess both kinds of freedom. Hence their good works: systems of communications by railroads and by seas, cooperation of commercial associations, and hot demand for vocational skills.[288] As I've myself witnessed it, he explains, countries reach prosperity in which freedom and constitution work in tandem with political planning and control. If a country loses its freedom, however, it loses its dignity and wealth; its people degrade to poverty and inflation while their consciousness, energy, and spirit weaken beyond repair.[289]

118

What, you may ask, is the thrust of al-Tūnisi's project? Well, simply this: where there's willing, thinking, saying, there's a way. And this way, as Vico would say, justifies change of institutions when circumstances are propitious. Al-Tūnisi views the West or Europe in this light: it has progressively changed and changes constantly for the better. Arab-Muslims can achieve the same if they

---

[286] Aqwām al-Masālek, p. 168.

[287] *Ibid*, p. 207.

[288] *Ibid*, p. 209.

[289] *Ibid*, p. 214.

want to without tainting the faith. In fact, they can become part of the modern
world while remaining Muslims. That's the spirit of Ijtihad, pure and simple.

What's more, when he touches upon political matters, Arab-Muslim
history abounds in ideas, procedures, concepts, techniques that can be combined
with those of Europe to create a viable, dignified quality of life for all Arab-
Muslims. The second Caliph 'Umar ibn al-Khattāb, taking over the helms after
Muhammad, pursues a policy that in essence differs little or none from the
practice of European political freedom and political debate. For example,
addressing his "state" council (*Majlis Shura*), he says: "if you see a crooked or
deviant part in me, straighten it out." As well, the practice of electing
representatives in a European country resembles that of *Ummah* presided over
both by a group of men (*'ulama*) and one ruler limited by law, natural or revealed,
and by consultation.[290] Consultation comes in the form of *'ulama* and men of
affairs. They speak to him freely, guide him in the right path and prevent him
from doing evil.[291]

From doing evil—that's uppermost on al-Tūnisi's mind. For he knows of
corruption both inside, within governments (political, moral, religious), and
outside where the would-be enemy crouches for the kill. This is as much evident
in Tunīsia as in all Arab-Muslim states. And for these reasons, and only when
such corruption (in all the senses of the word) is rampant, al-Tūnisi is willing to
entrust the affairs of government to one single tyrant.[292] But this is only a last
resort. It can be instantly abrogated if the government in place intends to
introduce progress. And to do so peacefully and knowledgeably. Yet as a prime
minister, he fails to bring it off, though he never abandons the principle of the
thing.[293] That's why his book is penned as a political theory with the intent of

---

[290] *Ibid*, p. 208.

[291] *Ibid*, p. 225.

[292] Let me quickly add that al-Tūnisi wouldn't wish this situation to materialize in any form or
shape at all. But since he monitors historical events carefully and consciously, his ideas and
statements prove prophetic of today.

[293] For this failure, see Horani's insightful analysis, pp. 94-95.

enlightening the public, eschewing violence, and insisting no less on the quality and practice of freedom.

Europe's portrait, you see, is profound, searching, constructive, and peaceful. Al-Tūnisi carefully monitors the history of the principles of European freedom and progress, and explicates its various causes and conditions of possibility. Europe, he feels, has paid a high price for them in the mud of battles. But he also isolates the non-combative methods that go into their making. For example, he links their ascent, or perhaps advent, to the good and practical planning of European stages of education, on the one hand, and the latter to the enlightenment of the men in power (the power elite), on the other. And this, he concludes, not only conforms to the limited resources underlying European progress; it also conforms to what he sees as the exigent needs of Arab-Muslim situation which, likewise, demands, now more than ever, serious effort in bettering teaching and education as well as ensuring the proper enlightenment of the power elites.[294]

119

You now have, I presume, a clearer picture of Europe as Ottoman and Arab painters etch its nineteenth-century contours. It's a somewhat slanted picture, of course: I mean slanted in favor of certain ideals that certain individuals desire for their own country—knowledge, freedom, power. The question is, are they wrong to want to change things in their world? Not at all. Knowledge, after all, is no property of an individual or a people? And our savants, being alert to it, privilege themselves and their fellow countrymen and women as equal partners. All they really want, impossible as it may sound, is to build bridges between East and West or, if you will, between Islam and Christianity. What's more, having grown up within strict, profoundly pious Muslim environment, they seem adept enough not to entertain doubts with respect to Islam's character's

---

[294] At this point I should say that al-Tūnisi is unable to give expression to the phenomenon of imperialism in Algiers which comes under French hegemony in 1830. Although Tūnis borders on Algiers, he isn't in a proper state to permit him to do so. After all, imperialism is best criticized, critiqued, attacked, or fought by those who experience it. Looking at things from this angle, and keeping in mind what as al-Tūnisi says about Arab-Muslim world in general, I feel there's no need for me to include Algerian view of the West.

malleability to coexist with the West. And yet despite the slant and the wish, the picture isn't that smooth. There are protests that anathematize both the reconciliation and modeling. Some are vehemently adamant in their call for ending it (Ottomans), and some are critical, cautious and more thoughtful about how to work with Europe or the West.

In eighteenth-century Turkey, inimical protests are rife. The reformist trend, then pioneered by some sultans and their aides, meets with acrimonious rejection by Janissary forces, on the one hand, and by religious apparatus, including Sufist orders, exercising authority over law, education, on the other. Though a few enlightened religious men support Sultan Selim III's reforms, for instance, the religious apparatus oppose them point by point, considering them heresy, unbelief, not to speak of imitation of "infidels' ways." Reality thus takes a wolfish turn, and makes an end of the sultan. The opposition, of course, continues well into the second half of nineteenth century and ends with the decline of Ottoman Empire altogether. Meanwhile society splits between power-elites and their families who pursue their life and education independently of religion and the masses over whom the 'ulama wield their hegemony. A paralyzing societal divide, to be sure, and divide within divide, which the Arab-Muslim world hasn't been able to rid itself of as yet.[295]

120

I bring up this circumstance for contrast with the more complex Egyptian experience. Egypt's religious apparatus remains placid throughout the nineteenth and first half of twentieth century; it puts up no fight against openness to European arts, sciences, and technology. This holds good for the power-elites as well. Unlike their Ottoman counterparts, they actually see to it that no situation arises which would drive a bitter wedge between liberal and conservative views of Europe or the West. This is because they and other advocates of European ideas never instigate a clash with Islam. Besides, no one points an accusing finger at their being unbelievers or apostates. They're dualists at best (if I may say so): Muhammad Ali and Isma'īl Pasha, as you saw, present themselves at once as

---

[295] Unis, Heyd, "The Ottoman Ulama and Westernization," *Scripta Hierosolymitana* IX (1961).

defenders of Islam and advocates of progress. What's more, learned men like al-Tahtāwi and Mubārak are students of theology at al-Azhar Universit, and their professors more than support their efforts. And yet there's a hidden irony in all of this. These men, among others, want to make Egypt a modern state, independent, progressive—but so fast, so precipitously that it ends up becoming a British colony instead.[296]

You may ask: how is it that openness to the West induces no major conflict in Egypt at this time? Well, it's simple: compared to Turkey's, the religious apparatus is weak and ineffectual. Beofre Napoleon's expedition into the country, al-Azhar Sheikhs remain out of the mainstream; they don't, as Brahmins do in India, participate in the political process either by way of advising, consulting, interpreting the law for guiding rulers, or even educating the populace. And during the expedition they co-operate with Napoleon; they even act as liaisons between the French and the populace. You see, these Sheikhs may be respectful of and have a warm place in their hearts for the populace, but they certainly, or perhaps curiously, lack influence: they're unable to play the role of leaders of the people vis-à-vis the expedition. (Incidentally, the same situation obtains today: the 'ulama want power, and only power—but no role as political consultants; they don't even educate rulers or insist on doing so when these get out of line.)

Which fact, consequently, enables Muhammad Ali to clip what remains of the wings of al-Azhar Sheikhs without the least opposition on their part. Later when Isma'īl restricts or undermines the Sufi orders, he relies on the legal opinions (fatwa) of the very Sheikhs themselves. That's why no struggle exists at the time. But soon, as you shall see, the movement for reform itself gets weaker and weaker by the day.

121

It all begins with a certain number of peaceful, conscientious objectors to European openness. This is then slightly reinforced by a bevy of al-Azhar

---

[296] This is true to form when it comes to Arab-Muslim ethos: it's as much manifest in their swift and sweeping conquests as in their equally swift and sweeping acquisition of Greek and Persian sciences. In all three cases—fast conquests, fast learning, fast modernization—they lose what they strive to acquire, so that the old saying "haste makes waste" applies to them lock, stock and barrel.

Sheikhs that, apparently, hasn't as yet either partially or totally lost its moral influence over the people, though it remains incapable, or let me say, intentionally incapable of putting up a fight against Isma'īl's more drastic reform measures, one of which is the extravagant notion of making Egypt a cultural piece of Europe. In any event, this bevy of scholars or Sheikhs keeps its mouth shut, and completely ignores the tendentious picture that has been drawn up of Europe. Why it does so is itself a fascinating story, but, unfortunately, there isn't enough space here to accommodate its full range. Let this example serve a legion.

One al-Azhar Sheikh named Husayn al-Marsifī is a rickety man. But his intellectual powers remain intact, with prodigious appetite for learning. For in his late, very late years, he tries to acquire the French language. He then writes an epistle titled "Risalat al-Kalam al-Thamān" (literally, An Epistle of the Eight Words) in 1881, at the beginning of the spread of the new European ideas in Egypt at large. In it he attempts to explicate the meaning of eight terms circulating in language at the time. They are "Ummah, wattan, hukūmah, 'adl, dhulm, siyāsah, huriyya, tarbiya," (community, country, government, justice, oppression, politics, freedom, and education) respectively. He says, "I implore the readers of this epistle to allot these words a huge portion of their care and devotion, for I explicate expressions currently circulating among the people who speak of them constantly."[297]

If you read carefully between the lines of this epistle, you'll hardly miss the very interesting, thoughtful expression and, what's important, deliberate avoidance of any mention of objection to the power-elites' openness to Europe. Yet in this very absence or what seems to be one, you discern the unmistakable battle that Sheikh Marsifī tacitly carries out against the advocates of the new trend of modernization who are deeply influenced by the various schools of Europe. But the Sheikh ignores his adversaries; he also guards as much against using the word Europe as mentioning anything in relation to it. This means that his explicatory epistle, despite its significance as a representation of a silent battle he's fighting, its author, whose behavior's typical of *ulama* in general, refuses to

---

[297] Husayn al-Marsifi, *Risālat al-Kalam al-Thamān*. (Beiruth: Dar al-Tali'a, 1982), p. 39.

join the circle of debate in vogue in Cairo at the time—except in the form of passive strategy or, if you will, passive resistance.

122

Al-Marsifī's passive resistance spurs me on to consider certain aspects of Jamāl al-Dīn al-Afghānī's work, even though he isn't an Arab-Muslim. Not only he contrasts with Sheikh Marsifī (he's actually everything the Sheikh isn't); as well he's the most outspoken, complex thinker the Muslim world has ever known so far. I also consider his work, though briefly, because he lives in Egypt for a while and works together closely with his student and colleague the Arab-Muslim scholar Muhammad Abduh. Finally, both al-Afghānī's and Abduh's thoughts are beautifully fused in the work of Sheikh Husayn al-Jisr, which, also briefly, I consider last.

Al-Afghānī, to say it again, is a multi-layered thinker, and far from being easy to pin down to something or anything palpably specific. Still, you could say that his project as a whole spans or comprises a two-fold thematic: to strengthen the arm of Egyptian-Indian Muslims, exploited as they are to the point of misery by English Imperialism, and to help Muslims everywhere, as they too are exploited by Western imperialism in general, to regain their unity and dignity. Much, of course, has been written about this double thematic, which obviates the necessity for me to repeat any aspect of it even in a summary form.[298]

Two specific aspects of his personality and project (I'm inclined to think his personality is pretty much his project) may be isolated for a better comprehension of both. To begin with, he's always admired the French Revolution's mottos of freedom, equality, and fraternity. And, like his contemporary Nietzsche, he thinks the French, before the revolution, are the civilizers of all European peoples.[299] But he doesn't admire Rousseau and, unlike

---

[298] See Horani, pp. 103-192, an excellent study; see also Nikki R. Keddie, *An Islamic Response to Imperialism: Political and Religious Writings of Sayyid Jamāl al-Dīn al-Afghāni* (Berkeley: University of California Press, 1983).

[299] If you wish to know and understand why Arab-Muslim savants are fascinated by the French people and French culture, see F. Nietzsche's brief aphorism on the French: *Daybreak: Thoughts on the Prejudices of Morality*, trans R.J. Hollingdale (New York: Cambridge University Press,

Nietzsche, Voltaire. Why? Because, claiming to remove superstition and enlighten minds, they overthrow duty, and sow the seeds of license and communism. They consider manners and customs superstitious, and religions the inventions of men of deficient reason. In a word, "they openly engage in denying divinity and slandering the prophets."[300] Though Nietzsche might concur with him concerning Rousseau, I don't think he would agree with him concerning Voltaire. Unfortunately, al-Afghānī doesn't consider Voltaire's free spirit, his bright, clever, sardonic smile—everything that's unromantic about him, particularly his celebration of the multi-faceted enigma of human reason.

123

In any event, what's interesting for me is al-Afghāni's multi-layered personality. I mean there are several voices that traverse him at the same time— Muslim (now Shi'ī, now anti-clerical); populist defending the cause of Islam, Westerner defending science and philosophy; also Indian, Persian, Egyptian. A kind of "internal" polylogue (he prefers to speak, not write) adapting to the occasion that requires one or the other voice. Put otherwise, he speaks in the first person while multiplying proper names, masks, signatures. That way, he comes, I think, as close as possible to Nietzsche's encomium of mask wearing: "whatever is profound loves masks... There's not only guile behind a mask—there is so much graciousness in cunning.[301] That's al-Afghani in a nutshell. It's as if he doesn't want to give up any of these voices or masks. Why should he? After all, they constitute his very "culture."

Let there be no misunderstanding: al-Afghāni's multiple voices hardly signify indifference or purposelessness; housed in one man or body, they make him no drifting iceberg setting with any current anywhere that wreck ships. Quite the contrary, he's the man who definitely knows his own mind, firm and steadfast

---

1999), section 192. Not that Nietzsche talks about Arab-Muslims, but that his insight into the French character and achievements is helpful.

[300] Jamāl al-Dīn al-Afghānī, al-A'māl al-Kāmila (Beirut: Dār al-Kātib al-'Arabi), p. 521.

[301] See F. Nietzsche, Beyond Good and Evil, trans. Walter Kaufmann (New York: Vinatge Books, 1989), section 40, p. 50.

as ever. So much so, in fact, you find a sense of dignity, a certain pathos agitating beneath these voices—which I just called "culture." And this culture pits his taste not against Christianity as such, but against what Christian Western oppressors have done and might do to Muslims and Arab-Muslims morally and spiritually. He wants to understand why these oppressors are bent on exploiting Muslims and Arab-Muslims; and he doesn't seem to find a sensible justification for it.[302] Which absence explains another thing: first, it incites him to speak for the behalf of early Arab-Muslims; secondly, it empowers him to apologize for their inability to accord the faculty of reason a guiding role in their lives—but instead to cling all the more to the tutelage of religion.[303] Something I already touched on in my brief historical review of the Arab-Muslim community.[304] There I express my sadness, too. Al-Afghānī and I are quite sad about this Western will to oppression. We feel it ought to transcend itself so that Arab-Muslims might find a way out of the plight (in all the senses of the word) in which they still find themselves.

124

What on earth attracts Muhammad Abduh to al-Afghani? Isn't it perhaps the latter's special pathos—his extensive knowledge of both East and West, so that he inhabits each with such ease and confidence? Isn't it, by the same token, his sympathy for the plight of Arab-Muslims? Isn't it, finally, Abduh himself, a scholar and a Sheikh of al-Azhar University as devout as he and, therefore, an equal in intellectual caliber? In short, isn't it simply the meeting of two minds? The answer to all questions is the affirmative yes. But then such meeting of minds hardly means two peas in the pod. In point of fact, here are two

---

[302] Of course, he's no philosopher of power; hence it doesn't occur to him, as Nietzsche says, that power must express itself; it assimilates everything it lays hands on for more power. See F. Nietzsche, *The Will to Power*, translation Walter Kaufmann (New York: Vintage Books, 1968), section 2. "The Will to Power as Life," pp. 341-347.

[303] See "Réponse de Jamāl ad-Dīn al-Afghāni á Renan," *Jamāl ad-Dīn al-Afghānī, Réfutation des matérialist,* trans. A.M. Goichon (Paris, 1942); also Nikki R. Keddie, pp. 181-187 in particular. The Arabic text isn't included in the complete works.

[304] See above, part one chapter one.

personalities and minds as much alike as they're different in their views of the East in relation to the West.

Now Abduh believes, as al-Afghāni does, that the way out of this Arab-Muslim plight is surely a return to the original and authentic teachings of Islam—but with the proviso that Arab-Muslims can no more afford to remain under the tutelage of religion alone than under the tutelage of reason alone, or philosophy alone or science alone. The two powers—religion and reason—must work in tandem. So that agreement and reconciliation may be effected between them. And that's precisely the point at which the two scholars differ. Al-Afghāni argues that no agreement and reconciliation is possible between religions and philosophy. "Religion imposes on man its faith and its belief, whereas philosophy frees him of it totally or in part."[305] It's a bit surprising that he himself never frees himself from such a mental binary structure. Anyhow, Abduh argues differently.

Reason, he says in effect, can't act independently as a guarantor of security and happiness for a people, nor can it even forge those two conditions without the guidance of faith. Just as no animal can perceive a physical object or phenomenon by the sense of sight alone but needs also the sense of hearing to grasp it totally, so no religion, itself like a general sense organ, ever fails to come to aid reason in what reason conceives to be the means to happiness. Reason and religion, then, are quanta of forces reinforcing, sometimes jostling, each other for a full comprehension of phenomena. In other words, reason, by nature a limited faculty, not only corrals faith, being unlimited, to unveils its beliefs, but also helps set them within the bounds of practical operations. "How could anyone," Abduh concludes, " deny reason its right in doing exactly that, that is, in examining and sifting through all the proofs (offered by religion) that eventually lead him to understanding it (religion)—understanding which God grants him."[306]

125

---

[305] See Nikki Keddie, *An Islamic response to Imperialism*, p. 187.

[306] See Muhammad Abduh, *Risālat al-Tawhīd* (Cairo: Dar al-Ma'arif Bimasr, 1971), p. 142.

Obviously, what Abduh attempts to do here, at least theoretically, is to exercise his *Ijtihad:* that is, to infuse religion and faith with the spirit of reason, so that religion, as it sits in the hearts of the populace, may be trained to free itself from the shackles of traditionalism and dogma. Which, of course, can easily be done if, according to Abduh, teaching and learning institutions get reformed as soon as possible.[307]   He waxes lyrical on the subject of the long forgotten exercise of intellectual freedom—*Ijtihad:* "the faithful have long been deprived of independence of will and independence of thought and opinion—without which no Arab-Muslim worth his/her salt can be happy as God intends them to be."[308]

Al-Afghānī, needless to say, doesn't see it that way: he thinks the masses "dislike reason and its teachings."[309]   And the two, the masses and reason, to cut corners, part ways. Obviously, he cares little for education of the masses. What's more, the distance between the two scholars gets wider and wider the more they touch on political issues, such as negotiations with the English. I mean al-Afghānī distrusts the English and will have nothing to do with them, while Abduh, disagreeing, argues that reconciliation or making peace with the English redounds to the greater benefit of the Egyptian people. And says so in the same breath with which he enjoins Arab-Muslims to hold the tool of critical understanding and delve deeply into the recesses of faith in order to uproot the causes of their decline.[310]

In fact, Abduh is quite clear about his attitude and view of the English. While he urges profound study and comprehension of the secrets of European accomplishments in science and technology and philosophy, it's mandatory, he says in effect, that we should compete with the Europeans, now more than ever, by manufacturing guns and rifles, warships in land, in the air, in the sea, among other military arts and gears. And that, naturally, depends on our rigorous

---

[307] *Ibid*, p. 151.

[308] Ibid, p. 151.

[309] *An Islamic response to Imperialism*, p. 187.

[310] *Risalat al-Tawhid*, p. 155.

learning of physics and mathematics. "This is a duty," he concludes, "imposed on Arab-Muslims in this age, because the obligation of our being prepared militarily can hardly be accomplished without these sciences."[311] Which explains the two birds he tries to hit with one stone: to reform the system of education and to excise what fantasies and superstitions still cling to the faith, on the one hand, and to express his suspicions of the teaching and learning institutions that Europeans have set up in Egypt.

126

The upshot of Abduh's position is this: he accepts wholeheartedly the notion of keeping one's rendezvous with Europe, so that clear apprehension in regard to its progress and thought might lead to the possibility of change here at home. At the same time, however, he rejects the opinion exhorting Arab-Muslims to imitate Europeans lock, stock, and barrel. Like Khayr al-Dīn al-Tūnisi, he'd rather trade on European attainment in science, military, and politics as sensible means to return to history—and to do so not only to review the rationality of Muslim dogma but also to inaugurate the project of reforming religious belief itself. This double-edged attitude in relation to the West and to reform anticipates Ali Mirsepassi's statement at the end of twentieth century, which, though quoted earlier, I'd like to quote again, since it's beautifully worded: "Fear of democracy in the Islamic countries is indeed a product of becoming alien to their own history and culture; and to achieve self-awareness, to re-gain insight into the most important aspects of their repressed history and culture, they have to face the West, walk through it, get to know it first hand, and then look back."[312] I think this is precisely what Abduh tries to do at the time.

And to do it knowing full well it doesn't any way signify total reconciliation between Muslim faith and European progress, or between Islam and Christianity. The feat is almost impossible as al-Afghāni has believed all along. And so Abduh's far from opposing him or anyone else on that score. But

---

[311] Paraphrased from Arabic translation of Charles Adams' book, *al-Islam wa-l Tajdid fi Masr* (Cairo: Da'irat al-Ma'arif al-Islamiyya, 1935), p. 128.

[312] See above, page 36.

it does mean that European progress incites him, in Mirsepassi's words, to look back in order to re-examine the dogma and elucidate whether its jurisdiction is appropriate for his time. A more rounded project of the same magnitude is taken up by the well-educated Sheikh Husayn al-Jisr who leaves no stone unturned in an effort to combine al-Afghani's insightful thoughts with those of Abduh.

127

Sheikh al-Jisr is a student of al-Azhar University, and influenced by none other than Sheikh Marsifi himself. He is also the Sheikh of education, of well-rounded education, that is, both Islamic and European or Western. For in the course of explaining the latter's resources for progress, he comes to learn to deem education the way to a people's advancement. I know, he says in effect, when Westerners have wakened from their long sleep of carelessness and risen from their thick-witted hibernation, they've found that the surest means to ascend the ladder of perfection and reach the summit of civilization is the widespread development and continued prevalence of sciences among them—of which rich and poor, great and lowly, old and young partake.[313] He also underscores European progress in the domains of industry and agriculture, and, therefore, he doesn't see any objection in emulating them in these fields. Indeed, he goes on to say, it's imperative that Arab-Muslims import modern sciences—industry, arts, commerce, agriculture, even their neighbors' (European) steam engines, then pursue them most rigorously so that they're enabled to confront them on an equal footing when the occasion arises.[314]

Sheikh al-Jisr also believes that Arab-Muslims, unlike Europeans, don't require six centuries to attain unto the realm of progress. They can, he concludes, and right away, get hold of the very tools the West has used (they're now available there) so as to set tem up and build on them. For while the West has struggled without a clear-cut goal and followed an unclear course, Arab-Muslims differ in that they have solid determination and resources (skilled technicians,

---

[313] See Husayn al-Jisr, *Riyād, Trāblus, al-Shām* (Tripoli, no date), vol. 1, p. 50.

[314] *Ibid*, vol. 2, p. 6.

proficient organizers, experienced politicians) to do the job and arrive at their goal in not time. In short, they can be on the upswing so long as they don't lose sight or overshoot the mark of what's immediately necessary for them now.[315]

Sheikh al-Jisr has all the respect and admiration for Europeans. But he doesn't forget that their achievements belong in the domain of materialism. Which explains his sharp focus on science and technology. He's also aware of European accomplishments in arts and philosophy, but he has no use for them in particular. For example, issues like freedom and equality which occupy his contemporaries' minds, stir up little or nothing in him. Actually, he isn't interested. Ultimately, he feels no Western political system matches Islam's. Consequently, unlike his contemporaries, he takes no interest in matters of imperialism or oppression or revolution. Nor does he, curiously enough, see any challenge posed by Western politics. You could say this fortification against Western politics resides in his unshakeable confidence that all that Arab-Muslims need are the tools to put them on the upgrade in the world in which they live and of which they form a part.

128

Al-Jisr's main goal in his fortified attitude to politics is that he really wants to set down the fact that Islam is a politics and a way of life and a religion-- all in one. After all, Muhammad's mission is an authentic one and *Sharī'a* is appropriate for all time since it's adaptable to all time. Now if scientific discoveries and knowledge contravene what the Qur'ān contains, then that's due to errors in textual interpretation. For these texts comport with reason. This is the same conclusion that Abduh has already reached: *Sharī'a* in no way disagrees with intellectual sciences. The difference, though, is that Abduh speaks intuitively or lyrically while al-Jisr reaches it by reasoning or argumentation. How so?

He demonstrates sound knowledge when he discusses his quarrel with modern materialist theories and refutes them. This is new in late nineteenth century: no one else undertakes that kind of project, not even al-Afghāni and

---

[315] *Ibid*, p. 7.

Abduh who dabble here and there with chatty, on the surface manner in Darwin's theories of evolution, but nothing like al-Jisr's argumentative exposition in his most important book which he designates as an epistle.

He begins the epistle with extensive marking of the important principles of the faith and of *Sharī'a*. The aim is to elucidate the truth of Muhammad's mission as well as to re-mark the continuity of *Sharī'a's* jurisdiction and its application through all time. If you ask why bother with such lengthy exposition and not simply come to the point immediately? The answer, it seems to me, is that he needs, before taking up his argumentation, spiritual ammunition with which to parry the theories of the materialists and evolutionists intelligently. That's not all, the exposition itself actually symbolizes, again as I see it, a necessary gateway to confirming his faith which brooks no doubt of the authenticity of Islamic faith. It also symbolizes his attempt to reinforce and foster the faith and Sharī'a principles and, in turn, to enjoin his readers to be always mindful of them and to understand their significations.

And when the time comes for him to respond to the materialist and evolutionist theories, he first sets his thought down in the form of a summary, or rather of a summary of how he himself understands those theories. I know, he says in effect, that our ancestors have developed various schools of thought in relation to the origin of the universe, the heavenly bodies, this earth and its variety of human beings, its flora and fauna. But what's been fixed now, what's been established and corroborated by evidence and experience is that the source or origin of this world, so they say, is two-fold: matter and force (motion). What's more, they say these two entities are so old, so indivisible one from the other that no one could by any stretch of the imagination entertain the fantasy of their ever being apart. Now matter is ether filling the entire space, and space is primordial matter in simplest form possible. Force, on the other hand, is the motion of the separate particles of matter which are identical but which are different in qualities and in form.

They say that this motion is self-caused, and that the heavenly bodies— planets, humans, plants, animals, objects—are formed from matter itself by means of its motions. And this formation has occurred not after the manner of the effect occurring from the cause in accordance with necessity. In other words, the formation hasn't proceeded according to the law of cause and effect or according to cosmic designer. Besides, neither matter nor its motion or force has consciousness and purpose in generating anything from itself. So then when these particles have combined in special qualities there occurs a nebulous matter, that is, small bodies that gather together by means of the law of gravity. And so research and experiments have shown that the combination of matter's particles by their force or motion and their mixing together in specific or special proportions metals are formed as are all material bodies.[316]

129

What, you may ask, does Sheikh al-Jisr accomplish by this exposition? In a nutshell, to unveil the fragility of materialist theory. If the first cause is immemorial as those theorists claim, how then is it possible to judge that its effects are under way when this cause itself exists since time immemorial. Put otherwise, if the cause of the variety of things which is matter and its force is immemorial, then its susceptibility to create would also be immemorial; and if its susceptibility is so, then the variety, too, would be so. But the fact is that neither the latter, nor the former, nor the first cause is so at all. Consequently, if before its susceptibility to create, what are matter and its force doing in the domain of time immemorial? And how could matter experience time when it's moving about without productivity? On the other hand, an event or what's under way must inevitably have something issue from it, something which would indicate its existence if it's absent, like something brought to light from darkness; otherwise it's bound to probability without being probable—which is decidedly self-evident and axiomatic.

It's an error to conclude that al-Jisr is attacking science and its important contribution to human knowledge of the universe and its function. Of which he's

---

[316] See *al-Risāla al-Hamīdiyya fī Haqīqāt al-Diyāna al-Islāmiyya wa Haqīqat al-Shari'a al-Muhammadiyya* (Beirut, 1889), pp. 162-167. What I present here are highlights of al-Jisr's thought. And I'm not completely sure that I've hit the mark. I'm hoping readers may get the gist of his thought by the little I present.

profoundly aware and quite appreciative. He's actually of the opinion that if what the theorists claim is true, then it behooves Arab-Muslims to interpret them congruent with *Sharī'a* texts. Notice also that he doesn't even denounce the evolutionists; in point of fact, he argues that if the theory of evolution is proven correct someday , then Arab-Muslims are bound by duty to interpret it in order to reconcile it with the faith so as to maintain the faith.[317]

130

In conclusion, Sheikh al-Jisr is no doubt a redoubtable associative thinker, and, perhaps the only in the Arab-Muslim world of the nineteenth century. His views of East-West relations, of the West, in particular, are, like al-Afghāni's, respectful, admiring, thoughtful—though cautious. Cautious because he doesn't wish science to overrun or overpower the faith nor the latter the former. He'd rather see them agree if he could manage it, only because such agreement redounds only to the enrichment and perfection of Arab-Muslims envisioned by God in *Sharī'a*. In this sense, he's very much in concurrence with Abduh. But, unlike al-Afghāni and Abduh, de doesn't return to the past, to the original sources—Qur'an, *Sunnah, Hadith*—for spiritual food or for reactivating everything he finds there. After all, it's impossible to find the solution of a problem in the solution of another problem raised at another moment by other people. I think he's quite aware of that. But one can return to these past monuments in search for tools for analyzing what's going on now or at the time— and to modify it.

Also, unlike al-Afghāni and Abduh who are ideologists without a following, al-Jisr speaks to a huge number of people. In point of fact, his epistle *Risala al-Hamidiyya...* has had profound influence at the time (it appears in

---

[317] *Ibid,* p. 305. I'm not sure if the devout Muslim Muhammad Iqbāl has in mind Sheikh al-Jisr's reconciliatory attitude when he makes the following remark: Einstein's theory creates a new way of seeing the universe and suggests new ways to see problems common to both religion and philosophy. It is hardly a matter of surprise that the new Muslim generation of Asia and Africa demands a new direction for its faith. With the renewal of Islam, it's necessary to examine without any preconceived ideas European ideas and the degree to which the conclusions Europe has reached can help us to rethink and, if necessary, reconstruct the theological concepts of Islam." See *Reconstruire la pensée réligieuse de l'islam* (Paris: Editions Adrien-Maisonneuve, 1955), p. 14. When you juxtapose the two men's ideas, you have insight into the tremendous flexibility of Islamic faith and its essence of peacefulness and moderation.

1888), particularly in relation to the thought or debate then going on with the theories of materialism and evolution. Finally, unlike al-Afghānī and Abduh who want to return to the sources, actually to the rule of *'ulama* lock, stock, and barrel, his work lends spiritual weight to the art of scholastic theology which has had no other sources but the volumes and compilations of anterior authors. I think that in a surreptitious way al-Jisr is very much in favor of *Ijtihad* and wants to see it resurrected from the dead.

The contradiction or, let's say, the incompatibility between science and faith is nothing new; it's actually still going on today, and quite fiercely.[318] It's certainly redolent of paradoxes, ambiguities, complexities almost impossible to resolve. But, to say it again, isn't the impossible by its very nature possible, if people would just let themselves observe how events or thoughts are inscribed in a chain or in a system within which one event or thought refers to the other precisely by means of no specific agent, subject, or a consciousness underlying it. For example, in the final years of the nineteenth century, someone like Sheikh al-Jisr appears on the scene of materialist and evolutionist theories, waylays them, but hardly knows beforehand he'd enter the debate with them and come out a different thinker. I mean while he begins his project by defining the limits of Arab-Muslim faith and *Sharī'a* based on his knowledge of traditional material, he ends, when he finishes his fray with the theories, by thinking or rather by re-thinking his faith inoculated with a disposition for rationality. All this without the least intervention of consciousness. In the long run, he comes to believe that he shouldn't sever the links between faith and whatever is proven scientifically true, including the theory of evolution and progress. Indeed, if this theory is proven correct, God's wisdom, he believes, is capacious enough to accommodate it.

131

The new coloring visible in al-Jisr's theological thought parallels that of many other Muslim reformists. Because of them Arab-Muslims in general begin to comprehend their religion in a new way. Reason appears like an agent mediating between text and epoch, and from this operation a fresh understanding

---

[318] See Niall Shanks, *God, the Devil, and Darwin* (New York: Oxford University Press, 2004).

occurs for the first time.[319] The persistence of Muslim reformists in challenging modern European thought urges them to charge Islam with what it couldn't do in its history. Consequently, Islam widens its scope for "democracy" and freedom through the restitution of *Ijtihad*, deliberation (*Shura*), and fairness.

In addition, al-Afghānī, Abduh and al-Jisr lay down what I'd like to call the principles of the brave new world of ideological dispute which develops with them in late nineteenth century. As a point of comparison, you could then say al-Tahtāwi, Mubārak, and al-Tūnisi (whom you met earlier) portray, as they see it, the picture of Europe as progressive and liberal, though uneager for the fray of debate. The former threesome, however, view Europe only through their view of themselves as Arab-Muslims, while they view themselves as such—and this is significant—only through putting up Europe as model before their eyes. This situation impresses its image, the image of a new vision of self-knowledge through the other, upon the entire next century. What, in a nutshell, both Plato and Mirsepassi have thought.

---

[319] See *Fahmi Jad'ān, Usus al-Taqadum 'ind Mufakīrī al-Islām fi-l 'ālam al-'Arabi al-Hadith* (Beirut: al-Mu'asasa al-'Arabiyya lil-Dirāsāt, 1978), pp. 200-228.

Chapter Three: The Modern View
Part One

132

For two hundred years, the gap between East and West (Islam and Europe) seems to get narrower. It'll be closed one day, I wager. This is due to the reform launched by certain Muslims (Ottoman and Arab). The dynamo of this reform is, of course, Europe. It energizes their heart and mind, even amid distrust of it; at least, it re-awakens them to a familiar history.[320] France in particular, though worldly, treacherous, yet fascinating, goads them to it, as does England to a lesser extent. These two cultures and their own rich, diverse history coalesce as a force to generate a new trend of thought that in the long run materializes in a political movement called constitutionalism. In a word, Europe or the West becomes that other against which Arab-Muslims measure themselves in their own mind. From this they come to know themselves solely in regard to their powers of intellect and debate.

This movement simply means the populace can now freely elect their representatives. It also means certain modifications in political structure are both imminent and necessary. That's precisely what transpires in Turkey. One major modification, for example, occurs between 1879-1908 when the sultan's authority gradually shrinks to a minimum, though not without disturbance or tension in its wake. This clears the grounds a decade or so later for the pro-European Mustafa Kamāl to make Turkey's political and in social life a piece of Europe. But this is too long and complex a story for me to take up here. Suffice it to say in Egypt

---

[320] You recall the age of philosophy and sciences that some Arab-Muslims introduce into their community in the ninth and tenth centuries. What Europe does is simply reminds them, at least those who care for their countries, to that history.

and Tūnis the constitutional movement leads to no hostilities or declared tension between parties. Kamāl's political reforms do stir up a bit of unrest in Egypt and Tūnis, but not so much as to corral or win the countries over to his side. Even the abolishment of caliphate in Turkey and its transfer to Cairo changes nothing. Ironically, the double act stimulates Tunisians and Egyptians, the latter more than the former, to do or think the opposite with respect to the issue of the caliphate and other related matters. But things aren't simple as you think.

133

Let one serve for legion. In the first half of the twentieth century al-Azhar Sheikh 'Ali 'Abd a-Razzāq stirs up some controversy around the notion of the Caliphate: does it deserve serious political or even religions attention or not? I think this kind of argument, if I may anticipate, opens up not a can of worms or evils (resentment, destruction, belligerence, and so on)—but rather discussion. Discussion, *Ijtihad*, negotiation, argumentation, debate—these desiderata of democracy in the most open sense of democracy (which is yet to come) constitute an early historical precedent for today's most urgent praxis in Mid-East politics or politico-religious structures.

The Caliphate, he says in effect, is innocent of or external to the Muslim faith. For one thing, the Qur'ān is too great, too spiritual to even mention or hint at it. For another, the *Sunnah* and *Ijma'* each honors it by thoughtfully keeping it at bay. "Well, given that, are there other religious sources available that refer to it if these don't? Not that I know of," he answers.[321] Besides, actual reality as made by history and endorsed by reason demonstrates that God's rituals and His noble Revelations are hardly dependent on the kind of government the *'ulama* call Caliphate. Hardly dependent, too, for that matter on any caliph designated by the people as such. After all, Muslim and Arab-Muslim ethics never hinge on the

---

[321] See 'Ali 'Abd a-Razzāq, *al-Islām wa 'Usūl al-Hukm* (Beiruth: al-Mu'asasa al-'Arabiyya, 1972), p. 124.

presence or absence of Caliphate either. Put otherwise, "Arab-Muslims have absolutely no need for a caliphate rule in their religion and life."[322]

Obviously, Sheikh 'Abd a-Razzāq, since he brings up reason and history, wants to see religion totally separate from politics. If we clip the wings of reason, he seems to imply, and inhibit rational inquiry into the nature of the world in which we live, there's no surety, no guarantee either that we can flourish as human beings under the hegemony of religion alone. That's why he characterizes Muhammad as no more than a devout warner and a man. This is simply remarkable, to say the least: here's a devout Arab-Muslim who, out of respect for Muhammad, the Qur'ān, the *Sunnah,* and *Ijma'*, *Shurah* assimilates so comfortably Western ideas about the separation of church and state, who also sees it conducive to his nation's prosperity and well-being to adopt and adapt, without being blindly imitative, those ideas to its socio-political life.[323]

133

But the will to such felicitous fitting of ideas rarely goes scot-free. It's in the nature of things. He now has a critic, another al-Azhar Sheikh named Muhammad Bakhīt. Sheikh Bakhīt also happens to be well versed in European Enlightenment and perhaps a secretive advocate for the practice of separation of church and state. His criticism, though, is a bit cagy, cautious, guarded and so, at the same time, most revealing of his innermost and, if I'm right, honest secret opinion. First, he tries to be modest about it: what is good for the goose (Christianity), if I read his mind correctly, isn't necessary good for the gander (Islam). But, taciturn as he is, he doesn't really explain why. Anyhow, he then turns to 'Abd a-Razzāq's ideas and generalizes some more: people need a governor and a ruler to hold them within prescribed limits, to avert oppression perpetrated against them, to administer justice among them, and to judge in accordance with the law accepted by them all.

---

[322] *Ibid,* p. 136.

[323] For further insight, see Horani, pp. 82-88.

Albert Horani, however, sees through all this. Looking, so to speak, over the shoulders of both Sheikhs, he observes that Sheikh Bakhīt actually espouses Sheikh 'Abd a-Razzāq's declaration that Arab-Muslim Sunni thought has always ascribed the caliph's authority either to God directly or to the people; he also explicitly avows that the correct opinion is that which says that the community is the source of the caliph's authority, that the caliph derives his authority from the community, and that the Islamic government headed by the caliph or imam is a democratic government—free and consultative. In saying so, Horani, further observes, Sheikh Bakhīt not only admits Islamic political institutions to be similar in detail to that of modern political institutions, but he also entertains the thought that the two types of institutions hardly differ from each other. We see, Horani concludes, conciliation between Islamic political conceptions and modern ones of which Arab-Muslim forefathers speak has been accepted today without question. Consequently, you see a sort of irony here: it appears that Sheikh Bakhīt doesn't realize that in saying all that he says and thinks, he actually paves the way for European rationality to penetrate Islam—yet by the same token he criticizes his colleague Sheikh 'abd a-Razzāq.[324]

134

Let's pause here at this point in time so as to put things in perspective. Medieval Arab-Muslim savants see Europe in terms of climate, topography, temperament and behavior; sixteenth- and seventeenth-century Ottoman-Muslims echo the same, up to a point. But soon the empire and Europe get to be neighbors, or shall we say, adjacent enemy-friends; then the view gets displaced into that of coveting Western domains of science and technology, for which nineteenth-century Egyptians extend their desire still further. This extension, in turn, leads, in the second half of the nineteenth century, to the view of the West as the hub of liberalism and as such a model for Arab-Muslims to emulate. In the first half of twentieth century, the portrait acquires yet more intricate features: The West stimulates new trends of critical thought, and permeates through every nook and

---

[324] See Horani, pp. 189-193

cranny of their psyche. I mean from now on they can neither tackle their affairs outside East-West nexus nor ignore Western infusion of philosophy, rationalism, and science.

In this connection you find the scholar Muhammad Farīd Wajdi the perfect exemplar of East-West critical rapprochement. On the one hand, he betrays an extremist attitude that's still prevalent today, namely everything modern already exists in Islam; on the other hand, he spurs Arab-Muslims to a spiritual and intellectual agonism with Western thought. In both instances, he, along with his critics, prefigures the integrative thought of cultural theorists in the second half of twentieth century. These theorists would hold in check the invasion of Islam by Western rationalism, and set up as their mechanism of rapprochement East-West critical debate.

135

To renew his faith in the purity of Islam, Wajdi must search for it in the heap of European Enlightenment now piling up tall and imposing almost irresistibly in the Arab-Muslim world. In so doing, though, he doesn't give up either. His purpose isn't just to reveal the delusions that Europeans are immersed in, which fact distresses him; he also desires to draw serious attention to what he calls "the potion seeping unctuously, as it were, into the blood stream of our Muslim youths." He means the spirit of enlightenment. For these youths imbibe this spirit so unwittingly, so unreflectively it unhinges "them from their community and renders them destitute, neither here nor there."[325] To safeguard youthful minds, he steers in a dual path: he elucidates the truth and benefit of European sciences and at the same time affirms the truth and rewards of Islam. And what's this truth?

Well, Islam and modernity, he argues, are one and the same; in other words, since Islam is everything modernity is, a person could be both Muslim and modernist. And he really believes this is quite possible. After all, Western

---

[325] See Muhammad Farīd Wajdi, *al-Islām fī 'Asr al-'Ilm* (Beirut: Dar al-Kitāb al-'Arabī, no date), p. 20.

epistemology is but a one-sided thing and leaves something to be desired. And to clarify this idea, he exploits this Western ideas: if sensualist-materialist philosophy (a la August Comte) proposes the principle that any intelligibility incommensurate with emotional reality is probably illusory; and if this philosophy occupies a space in today's social fabric that's almost impossible to dislodge it from, how, then, "could one believe in religion in an age founded on the assumptions of this kind of philosophy and those principles?"[326] Obviously, the answer would be no one could. So Islam could fill the void.

At the same time Wajdi doesn't neglect to state his position precisely. He neither takes a stand against science nor fulminate against it: "I'm no enemy of true epistemology, nor an opponent of any of its sound branches."[327] Yet, having said that, he hardly explains what he means by true epistemology or sound branches, though he gives a hint or two. He contextualizes this position in Arab-Muslim ethical experience. Islam, he says in effect, is both a religion and a way of life with the sublime goal of liberating humanity from all malicious chimeras and false convictions that have clung to its moral constitution like poison ivy. Its goal, therefore, and perhaps its ideal, too, is no different, for example, from that of August Comte or Francis Bacon, and others in their effort to cleanse human perceptions of untruth, simulacra and injustice. In short, it's a complementary vessel of provisions for humanity's long journey to perfection in all aspects.[328]

136

Having cast Islam in an exemplary mould—the champion of human equality, of intellect and science, of discussion and freedom, of principles of progress—Wajdi concludes: today our illness in Egypt, also in the Arab-Muslim world, is that which results from blind adherence to tradition in all its aspects. It's what makes Islam, confronting modernity, weak from within, vulnerable,

---

[326] *Ibid*, p. 21.

[327] *Ibid*, p. 22.

[328] Ibid, p. 22. Wajdi strikes a chord in me: although he might not have read Nietzsche, he agrees with him about Comte's mandarin and hypocritical philosophy. *Will to Power*, p. 78.

unable to resist temptations. Hence the tinsel world of the West infiltrates our midst under names and appearances at once charming and veiled, or rather charming because veiled—and, for that reason spiritually dangerous. Therefore, and this is as much necessary as destined, we must resist it with our truths and laws. Resist here signifies becoming equal; we, too, he continues, possess in these truths and laws what it takes to be progressive; we must carry on, for our sanity and health, our agonism with the West.[329] A call which doesn't, I think, go unheeded in the second half of twentieth century. For you can hear it echoed by the four cultural theorists of the second half of twentieth century.

Wajdi's views clearly identify certain common grounds between East and West, especially in the domains of thought and knowledge. But, and here Horani hits the nail on the head, he, unwittingly, finishes by dissolving Islam it into modernity.[330] However, he, though Horani may be unaware of it, countervails by stressing East-West on-going debate at all levels: it would, he speculates, plant the seeds for profound intellectual jousts. "Profound" may have been responsible for the later characterization of such jousts as clash of civilizations, or, the most current, "clash of monotheisms."[331] Hence the unfortunate reduction of East-West to unilateral rather than multilateral relations. This is the incorrect or simplistic focus, as I tried to show before, and would, if not abandoned, make matters worse. After all, the West, you see, is as many-sided, complex, and culturally diverse as is Islam, as Djait and Saīd have already said.[332]

137

Unlike Wajdi, the Lebanese Rashīd Rida attempts to restore to Islam its center of gravity. For he wants it to negotiate from a multiple position of strength, character, and intellect, the better to bridge differences between East and

---

[329] *Ibid,* p. 694.

[330] See Horani, p. 162.

[331] See Reza Aslan, *No God But God: The Origins, Evolution, and Future of Islam* (New York: Random House, 2005), Prologue, p. 15. The entire book centers around this notion of clash of monotheisms with the intention of refuting it, of course, for which I couldn't but be moregrateful.

[332] See Djiat, pp. 130-136; also Said, *Covering Islam.*

West. And for this to be at all, Arab-Muslims must perform two daring feats: put down Sufism for teaching abject submission (which contradicts the essence of *Jihad* and *Ijtihad*); and merge cautiously with the spirit of the age. You can see Rida has a lot on his plate. He lives through the abolishment of the caliphate, then the break-up of Ottoman-Muslim Empire, and finally the parceling out of its remains by European colonizers. So he knows of the danger of Europe, its policy of encouraging particularism only and, as a corollary, of the shaky grounds on which Egypt and Lebanon stand. Besides, being an advocate of religious reform, he adopts the policy of careful reformism and furthers the religious work of his masters al-Afghāni, Abduh, and al-Jisr, without stirring up the rancor of intransigent conservatives, even in speaking of women's suffrage, *Jihad* (self-overcoming), *Ijtihad* (freedom of thought), or caliphate.

Such merits, among others, stand him, let's say, stand Islam, in good stead for East-West conciliation. Of course, he's, again, aware of Europe's threat and power, also of the difficulties relating to the hard-nosed intentions of European colonizers who, he feels, refuse to pursue a lenient policy with Muslims and Arab-Muslims. In effect, and because of this European colossus (in all the senses of the word), he possesses (and knows it, too) only one intellectual force (at least at the time): namely *Shari'a* tempered by positive law or a system of just laws appropriate to the situation in which its past history has placed it and with which to joust European thought, especially that of the English "who of all jinn and human on earth are the mightiest in deception."[333] And yet that meager arsenal for debate hardly daunts him; in point of fact, it goads him, daring him all the more to ply his peaceful trade.

138

And so he directs his efforts toward the possibility of face-to-face exchange with the liberals of Europe, those national minority peoples who practice autonomy of conscience and opinion. He reasons: what might be the best way to ward off, if not end once and for all European vampirism of our lands?

---

[333] Rashīd Rida, *Rahlāt* (Beirut: al-Mu'asasa al-Arabiyya, 1971), p. 311.

Requiting evil with another? Not at all. Or not yet. Diplomacy, he reasons, comes first. We must, then, have recourse to dialogue, to the art and skill of argumentation. The aim is to persuade the wielders of power directly or indirectly by appeal to their houses of representation and public morality. And what could be a priority topic of these diplomatic negotiations? Freedom, of course, and sovereignty to rule over ourselves. What's more, the entire procedure, if Europe guarantees such inalienable rights, would contribute to mutual profit: Europe trades foods and raw materials for all necessary tools and machinery for us to rebuild our lands.[334]

You see, Rida is certainly no political philosopher in quest of some epistemological harmony with Europe. Rather he hitches his temperament to the mundane and materialist wagon of commensurability between East and West. As to the political problem thereof, he sums it up in similar pragmatic terms: we in the Arab-Muslim world want to construct manufactories and industrial facilities which would enable us to dispense with foreign ones, since these impose economic strictures that strangle us. We ask the West to give us the tools to finish the job of exploiting our soil and redoubling its yield. We know our deficiencies and how to redress them. Therefore, we request Western liberals to be our ombudsmen to facilitate better East-West relations. Colonial governments won't let us get on with the business of preserving our culture and educating our public for maximum benefit to us. At one point we've been quite naïve, not to speak of ignorant, about the nature of these governments' ambitions and secrets of their policies. Now we know. We've been asleep. Now we're awake.[335]

139

Rida's centerpiece is the issue of parity between East and West at the level of industry and, naturally, of progress. But it remains unresolved and so troubling. He tries to set up the proper platform for it to serve as an argument for his trump card: Arab-Muslim sovereignty. You see, he's staking out a claim,

---

[334] *Ibid,* p. 369.

[335] *Ibid,* p. 373.

knowing well in advance it rests on Arab-Muslim present alertness. And he counts on it. In fact, he adduces evidence to show it can be the basis (for his platform) of fruitful dialogue with the West (something not possible a quarter of a century earlier). One overarching piece of evidence is this: Arab-Muslim senior leaders—political and legal experts, orators, writers, philosophers, and generals— and their young aides—the new educated crop of society, who follow their banner—are ecstatically resolute to be free: free to take the helm of their governments, with the laws of the land their only masters. Such leaders and aides would see to it that justice prevails among all peoples, natives or immigrants.[336]

What Rida recommends here, and does so in a subtly way, verges on a sort of mild warning. Though still advocate for East-West parity, he lets on that that mild warning might morph to hostilities if Europe or its liberals ignore Arab-Muslim rights. It would then be a bolshevism more destructive than the Russian one. And what would the consequences be? Nothing but Arab-Muslims' shaking their fists in the face of all European peoples. Which means, Rida imagines, the two forces struggling—Arab-Muslims united (and he has no illusions about that) against European peoples—this time not to achieve parity but to inflict mutual damage. Well, you wonder about this. After all, history has shown—even recently (Sadam Husein's invasion of Quweit through which, as his primary, though hidden objective, he has hoped to rally Arab-Muslims behind him)—the dream of unity isn't easy to fulfill. Not militarily, for sure. And yet Rida's visions of unity and parity remain acts of faith never to be abandoned or undercut by menacing fists.[337]

140

Shakīb Arslan, a formidable scholar and diplomat, is an old friend of Rida's. He follows his banner of Arab-Muslim unity and self-rule (*Jihad*), though he conceives of them a bit differently. For him they mean Islamic reformation

---

[336] *Ibid*, p. 383.

[337] See Horani, pp. 222-244. These pages discuss with profound insight Rida's approach to the issue of Islam regaining its center of gravity.

and Arab nationalism, and the two never part ways. Now the only means to both ends is nothing short of a movement or revolution that would provide a grid of ideas and principles, a point of leverage from which to launch on-going face-to-face negotiations with European imperialism. He himself, in fact, sets an example by taking the lead in these negotiations in France, England, Germany, and Italy more effectively than his friend Rida who has rarely visited Europe.

As to his call for a revolution—and not, say, like al-Afghāni who, when necessary, opts for a one-man rule or even a tyrant to kick off religious reform—it reflects his profound awareness of the decline and disunion of Arab-Muslims, particularly when compared, as he sees it, to the bonding and cohesion of each European nation. Both recognitions lead him to negotiate internally for an Islamic united political front so as to stand up for the latter's rights vis-á-vis imperialist forces. Unlike Rida, you see, he has nothing like bolshevism in mind, nor does he limit his diplomatic discussions, at the level of East-West bridge-building, to appeals to the liberals of Europe—though the appeal itself may be an epiphenomenon which could be usefully combined with political confrontation. In any event, Arslan's plan is an all-out religio-political struggle, keeping in mind the highly organized European political power, first of all.

Arslan, then, is a dualist thinker with East-West polarity as centerpiece of his thought. Which, once more, distinguishes him from Rida. Rida, you see, argues in terms of parity (West and Islam are equal, each a piece of the other historically), Arslan, perhaps more articulate, thinks in terms of polar opposites with many grades between them that could conduce to mutual understanding and bridging differences. An example, which lets him in on that polarity, may help clarify the point: why, he asks, do Arab-Muslims, compared to Europeans, lag behind today? Once Muslim East is progressive while Christian West retrogressive; again, today Western armies penetrate Arab-Muslim world; formerly, Arab-Muslim armies penetrate Europe. What has happened? Well, Arab-Muslim present situation everywhere shows abject decline. This is mortifying, most distressing and, given their glorious history, makes no sense whatsoever, neither from a religious and existential perspective nor from that of mind and matter. And he repeats the same question: why do Arab-Muslims shine brilliantly in the past but live in a state of decay at present?[338]

141

His answer, though echoing others before it, waxes more lyrical: Arab-Muslims' one-time brilliance and strength take off from deep piety and faith and hunger for knowledge. Given that, their ancestors prevail in the world; now the heirs have squandered that spiritual treasure, forfeiting thereby their animalism and enthusiasm which in others create unity (Germany, France, Russia, England). They've lost, too, their spirit of sacrifice and resolve. More than that, their present decline hinges, I wager, on their ignorance that, unbeknown to them, breeds, like maggots, despondence and despair. Hence their unethical and cowardly behavior as well as (and here, in the 1930s, he speaks as if prophetically of today) the corruption and tyranny of their rulers.[339]

All this lyricism leads to the contrast with Westerners. It's not true, he says in effect, that Europeans, the West in general, triumph because of their science, artillery and planes; rather they succeed because of their energy and spirited enthusiasm; indeed, knowledge without enthusiasm is nothing; the two go hand in hand. At this point Arslan gives many examples, but one of the most important is Japan. In 1868, Japan barely counts as a power; look at it today, after fifty years; it takes over all forms of European knowledge, makes them its own, and competes with all European nations combined. It does so while still preserving its religion and traditions. Well, what's the secret? The will: that's the secret: in short, where there's a will there's a way.[340]

However, Arab-Muslims, he continues, are devoid of both will and way. They're divided and subdivided between apostate and passive. The apostates

---

[338] Shakīb Arslan, *Limādha Ta'khara al-Muslimūn wa-Limādha aTaqadama Ghayruhum* (Beirut: Maktabat al-Hayat, no date), p. 39.

[339] *Ibid*, p.77.

[340] *Ibid*, p. 79.

abandon religion; they also split apart, spurning the community, and blindly following European ways. To be sure, these renegades not only deny origin and faith; as well they defy every natural and moral law charging them with preservation of the community's character and fundamentals. The passive give way to imperialism, as if beckoning it to come up and rescue them from themselves; for they feel, as every gesture signals it, they can hardly tolerate themselves anymore. They need a new inoculation to imbue them with a fresh lease on life: the West may be that serum in disguise. So let it invade and dominate if it wills.

And the West, shrewd, calculating as it is (something inherent in its nature) heeds that thought. It sees through all despondency, apostasy, passivity, and moral degeneration; like an eagle, it then swoops down, interpreting these weaknesses as signposts and alibis for domination, sometimes, which amounts to the same thing, even for missionary work. And again, among the apostates there are those who pose as the pious ones. But they're in mask; they hide in religious cloaks and, to justify themselves, declare war on the sciences and arts, on philosophy and knowledge; they even exploit the latter as an excuse to execrate the infidels. In so doing, they unconsciously contribute not only to their community's stagnation; they drive the last nail into its coffin as well.

Arslan, however, never forgets that those agents of degeneration or death aren't alone. And this perhaps sharpens further his ideas of polar opposites. Christian West, too, he thinks, has its apostates and passive elements as well as moral degenerates—some of whom are members of the power-elite. And like their Arab-Muslim counterparts, they saunter around in religious disguise, denouncing right and left every single innovative effort, whether in philosophy or in science. But here they differ somewhat, though that doesn't make them less frightening: these Christians think and speak in terms of good and evil, which permeates every nook and corner of their life; accordingly, they encourage their countries to invade Arab-Muslim ones, African ones, Asian ones, kill their leaders and convert them to Christianity. Arslan, you see, is quite astute: he looks around (after all, he knows Westerners and how they think) and sees things as they transpire—for example, he sees those among Christians who make it a point to execrate every person who, in word or deed, deviates from what the bible teaches about creation.[341] Is he far from announcing a future trend here? Not at all. Today, global resurgence of Christian fundamentalism and the enormous concomitant damage it causes both psycho-socially and educationally, even scientifically, are far from trivial or simply fashion of the times.[342]

142

What, then, could Arslan's hope for Arab-Muslim renaissance be? And subsequently for East-West reconciliation no less? After all, he can't but hope. First, East and West are alike in many good and bad ways. Apostasy and passivity may come and go in the Arab-Muslim world as in the Christian world, but they can't touch either world's fundamental culture. For this culture's rooted in solid earth; also it's been, and recognized as such, the broker of Western knowledge in many aspects; and the same holds for Arab-Muslim culture. If so, how explain the soaring progress of the former and regress of the latter? Is it religion? Well, it seems Protestants point the finger at Catholics as stumbling block; Voltaire sees Christianity in general as huge barrier in the way of progress. The list goes on.

The truth of the matter is otherwise, however. Christianity, despite certain sectarian streaks, has never been the reason for Western lag, as Voltaire claims; in fact, it has cultivated, if not disciplined, Westerners after these have embraced it. Think of Newton, Descartes, and others. But really to burden religion with this kind of accusation stands the truth on its head; besides, it isn't fair at all.[343] Therefore, taking their cues from this—that religion is no barrier—Arab-Muslims

---

[341] *Ibid*, p. 116.

[342] Niall Shanks, *God, the Devil, and Darwin*, pp. 3-15.

[343] It's interesting to speculate at this point: if Alfred Crosby could read Arabic, mightn't he find in this idea of Arslan's an incentive to write his book? It's also interesting that he begins with a couple of quotes from medieval Arab-Muslim historians, which lead him to the exposition of his theme. See *The Measure of Reality*.

can forget and forgive Sunni egoistic conservatism for closing, in fear for itself, the doors of *Ijtihad*. But are the doors closed now? No. Therefore, Arab-Muslims can join the race to progress (in all the sense of the word) as every Western nation has done. What's needed is effort and sacrifice; Islam's role, like Christianity's, is to enhance and sharpen their vision. They can search high and low if they want to, but they can never find a better incentive to learning and knowledge than Islam and the Qur'ān.[344]

143

The foregoing paragraphs relate briefly the work of four outstanding Arab-Muslim scholars. These scholars, as you saw, are thinkers and historians, forecasting an event that hasn't yet happened except in imagination. Put otherwise, they each, based on social and historical realities (heterogeneity, sectarianism, arts and areas of knowledge) fiction a truth that could produce or induce the event. This fictioned truth lies, of course, behind the event East-West rapprochement. To that extent they perform certain interpretations, for the most part correct ones, with no lapses of the intellect.

To begin with, they know Western thought well—enlightenment, progress, science, rationalism, empiricism; domains which pose a challenge to Arab-Muslims. For example, on the negative side, the Qur'ān, the *Sharī'a*, the whole tradition pales when juxtaposed with Western epistemology, like night light in the dawning sun. And yet, on the positive side, they think all isn't lost. For a thorough knowledge of the Qur'ān and Sharī'a, along with a thorough knowledge of European epistemology might lead to the establishment of a new, daring way of thinking, call it associative thinking, if you will, whose avatar would then be, again, East-West rapprochement. Their idea is that if Islam is firmly lodged in the context where it belongs and has always belonged—global community (something Arab-Muslims have never considered or broached before or yet)—then the possibilities for East-West bridge-building become greater than ever. This is a little like the origin of religion: first, under the rule of religious

---

[344] Shakibī Arslan, *Hādir al-'ālam al-Islāmi* (Beirut: Dar al-Fikr, 1973), part three, p. 339.

ideas, you get used to the idea of 'another world' (below, above, behind) and feel
empty and deprived if you get deluded about it; then from this feeling grows now
'another world.'

144

There are signs pointing to that event, actually. Many young Arab-
Muslims are truly hungry for knowledge, especially under the influence of
Western ideas. This, of course, is no defect or flaw. On the contrary, it's an
atavism of former intellectual curiosities distinguishing many medieval Arab-
Muslims philosophers and geographer-historians who roam the continents
learning about other societies and in the process about their own. And not only
that. The four scholars think that the very development of Western thought could
be a great stimulus for Arab-Muslims to examine the consequences of European
thought itself. (Which possibility, speaking in anticipation, materializes in the
second half of the twentieth century.) And this examination itself, in turn,
perhaps by a process of osmosis, as it were (and giving it time is of the essence
here), could become a stimulus for Arab-Muslims to re-visit Islamic religious
thought itself, perhaps even also re-build it anew or reconstitute its diversity and
rights to be a partner in the world. This is no doubt a courageous, unprecedented
way of going about putting Islam on a rock-like plinth as unshakeable as the sun
itself.

Which, as our scholars further speculate, entails on Arab-Muslims to
acknowledge two significant issues, first, the credibility of development of
European thought, at least in certain of its aspects, and, secondly, the restoration
of the Islamic intellectual system on the basis of the consequences of development
of European thought, which could either be adapted, utilized, or commissioned to
clear the grounds for a deeper understanding of the spirit of the Qur'ān, the
Shari'a, the Hadith, and other aspects. This has been the case once in the twelfth
century. Since then, it's no exaggeration to say that the Qur'ān has suffered and
still suffers from misinterpretation of its content—not only because of several
centuries of stagnation in the domain of thought, but also because, during the

centuries of the heyday of Arab-Muslim thought, the intrusion of Greek philosophy leads to distortions of the Qur'anic spirit and the man's behind it.[345]

145

All due respect to Medieval philosophers, our scholars argue, Greek philosophy cast a veil over their eyes when it comes to the holy book. The two diverge in content and method. If you must live, then be moderate, rational, self-controlled—in short, "Know thy self." This is Greek dictum par excellence, and individual's philosophy, to boot. The Qur'ān has it differently. It calls for self-overcoming (*Jihad*), for balance between individual's interests and community's, and for knowledge of the universe from the most trivial to the most exultant. It thus spares nothing, and takes no human being as the measure of all things. Besides, its main aim is to awaken in humans the sublime feeling integral at once to their relationship to God and to the universe. Accordingly, it enjoins meditation on nature in that it stirs the experiential spirit in an era when the visible world is too impoverished to be a vehicle for comprehending what's behind, below, above creation. And what's there is another world, the metaphysical world. But this world constitutes no explication of the principles of experiment which are the subject and content of natural sciences. Religion is no science of nature like chemistry seeking to unlock nature's secrets based on laws of causality. Religion's aim is the explanation of one of the major domains of human experience: spiritual exercise. Which, needless to say, differs from the domain of those sciences.

European rational philosophy has failed to adduce evidence demonstrating religious experience. As has Christianity, too, for the simple reason that it preaches and teaches flight from reality. Islam fills the gap by preaching and teaching that mind or spirit corresponds to reality. One doesn't renounce the

---

[345] To this day issues like compulsion in religion (Qur'ān 2: 256) or polygamy (4: 3; 4: 129), just to mention two outstanding ones, haven't yet been freed of malicious interpretation and even deliberate distortion. How could that be when Franklin Graham, for instance, denounces Islam as an evil and wicked religion? Now if he really means that, then the onus is on him to prove it. But if he's playing a political game to please the ears of the ignorant and naïve (and there are millions of them), then I challenge him to prove it isn't so.

latter to reach the former; they're one and the same. This is precisely the significant point our four scholars are in agreement on. Consequently, Arab-Muslims don't renounce the world, but rather live and develop in the world, while the world, far from being fixed, constantly changes—which the Qur'ān affirms. Given this perspective, spiritual exercise or, what amounts to the same thing, emotional experience moves from one state to another. And Arab-Muslims, who embody this experience, undergo change all the time. What counts in essence is the emotional experience itself. Particularly that in it which doesn't get stuck on what it knows, but rather has the appetite for and enjoyment of the chase and intrigues of knowledge, from here on earth up to the highest and remotest stars. This is the spirit of Islam.

It's easy to criticize our four scholars for being either-orists: I mean for rejecting rational philosophy in favor of the principles of irrational philosophy. If this is the only criticism, though, then it fails to see and appreciate the Muslim way, namely spirituality tied to this world, not to the next. Moreover, since this world constantly changes, that spiritual relation to the world does, too. To clinch the point, they offer this telling analogy: a snake that can't slough its skin, dies; so do humans if they prevent or are prevented from changing their opinions.

The point is clear: our scholars are doubly informed, or let's say they've cultivated a double wham of power: European philosophy and knowledge of the Qur'ān and Islam. With this dual arsenal of knowledge they can fight the West, not militarily, of course, or atrociously but—intellectually. Actually, the time's come for this kind of fight: fighting the habitual, experiencing the insecurity of independence, and the frequent wavering of their feelings and even their conscience. They don't seek rest and peace and pleasure in their inquiries. No, only truth, even if it's the most abhorrent and ugly. What's more, they urge the West to do likewise, so that each side recognizes itself and its value in the other: each side sees in the other a sort of challenge, and each side takes account of and lives up to that challenge—and thus comes to know itself in regard to its powers of intellect and endurance. The very sort of thing late twentieth-century Arab-Muslim cultural theorists would learn to do.

146

But before I get to them, a word concerning the implications of that challenge is in order. Which, I think, it's also a way to come to them. The word refers to the new approach to education that's been spreading in the Arab-Muslim world. It's based on the principle of *tawhīd* (unity). Something, let me quickly add, I'm still in process of teasing out from the texts of our four scholars. It's as if I'm still dwelling in a great stream of their thought and feeling, wishing to pursue this stream even in nocturnal dreams.

Unity of Arab-Muslim world can only be achieved, these scholars suggest, if Arab-Muslims realize once and for all that since humans make the world in which they live, that humans by definition and by their very nature change also, then this world doesn't and can't stay the same for all time. No philosophy, religion, spirituality, ethics, or law indeed stays or is for all time. A man-made thought may develop into a principle which itself, in turn, may become eternal; yet by that very fact it undergoes change; that's to say, new events, even if accidental, compel the principle to appropriate changing aspects of itself while itself, the principle in essence, remaining permanent or same.

That's precisely *Ijtihad* at its very core: whatever principle it deals with (Hadīth, law, *Sharī'a*, jurisprudence, ethics, spirituality, etc.), it doesn't destroy; it simply introduces or adds a new aspect to it while the principle itself remains permanent. In a word, it becomes the changing aspects of the permanent. And so, despite Sunni truculent attitude, it's impossible (and here the impossible can't by necessity be reversed) to slam the doors of *Ijtihad* shut for ever, for that would otherwise deny what it means to be human—if not deny Islam, pure and simple. Sunni orthodoxy, as you saw, entrusts everything to *Sharī'a*; well and good, but it does so to the exclusion of personal inventiveness, and so *Ijtihad* becomes an anathema. Even at the expense of everything that's human. But you know now why it proceeds with this contradiction. Orthodoxy derogates *Ijtihad* because it fears for itself (no one shall have power over its intellect), and it fears for itself because it wants to maintain itself (it feels it has come to a halt before its own teaching). These are its secrets or secret fears. In this case, needless to say, it neither welcomes nor helps to create the conditions whereby great culture thrives productively as a beautiful fruit tree on a trellis.

A brief, schematic history shows that orthodoxy's dream of maintaining itself at any price, of domineering as a politico-religious state is unfulfillable. Recall the different philosophico-theological schools that *Ijtihad* makes possible, including the short-lived dissemination of Greek philosophy among Arab-Muslims in the ninth and tenth centuries.[346] Now the plant grows, an offshoot, Ibn Taymiyya, a theologian of the thirteenth-century, introjects the image of *Ijtihad* and critiques all dry husks that have overlain and distorted the fundamentals of Islam.[347] Then another offshoot, al-Sayūti of the sixteenth century, of the same caliber as Ibn Taymiyya, comes along and gives *Ijtihad* added wings, as does a third offshoot, Abd al-Wahhāb of the eighteenth century, a reformer in the tradition of both theologians.[348] These Arab-Muslim philosopher-theologians, among others, affirm their right to *Ijtihad*, thereby sharpening their intellect, the better to be the good Muslims they want to be.[349] You see, the gush of thought-*Ijtihad* is unstoppable, and breaks down every obstacle in its path.

147

Ijtihad is also evidently influential, as you saw, in Turkey, in Egypt, then Lebanon and Syria (our four scholars). Well, this brief history speaks loudly and clearly, despite Sunni objection or concealment, of the urgent need Arab-Muslims

---

[346] In addition, I'd suggest a chapter, though short, outlining the daring thought of a few medieval Arab-Muslim philosophers and doubters. After all, the history of Arab-Muslim "enlightenment" (if I may say so) doesn't pale before orthodoxy, although the latter wins in the end. See Jennifer Michael Hecht, *Doubt* (New Yortk: HarperCollins, 2004), pp. 216-239.

[347] See al-Suyūti, *Tarīkh al-Khulafā'* (Cairo: al-Maktaba al-Tijāriyya, 1970).

[348] See Karen Armstron, pp. 14-15.

[349] For further information and expansion on the practice of *Ijtihad* in Ibn Taymiyya, see Rudolph Peters, pp. 42-53; and for a fine, brief historical review of the true meaning of *Jihad*, also of *Ijtihad*, see Reza Aslan, pp. 75-106.

feel to start to re-educate themselves both in their very own intellectual heritage and Western heritage. For example, they may begin with examining the abolishment of caliphate in Turkey and the support it receives in Egypt. This is the first step in the direction of reform, not terribly different from that initiated by al-Afghāni and Abduh, though not as daring. When the two forms of reform are combined, Arab-Muslims discover that replacing the caliphate with a republican rule not only agrees with Islam, but it also has become one of the modern necessities in view of the new forces released in the Arab-Muslim world. This is most important intellectual movement stimulated by exposure to European thought and sanctioned by *Ijtihad*.

Ijtihad is now a force not to be or can no longer be resisted. This is because a move like abolishment of the caliphate, which it sanctions, meets with no objection in the Qur'an. Which, in turn, means the return to origins (*salafiyya*) isn't only a form of renaissance in the Arab-Muslim world; it challenges the very traditional but stagnant forces that claim the same return. The latter argues that the caliphate is the essence of Islam, which conforms only nominally or formally to the tradition, the former comports with the very life-giving principles of Islam—exactly as has been said concerning democracy as *Sharī'a*'s mind and soul and equality justice itself. Though the Qur'ān doesn't explicitly refer to republican rule, the latter has become, thanks to *Ijtijad*, a necessity born of the very spirit of Qur'ān.

So the end of the Caliphate means Arab-Muslims as a collectivity can take the helm in their own hands. This is called the right to self-determination—a new empowerment of *Ijtihad*. New not in the sense of being absent from Islam, and now it suddenly appears from nowhere. But new in the sense of re-emerging from orthodoxy's having excised it from the community's body. The community wants to take back that right. Which orthodoxy can do nothing about: its old wings are clipped, and the march is on. Indeed, if every Arab-Muslim nation takes care, through *Ijtihad*, of its affairs, minding its business until the people become strong and capable, the day would dawn when all nations bond not exactly into the same *Ummah* Muhammad dreams of, but into another community based on similar principles. This could be a federation of states transcending sectarian boundaries, the better to open up a fresh socio-political horizon common to all.

You see, this upcoming federation would hold as its principle independent self-rule. For that, thanks to *Ijtihad* which, in the light of the exigencies of the age, may yet trail paths long unforeseen. However, there are obstacles in these paths. The most troublesome happens to be the kind of fundamentalist nationalism now in full force. For it possesses the power to corrupt and destroy; another is Arslan's notion of sacrifice which dissolves individuals into the community, coercing them to think under the spell of custom, established judgments, established causes, and of no other reason than those of authority. But *Ijtihad* as personal endeavor, as resistance to this formulaic imitation can take care of that, as can education and re-education. For then Arab-Muslims can look into the *Sharī'a* and recognize its amazing malleability, its pliancy to change, as the history of jurisprudence testifies.[350] Besides, because the Qur'ān's no book of law, and because it sees the world as becoming and change, it won't block the idea of individual initiative. Even the four schools of theology never consider what pronouncements they make as the last word on a subject. This is indeed as it should be, for constant elucidation of *Sharī'a*'s content vis-à-vis a time and place is the very lawful act itself to perform.

Once again, the idea of development and renewal in Islam and its traditions takes off from the positivism of presence of the other. And it all begins in the ninth century and continues until this moment. Indeed, this confrontation has been most conducive to the awakening of Arab-Muslims to their role in the world. In the twentieth century in particular, the pressure of new global factors—politics, commerce, technology—has exerted tremendous influence, so that Arab-Muslims, even if they don't admit it, realize the importance and value of dialogue

---

[350] See Fazlur Rahman, pp. 74-138

and personal initiative or *Ijtihad.* The burgeoning of republican spirit and the gradual establishment of legislative assemblies are emblems of real progress in this regard. Even if political opposition increases (after all, one needs one's political adversary), it would still be a good thing to welcome. Indeed, it would most likely facilitate the transfer or transposition of *Ijtihad* from individuals representing the different schools of theology to a legislative body—in which case *Ijtihad* would guarantee to these legal and theological discussions the benefit of judgment of those who aren't theologians but ethical positivists.

149

If anyone comes within close range of Plato's ontology of self and other, of knowledge of self through the other, it's probably the Algerian thinker Mālek Ibn Nabī. A prolific writer, Ibn Nabī composes his controversial ideas under duress: Algiers is in the second stage of French imperialism, and political pressure against intellectuals is quite severe. Allow me to run quickly through a few ideas before detailing their signification. One idea concerns the great problem of culture. He argues that thought, if it's to be worth its weight in progress, develops as part of that problem alone. Another is that politics and culture are antagonists; the one lives off the other and thrives at the expense of it, but never the two shall keep in harmony. A third and final idea is that all great ages of culture are ages of political decline; what's great culturally has always been unpolitical, even antipolitical. All in all, you see, he appeals to Arab-Muslims everywhere to take responsibility for themselves, to resurrect the practice of *Ijtihad* and ethic of self-discipline, the better to resist imperialism and get hold of their identity.[351]

From these ideas he draws one brilliant conclusion which, I think, brings them all into harmony with each other. He effectively demonstrates how imperialism can never colonize or coerce a people—if this people possess no disposition for or susceptibility to being colonized. The contrary of his truth, however, and sadly so, characterizes as much Algerian-Muslims as Arab-Muslims

---

[351] Malek ibn Nabī, *Ta'mulāt* (Damascus: Dār al-Fikr, 1979), pp. 87-89.

in general. As a cultural force, Islam, he thinks in effect, has lost its spirit of resistance since the battle of Saffīn.[352] While its susceptibility to imperialism starts to develop since the end of the era of Muwahidīn (the era of the first four caliphs, unifiers of *Ummah*, after Muhammad).[353] Imperialism, then, isn't the primary cause of impotence, apathy or intellectual indolence of the different peoples of the Arab-Muslim world. To believe otherwise means one hasn't yet formulated a sound judgment in this regard. One must, therefore, investigate the root causes of the movement of imperialism, not just accept it as fait accompli. In other words, one must investigate it as a sociologist, not as a politician. In doing so, one comes to recognize how it wiggles its way into the life of a naïve people and exploits their weakness or inability to overcome it. (Here he has in mind what happens to the Abbasid dynasty as foreign elements begin to infiltrate it.) Consequently, there's a positive side to imperialism: it liberates the energies that have long lain suppressed, dormant, or inactive. Perhaps this is the sole reward that a colonized people receive from the colonizer.[354]

150

Seen in this light, how does Ibn Nabī view Europe or the West? He sees it, of course, through its relation to the Arab-Muslim world. The Christian-European spirit turns into realpolitik or colonizing spirit. Even so, the impact is positive if examined sociologically. Accordingly, Ibn Nabī argues that for two centuries the West, contrary to appearances, plays a beneficial role in the history of the world. True, it isolates itself from the rest of mankind, turning up its nose at the latter as if it's no more than a ladder to its glory, but still it saves the Arab-Muslim world, for example, from sinking into the chaos of its secret powers. How so? Well, its colonizing activities infuse the colonized not only with a sort

---

[352] The battle of Saffīn in Iraq is the site of he downfall of the fourth Caliph Ali Ibn Abi Tālib at the hands of Mu'āwiya Ibn Abi Sufyān in the middle of the seventh century. Ibn Nabī evokes this battle to call attention to the division and divisiveness in Islam early on and, therefore, to mark them as a sign of its going under as an ethical force.

[353] This is the era when Islam is still a formidable unity against which no external force prevails.

[354] Malek Ibn Nabī, *Wajhāt al-'Ālam al-Islāmi* (Damascus: Dār al-Fikr, 1981), p. 85.

of afflatus of its social values; it's like dynamite exploding and dismantling the latter's encampment of silence. In a word, it's an awakening call. As such, colonization may inflict agony and create confusion in the colonized; yet it's actually blind to such agony and confusion, as if fated to lose consciousness of them; but by the very fact of losing consciousness of them it lifts the darkness and lets a new dawn come.[355]

Time, Ibn Nabī continues, has fastened on the West certain habits and tinctured its life with them. And being the top dog, it's quite difficult to modify or change such habits. Put otherwise, it isn't an easy matter for Western national psyche to amend its ingrained habits—which is the source of chaos it finds itself in. Today Europe's crisis is a crisis of ethics, more specifically, of separating knowledge from conscience. Indeed, while the sciences flourish in Europe, the imperialist tendency waxes greater and greater until it dominates Europe itself. Thus it gives birth to chaos at home which, from there, spreads to the rest of the world. The phenomenon of Nazism is a case in point. In addition, unemployment, corruption, espionage, treachery, treason, deception—these, not only multiply and intensify daily; they drag this arrogant civilization to the abyss. And so long as it ostensibly professes justice but actually uses it as a means to oppress and coerce the colonies, its high values devalue on its own soil and the meaning of its conscience vanishes. In a word, Europe is tearing itself apart, more so indeed than the colonies are being torn apart by it.[356]

To understand this state of affairs is to enlighten and empower oneself to resist. No wonder, Arab-Muslims wax averse to follow the West's example in every way. Particularly when the latter's decline and crisis verge on certainty day in, day out. Which means Arab-Muslims can't look for right guidance outside their own borders. They must, therefore, blaze new trails in search of fresh springs of inspiration at home (the divine and intellectual afflatus Ibn Nabī just

---

[355] *Ibid*, p. 113.

[356] *Ibid*, p. 127.

spoke of). But, let it be clearly understood (and this is the important balancing point), they can't live in isolation either, especially when the entire world is currently in quest of some form of unity or cooperation. Put otherwise, Arab-Muslims must never sever their relations with Western culture which, after all, represents one of the great experiences of mankind. Rather, they must see to it that they keep these relations with the West in constant state of renewal.[357]

151

All this may sound like a double bind; but it isn't. Actually, it's more like a paradox, and the point Ibn Nabī wants to emphsize. First, the year 1369, ushers in the stagnation of Arab-Muslim culture;[358] then, the imperialist West is itself in decline and steeped in chaos. These are ugly realities, to be sure. But what about prior to 1369? What about European Renaissance? Aren't these spots of history where efflorescence of Arab-Muslim intellectualism in all aspects and European intellectualism bask in the sun? In the case of Arab-Muslims, by taking cues from that bloom while investigating the history of this ugliness, they can, like the phoenix, resurrect themselves to life again. This is beauty, if there's one, and source of happiness, if there's this, too. People may differ as to what constitutes happiness, not only for them or for mankind but in itself. But there's only once place to find it: in knowledge, in the activity of a well-trained inquisitive and inventive mind—not in the intuitions of theology alone or in the visions of mystics alone. And this, of course, isn't without danger to them who take up the lead beyond the boundary-stones of the latter. It involves taking risks of all kinds.

In plain language, Ibn Nabī knows that Arab-Muslims, thank goodness, haven't yet mummified themselves by displaying above themselves their own death certificate. From now on, their spirit may develop farther, time hasn't run out for them, the clock hasn't stood still. After all, Western presence has made at least one thing possible, if not an actual fact: today Arab-Muslims everywhere are

---

[357] *Ibid*, p. 128.

[358] This is the year Tamurlane ascends the throne and puts an end to Arab-Muslim culture.

on the brink of a renaissance of which manufacturing and industrial facilities form a part.[359]   Again, thanks to Western presence, Arab-Muslims realize that faith and spirituality within a material world condition behavior and set up a definite cultural goal to be maintained and renewed from generation to generation and from class to class.   Thus society continues to live as it learns to balance spirituality, which is communication with God, not knowledge of God, with material progress.

As you can see, Ibn Nabī's understanding of culture scintillates a sort of rejoicing over his new-found invention of rational thinking. To that extent, it's a far cry from politics. Rather, it recalls, at least to me, medieval Arab-Muslim rigorous and sober joy of discovering (in all the senses of the word) the mind as gifted with an inner sense or with intellectual intuition. A mind, to be sure, that never comes to believe in itself as in complete fully-developed facts. For example, he has an idea how culture develops. Three fundamentals structure culture: humans, soil, time. Humans embody a three-fold directing power: education, work, capital. As to soil, it disintegrates when people living on it lack the education and technology for cultivating it—which are the primary means to paving the way for culture to come. Time, on the other hand, is almost a nonentity because Arab-Muslims haven't yet learned to value its constituent elements, namely it never runs out. But when they do, and they get to define its impact and its proficiency, then their present life would take on the meaning and value due to it.[360]

152

Besides, culture, he feels, forms and re-forms in a cyclical pattern. As such, it resembles an element in the eternal recurrence of things. As does the mind in history: it operates and functions circuitously and successively in the life of a people. Now it records their glorious and honorable deeds, now it dishonors them and delivers them to deep sleep. And the whole pattern repeats itself

---

[359] See Mālek ibn Nabī, *Shurūt al-Nahda* (Damascus: Dār al-Fikr, 1981), p. 122.

[360] *Shurut al-Nahda*, p. 72.

eternally. The idea underlying this interesting thought about culture is that every culture comes to an end after it completes its cycle, just as Arab-Muslim culture does in 1369. By comprehending this cyclical pattern and acting upon it Arab-Muslims can regain their glory once more, though not so much in terms of physical conquests as in intellectual, spiritual and ethical ones.

And what Ibn Nabī himself comprehends is this: we're, he says in effect, living in the twentieth century, in a world in which the hegemony of Western civilization seems to be uncontested and almost a historical law. In the little cubbyhole in which I sit penning these thoughts, I'm surrounded by everything Western through and through. "Therefore, it's futile to erect an iron curtain between the culture the Arab-Muslim world wants to realize and Western culture."[361] In fact, this all-enveloping Western culture, as much enveloping him as the Arab-Muslim world, is here to stay until it runs its course; and he, while feeling it as a strong impetus to his thought, wants to awaken Arab-Muslims to the benefits it may bestow on them if they learn to study, to investigate, to seek the truth. His search for causes leading to a revival of Arab-Muslim culture is a reflection of what he observes Western civilization ultimately to be: oppressive but stimulating.

Part Two

153

Recall the concurrent but opposed views of Europe in late nineteenth and early twentieth centuries. Certain Arab-and Ottoman-Muslim savants are disposed favorably toward it, deeming it a liberal model worthy of emulation. Other savants think differently: to them, Europe is an imperialist power both unethical and to some extent even godless. This view compels them, naturally, to return to the origins (the tradition or *salafiyya*) for ideals and principles comporting with their peculiar understanding of liberalism and progress. And yet

---

[361] *Ibid,* p. 43.

the former view, the liberal current, wins out, and gradually gains momentum in the second half of the twentieth century, particularly in light of the political decline and scientific backwardness. These slumps spur more Arab-and Ottoman-Muslim leaders and savants to look to Europe for ways and means to lift the region to a higher level of progress in all aspects.

The 1908 constitutional revolution in Istanbul, for example, draws ample support from various corners. Ali Yūsif comments on the event just a few days after its occurrence. Absolutist governments, he says in effect, have been resorted to everywhere in the past as a matter of necessity, and to that extent there's no distinction to be made between East and West. Now, however, in the wake of the Enlightenment, history alters its course. It replaces the old tyranny with the practice of constitutional government in which people grants itself the privilege of governing itself as it sees fit, and to do so with all due respect to the High Sultan who shall remain a nominal king, no more. This is the invention of the West in the last two centuries.[362] The Egyptian Rūhi al-Khālidi argues that what gives birth to revolution is despotism, and despotism is, of course, the root cause of social ills, backwardness, political decline which lead to revolution. But, let's be careful, he says in effect, this monster isn't to be ascribed to Islamic dogma at all. It's rather Asian by origin. Sift through the sheaves of Islamic histories in both East and West, and you'll see that Asian monster with scales tinged with a bit of African slavery, to boot. There's thus nothing in it either of Islamic freedom or of *Shūrah* as decreed by Qur'ān and Hadīth. Islam, as a culture, is, therefore, innocent of culpability.[363]

Another Egyptian savant, Walī al-Dīn Yakun, who has had several years of formative European education, also comments on the event of 1908. His commentary has a little lyrical quality about it. Yesterday, he rhapsodizes, we exclaim: oh, freedom, freedom, you captivator of nations and enemy of despots,

---

[362] Reported in Abdul Massīh al-Antāki, *Neil al-Amāni fi-l Dastūr al-Uthmāni* (Cairo: Matba'at al-'Arab, 1908.

[363] *Ibid*, p. 194.

you breeding ground of hope. Oh, how comforting to Man, delighting his spirit and giving life to nations. When she answers our call, coming with her friendly favors to bestow on us, we clasp her and pull on her hair and snatch her jewels from her. Then we fasten the chains she undoes from our arms onto hers.[364] You see, the idea of freedom shining through these words, despite its foreign provenance, captures Arab-Muslim mind and soul. It's a European invention, experience, and impetus of progress—to which, at least, informed Arab-Muslims are well disposed. But that hardly means Arab-Muslim societies should give it the cold shoulder, or better, not exert effort to harmonize it with Islamic *Shura* and justice. True, the constitutionalists' failure in Istanbul and the disclosure of European ambition may have diminished the surge of verbal enthusiasm accompanying the revolution. But the liberal current might have picked up momentum from political experience, or at least acquired force from persuasive argumentation.

154

One of the many prominent liberal thinkers of Egypt is Lutfī al-Sayyid who flourishes in mid to early second half of twentieth century. The articles he writes for his own newspaper (al-Jarīda), also the teaching of philosophy for a quarter of a century at Egyptian Universities—these, among other activities, exercise profound influence on youths and the country's public life in general. He and his students study the developments of European liberal thought, which is pretty much a reenactment of the intellectual drive his professor Muhammad Abduh, the liberal thinker and religious reformist, generates in him as his student at al-Azhar University. At the time the bond of freedom draws together a number of young men, al-Sayyid among them, who want to break through all intellectual and emotional manacles imposed by traditional academic departments. Though he never gives up on Islam, he plies the laboring oar to attain for his country freedom, civil rights and civil liberties as he learns to appreciate their significance among Europeans.

---

[364] Walī al-Dīn Yakun, *al-Sahā'if al-Sūd* (Beirut: Beit al-Hikma, 1970), p. 142.

Man is free, he says in effect in one of his numerous articles. Man is born free to think and to feel, to live or to die, to act or not to act. He fights tooth and nail to preserve all those liberties. But this natural freedom is utterly useless when other inimical forces tie off its sustaining veins. For when man is jailed (and unfree society is jail), or deprived of his right to speak and write, in short, to express his feelings and thoughts, then he absolutely reaps no benefit; he loses his political liberty.[365] What's more, natural freedom has no meaning or finds no expression except within the grid of civil liberties and civil rights of which freedom of speech and freedom of political participation are paramount. After all, political freedom is the guarantor of personal freedom; that is, it affirms and secures the existence of natural freedom. Anyone wishing to preserve the latter must enjoy the freedom to speak and to work: and the more man enjoys this freedom, the more he clings, with God's blessing, to his political freedom which is the be-all and end-all here.[366]

Al-Sayyid, as you can surmise, exerts heroic efforts to achieve profound understanding of the basic ingredients of human rights. In time his total ideas coalesce into something like a dogma, if you will, to which he clings to the end of his life in 1963. In many other articles, you'll find him at it again and again, perusing the causes of failure of constitution in Egypt: he believes it all boils down to the lack of securing the maximum number of freedoms for the maximum number of individuals. This belief underscores the fact that for him the principle of freedom, in addition to being a political procedure, is also a philosophical program. With respect to his position vis-à-vis authority, tradition is to be venerated, but democracy more: best, of course, when the two come together in harmony. Government, he says, is a deputy; citizens put it in place so that they may carry on with their daily affairs; they support it, and they protect it by sacrificing their lives and those of their children for it. But let this not bring men

---

[365] Lutfī al-Sayyid, Mabādi' fi-l Siyāsa wa-l Adab wa-l Ijtimā' (Cairo: Kitāb al-Hilāl (149), 1963), p. 133.

[366] *Ibid*, p. 139.

to the brink of revering government personages, according them higher regard or veneration over the rest of the people. In point of fact, when citizens do the opposite, they keep themselves at a far cry from attaining independence (in all the senses of the word).[367]

155

Liberal Europe isn't sufficient to inspire Arab-Muslims to build the political system and society they'd like in their world. Another dimension is needed to round off the portrait: scientific Europe, the emblem of progress. This total portrait now stirs up many new ideas concerning how or what global development and progress might be like in the future. Once again, recall the two formidable scholars, al-Afghāni and al-Jisr, and their critiques of Darwin's theory of evolution, particularly the effort they exert in showing how this theory stacks up favorably or not with creation theory. These scholars are indeed the great heroes. They set the tone and strike news paths for today's Arab-Muslim world to follow. What this world needs, they say prophetically, and perhaps even hungers for, is intellectual debate—that which awakens it from its long lethargic sleep and lets it see the light of modern world. The light that shows war and destruction are passé: but that debate and argumentation, those creative endeavors teased out from the jumble or joust of great ideas, are in.

Well, in this connection, you have a very interesting and dynamic scholar Isma'īl Madhhar. He writes a book in which he defends the theory of evolution by advancing the (perhaps) shocking thought that it hardly differs from or contradicts Islam. Faith and evolution can't be lumped into a single entity: human evolution isn't part of God's plan of creation, for He has created man whole and complete. Accordingly, Madhhar, on the one hand, rejects the tendency of pure unbelief which he identifies with another scholar Shablī Shamīl who advocates evolution only to justify his materialist apostasy. But he also, on the other hand, objects to al-Afghāni's who rejects evolution believing it to be contrary to the faith. In a word, faith and evolution must be kept separate. Most significant of all

---

[367] *Ibid*, pp. 60-61.

is that Madhhar assigns a positive role to both science and evolution. He treats them as a unity. Evolution, he says in effect, is a branch of modern scientific developments that are worthy of pursuit, especially by Arab-Muslims; they're called upon, as a matter of conscience, to study this important theory carefully and then to translate it into Arabic. After all, they're on the verge of a scientific and literary revolution whose pickaxes dig into the old style of thought to make room for new edifices of thought.[368] He finishes by affirming that the modern age owes much to Europe which, despite its imperialist agenda (this is separate issue), is still the power house of new ideas and new techniques for all nations. And what's all this the result of, he asks? It simply begins in the grey matter of the brain.[369]

156

You can detect a reproachful tone in Madhhar's words as he reflects on Egypt's ill-developed society as on the various societies of the Arab-Muslim world. Egypt, regretfully, abandons its antiquity without mastering its modernity; it seems unable to learn from that ancient culture—its talent, learning, experience, practice, appropriation, incorporation—nor tries to put in place a standard, a philosophy, a politics, an ethics that would as a beacon light the way through the thick, floating dust of global revolutions and their suffocating smoke. Put otherwise, Egypt fails and has failed to sift through the great volume of sundry modern ideas for that which comports with its own talent and temperament.[370]

Madhhar is certainly a daring spirit and a free spirit at that. One of the few to grow on the sunny soil of Egypt. At one point in their history, Arab-Muslims, he submits, have had their hands on science and philosophy (philosophy is the queen of sciences, says Ibn Rushd), and the few innovative, daring spirits among them are never plagued by the fear that they might be incapable of

---

[368] Ismaï'l Madhar, *Malqa al-Sabīl fi Mathhab al-Nushū' wa-l Irtiqāa'* (Cairo: al-Matba'a al-'Asriyya, 1926), p. 4.

[369] *Ibid,* p. 11.

[370] *Ibid,* p. 12.

knowing the truth. What has happened? Is it because suddenly that daring spirit
deserts them, and just as suddenly they no longer understand themselves, as if
assailed by timidity? Mustn't Arab-Muslims, then, learn today to generate the
warmth and enthusiasm to do justice to this thing of thought that still dwells
within them? I think they must, says Madhhar, and needs must do become free
spirits again.[371]

Instead of muddling aimlessly between old and new, Arab-Muslims will
do better to let go of the old for a while and to turn attention instead to imbibing
fresh ideas. After that they may look back, as Mirsepassi would later say, and
perform a comparative assessment of their findings.[372] This could easily be
accomplished by establishing scientific institutions and embracing the spirit of
criticism like a doctrine. Indeed, the age of criticism, of critical philosophy, is
upon us, says Madhhar, the age in which the spirit of criticism assumes the role of
guide in human endeavor: the latter prides itself on reaching the level at which it
no longer drags its feet uncritically behind old traditions. In defending the theory
of evolution, for example, Madhhar forthrightly, and perhaps radically, calls for
the introduction of Latin nomenclature into scientific classification and exposition
even as these are translated into Arabic. This act, of course, signals reverence for
freedom of knowledge: it constitutes a medium of communication between
international communities, on the one hand; and it gives no sanction to any nation
for monopoly on terms, on the other. Besides, if only Arabic translations are
retained, Arab-Muslims would be deprived of the benefit of a sort of lingua
franca, that is, the experience underlying common global scientific discoveries
and philosophical insights.[373]

The upshot here is this: the theory of evolution poses no problem for
Madhhar. In so far as he's concerned, it has nothing to do with religion; it doesn't
even touch on the issue. Actually, Darwin now and then goes out of his way to

---

[371] *Ibid*, pp. 138-144.

[372] See above note 165.

[373] Ibid, p. 267.

express admiration for and awe of God's work. So does Einstein. Besides, if science and religion are opposites, so be it; opposites are necessary and thrive on each other. Religion needs science as much as science religion in order for each to affirm itself. Quite frankly opposites are what structures life and the universe. So if Darwin critiques religion at all, he never intends to undermine belief, but rather to show that evolution is a temporal process, and a long one, to boot. Religion, too, evolves like every living organism, like science itself; though inspired, it hardly ever mature instantly or by fiat. There's thus a domain of science, and another of faith: the two mustn't and can't be confused, just as the limits of each must be carefully known and observed.

157

We're approaching mid twentieth century. Meanwhile Arab-Muslim portrait or view of the West keeps on acquiring intricate configurations, also brighter, denser shades and colors. Madhhar's creative, daring spirit, and other spirits before and contemporary with him (some of whom you already know) pass on the torch to a new spirit, kindling it in turn to high flames. This is Taha Husayn, a scholar and avatar of an entire culture in miniature—psychology, education, theory, philosophy, criticism, history.[374] His first major and controversial work, for example, treats of literary criticism. It applies Western critical theory (empirical, psycho-social, textual, hermeneutic) to the study of pre-Islamic literature. Long story short, the work's bull's eye, if I may put it that way, is to set up a standard, relatively new, for Egyptians and Arab-Muslims alike to follow: rigorous re-examination of the self. In this sense, the work shakes the venerable heritage of tradition and faith.[375]

It's not the only work that does that shaking. There's another, a sequel, if you will, that draws up a larger, clearer portrait of Husayn's view of the West,

---

[374] These spirits aren't dead. Nor will they ever die. Arab-Muslims everywhere can reach out to them and listen to their sweet words imparting insight, courage, and, of all human endowments, common sense.

[375] For an informative, balanced, and insightful critique of Husay's book, see Yusuf al Yusuf, *Maqālāt fil Si'r al-Jāhili* (Algiers: Dār al-Haqā'iq, 1980), pp. 83-113.

and, for that reason, falls into line with my narrative here. After all, my theme isn't literature and poetry. At any rate, the book appears in 1938, thirteen years after the first. In it you find unparalleled density of shades and lights and colors accruing in the portrait which, to repeat, has so many ties not only with the other shades and colors you already know about, but also with a whole panoramic vision of history.[376]

158

To begin with, such issues as political freedom and scientific progress, curiously enough, aren't Husayn's primary focus. Rather, his number one concern is culture. He purports to show Egyptians and Arab-Muslims what it is to feel and think culture—from now on. He starts off with what may be a shocking question: does Egypt belong to the East or to the West? The question, if I'm right, underscores a sort of orientation program for a fresh mode of life. Then another one comes on the heels of it to reinforce it: does the Egyptian find it easier to communicate with an Easterner or with a Westerner? For answers, Husayn, naturally, has to delve into Egypt's past. The past unveils extraordinary things: strong evidence of Egypt's links and affiliations with cultures that have as well influenced modern Western civilization and renaissance. For example, the Aegean and Greek cultures need no mention at all. In fact, to repel a one-time Persian onslaught, Egypt seeks the aid of a Greek volunteer army. That, if anything, means Egyptian mind, right from its dawning consciousness, is of a piece with Aegean-Greek history and thought. Other Mediterranean regions or countries contribute different benefits, such as commerce and shipbuilding.[377]

To prove his point, Husayn singles out Egypt and Greece. Their interchange is unique, unmatched by any with the Far East. More than that, there's a sort of mutual affiliation between them: each, as it were, gives birth to the other, and both in their mature enlightenment destroy religious and linguistic unities which, to begin with, possess no efficacy whatsoever either as factors in

---

[376] Taha Husayn, "Mustaqbal al-Thaqāfa fī Misr," vol. 9: al-Majmū'a al-Kāmila (Beirut: Dār al-Kitāb al-Lubnāni, 1973).
[377] Ibid, p. 21.

forming political unity or as principles in building nations. That makes one thing clear: Egypt and Greece have exchanged knowledge since the time of Alexander. The city of Alexandria testifies to that, which isn't an Eastern city at all but a Greek city in the strict sense of the word. Now if Egypt welcomes Islam; or better, if it accepts Muslim faith and the language that goes with it, the gesture and embrace alter nothing of its consciousness. In point of fact, just as Christianity changes nothing of Europe's mentality, so Islam alters nothing of Egypt's. And far from displacing Greek culture, Islam actually extends the latter's influence into the Mid- and Far-East as well.

159

This exposition permits Husayn to advance two axiomatic truths. First, Islam and Christianity are affiliates; there's a sort of inner resemblance between them: both religions belong to the Abrahamic tradition; both have had intellectual intercourse with Greek philosophy, and both have been as much influenced by it as it by them. Put otherwise, the essence and source of Islam are also those of Christianity, and the relation of the one and the other to Greek philosophy is the same. Well, if that's so, then aren't the two religions as like as two peas when it comes to the influence they've both had on reason's formation that humanity inherits from Mid-East and Greece?[378] Some, like Muhammad Iqbāl, think that Greek influence in Islam has alienated Muslims and Arab-Muslims alike: that is, it has put them back two centuries, and now they can hardly, try as they may, comprehend Qur'ān or assimilate its spirituality. The truth, however, is otherwise. Husayn argues that the most decisive moment in the history of Islamic thought resides precisely in its affiliation with Greek philosophy.[379]

---

[378] The meeting of minds like Husayn's, Derrida's, and Arkoun's is no accident. And I don't mean to imply anyone of these savants has learned from the other. But I do suggest that perceptive minds do ultimately see or come to the same truth, and the same historical truth at that, namely Christianity, Islam, Judaism being one and the same originally. See Derrida's observations on the Abrahamic tradition, above, pp. 54-55; see also Arkoun's book *Rethinking Islam*.

[379] See Muhammad Iqbāl, *Reconstuire la pensee religiuse de l'islam* (Paris: Editions Adrien-Maisonneuve, 1955).

Surely, there's a difference between peoples living west of the Mediterranean and those living east of it. This difference, though, may be ascribed to a disparity in intellectual preparedness which can easily be explained in political, economic, climactic, and physiological terms. But the fact is that An Egyptian, or an Arab-Muslim is as much intellectually competent as is a Westerner. Consequently, it's absolutely incorrect, even downright unhistorical, to say or think, as Rudyad Kipling has it, that the East is East, the West is West, and the two shall never meet. But it's absolutely correct and historically sound to say or think, with Madhhar, that Egypt is part of Europe—a thought meant neither as encomium nor vainglory. This is because Egypt has always been a part of Europe in everything pertaining to educational and intellectual life in its various colors, branches, and forms.[380]

160

The second axiomatic truth is this: Arab-Muslim culture, Husayn observes, starts on the slippery slope about late eighth century. It comes to the abyss of misery in 1369 when next it all but gives up the ghost. What with all the resources it possesses in plenty which could've revived it—philosophy, *Ijtihad*, Ibn Rushd's heroic attempt to reconcile philosophy and Islam, and so on). But fate has planned otherwise: rigid, fear-ridden Sunni orthodoxy swoops down and bars the way. Which prolongs the death agony till the Ottomans, self-designated Muslims, pounce upon it, transfigure it, and then launch it, so to speak, into eternity. And yet the idea of culture, the bright embers still smolder and need only a fresh breath of life to fan them to flames again. And this is what I must do, says Husayn: it's time Egypt recouped its tenth-century long Greek heritage and reconciled it with itself and Islam. For Islam is and has become in time amply furnished to accommodate both.

Since Greek culture, Roman republic, and Christianity all combine to form the fertile soil where European mind has grown and still grows, then Egyptian mind is also the effect of Greek philosophy combined with Islamic faith

---

[380] Taha Husayn,, p. 36.

and jurisprudence which itself is linked to Roman law. This is the case in former times. In modern times, however, things are different. Egypt-Europe long-standing cultural affiliation constitutes the primary or basic factor in the formation of that mind. For example, our material life in Egypt, says Husayn, especially among the upper classes, is European through and through. In other social classes, it's also European, but differs according to how far from or near to European mode of living it is—in which case it all depends on the capacity of individuals and groups of individuals to assimilate, also their wealth, and their demeanor. Still, the essential truth obtains: how individuals determine their day-to-day life matches, if not exactly, at least pretty much how European individuals determine their day-to-day life. Except in degree, and a minor one at that, there's relatively no distinguishing the one from the other.[381]

161

But such affiliation between the two cultures isn't simply confined to material things. It partakes of non-material modes of life as well. Consider the political system, for example, or the judicial system: both follow European models. More than that, al-Azhar University finds itself in a race to modernize quickly along similar lines. Even the educational system in general, its edifices, methods of instruction, its programs are all founded upon European models.[382] The irony of it all, though, is that, we (Husayn now identifies with the entire society), we Egyptians still lag behind, perhaps too indolent to catch up with the means of modern Western civilization. Are we incapable? Not at all. Compare Japan. Japan has hardly had any intellectual or cultural affiliation with Europe as we do. And yet it now competes with Europe itself in the domain of science. Why? Because we, unlike the Japanese, have failed to reconstruct or refurbish our institutions.

---

[381] *Ibid*, pp. 40-41.

[382] Incidentally, the same holds true for many other countries in the Mid-East, Syria, for example, and Jordan, even Iraq.

Once we do, once we begin blazing that trail without any doubts or hesitation, we can reach the high status of a nation having its weight internationally. Inaddition, by participating in Europe's constant forward march toward new horizons of knowledge and open paths of truth we can not only or inevitably become Europe's equals, but also its partners in the business of sustaining culture in all its aspects: whether in good or ill, in sweet or sour, in like or dislike, in praise or blame. For that, it's obvious what we need: as much military power as economic independence—but also scientific, artistic, literary, intellectual, and psychological independence. And the means to attaining this end is for us to learn as Europeans learn, feel as the Europeans feel, govern as the Europeans govern, work as the Europeans work, and live and love as the Europeans live and love.[383]

162

But that doesn't mean we become merely copycats of the Western ways. As the body remains the same underneath what color or shape of clothes a person wears, so Islam remains the same donning the airs of modern life. Besides, there are differences. For example, modern Western science takes off in the face of clerical adversarial attitudes. Islam never stands in the way of knowledge; it also has no clergy and doesn't differentiate religious people from other classes of the population. These facts, if anything, indicate its adaptability to life's exigencies. And if Islam acquires modes of living and thinking from Persians and Greeks, it would be hardly discomfiting for it to follow Western models. At this point, Husayn proposes a choice: either we deny our history, that is, reject or refuse to recognize our ancestors as forgers of our Arab-Muslim culture (though I don't think we're prepared to go to that extreme); or we look up to these founders and, at the same time, follow Western ways without being slavish about it. If the latter is our choice, then we become strong as the West itself has become strong by assimilating much from Persian and Byzantine cultures.[384]

---

[383] *Ibid*, p. 5.

[384] *Ibid*, p. 58.

You can hear Husayn's tenor of thought loud and clear. Egyptians know Egypt's relations to the West, past and present. What they don't know, though, is that they fear it, or that they fear acknowledging their acceptance of it. If so, why suffer tacitly, he asks? Why deny our senseless suffering? Let's be honest with ourselves; let's take the bull by the horns instead of lazing the days away in dreams. There's no threat to our existence if we act; if we and the West keep abreast of the latest developments. Japan, for example, has never lost its grip on itself and its culture for espousing Western science; today, it's an equal. We, too, won't forfeit our national character, given its spirituality and deep roots in history. Besides, to say Western culture is pure materialism is untrue. If it is, then it's the Far East, not our Mid-East, not our Egypt. Again, the West embodies one of the great spiritual forces the world has ever known: sacrifice for the sake of knowledge and nation. And yet some Westerners, for many reasons, may feel vexed or troubled by their own culture. Nevertheless, this feeling hardly means they're discontent with it. If they are, it would then be a sure sign this culture is doomed to extinction.[385]

You may ask, what does Husayn's seminal thought ultimately yield? Well, it's only a portion of Arab-Muslim view of the West—and a multi-tiered one at that. To this extent, it's a three-dimensional thought: Greek mind, modern knowledge, and order, all rolled up into one thing: Western civilization. Now if this civilization appears materialistic, it isn't a sign of the times, Husaysn says; rather it's in the nature of things called Western. Its prosperity depends on knowledge, on the one hand, and on modern applied arts and sciences, on the other. He then waxes a bit lyrical. The various technical innovations, he says in effect, accruing from this combination changes and has changed both earth's face and mankind's life in general. But it's the ignorance of ignorance and the wrong of wrong to say or even think this materialistic civilization issues from pure matter itself. Rather it's the consequence of reason, of imagination, of free spirit.

---

[385] *Ibid*, p. 76.

It's the consequence of inventive, rich, fertile mind. Finally, it's the consequence of a living spirit in touch with orderly reason, nourishing, promoting, and spurring it to think, to produce, and to exploit its products.[386] We have what it takes to be exactly that

163

No doubt, Husayn is the "pivotal man" no twenty-first century Arab-Muslim people can afford to ignore. He knows what the Arab-Muslim world suffers from: laziness and dependence. As a man of culture, he can't sit idly; he can't help but pass on the torch. And now he invokes the concept of democracy in education and calls on the state to monitor practices of teaching and learning as well as to take charge of national education.

What dominates his program is the designation of the government as the only cultural entity responsible for guiding the future of culture and cultivating what he refers to as Egyptian mentality. In connection with this program, his most significant and perhaps daring invocation is this: al-Azhar University must help not only to incorporate modern techniques of thinking; it must also teach the distinction between the concept of nationality as understood by its professors and the new concept which both its youths and Egyptian youths at large ought to learn and assimilate. There should be a line of continuity between them, especially in view of the new understanding of nationality on which the life of nations and their interrelationships depends. The latter, along with everything else, has crept into to Egypt through modern global exigencies. It's inevitable that this understanding should find its proper habitat in al-Azhar's lecture halls and by extension in primary and secondary classrooms as well.[387]

Like Madhhar, he also calls for the teaching of Greek and Latin languages as integral part of this modern and necessary cultural planning. Not to do so would simply mean dooming Egyptians, perhaps also Arab-Muslims in general, to

---

[386] *Ibid*, p. 99.

[387] *Ibid*, p. 99.

ignorance, powerlessness, and blindness. It would surely augment the languor and indolence of the people. More than that, it would in the long run induce weakness of the will that would otherwise be fortified in imbibing the fertile history of relations and affinity not only between their own country and ancient Greece, but also their country and the West. As well he calls upon al-Azhar University not to specialize in the teaching of Arabic language and literature only, but to diversify its programs and course offerings. Above all, the teaching of religion at al-Azhar should be subordinated to the principles or conditions of civil instruction.

The future path of education, among others, happens to be, as far as Husayn is concerned, the same path Europe has mapped for itself and for its own development. And so Egypt, inevitably, has no other recourse but to reach for what Europe and the West have reached for and attained. Egypt has maintained strong bonding with Europe, along whose same path, he says, we're still marching, watching the same crises and obeying the same strictures as it has, compelled to achieve what it has achieved. In doing so, it has spread throughout most developed regions and the globe its irresistible, catching, invigorating vigor—the rights of man: freedom, justice, equality. In point of fact, peoples everywhere have sampled this goodly medicine and found it tasteful and tasty, and now they want more. Reason enough to say this goodly medicine is unstoppable, so that it behooves Egypt to get on with its progressive move on its own, to pursue the journey obediently—before anyone coerces us to it grudgingly or reluctantly.[388]

164

The foregoing paragraphs sum up Husayn's vision of Egypt's future and that of Mid-East no less. It comes into being almost on the eve of World War Two, during his maturity as a cultural theorist. Obviously, the idea of liberal Europe as a model (in all the senses of the world) informs and frames that vision. Does he smell a whiff of future imperialist omnipotence or threat? It's hard to

---

[388] *Ibid*, p. 165.

know, though something vexes him. At any rate, he urges Egypt not to delay its getting hold of Europe's tools of enlightenment. The urgency echoes al-Tūnisi's call some seventy years earlier. Yet there's a subtle difference, almost unnoticeable. Husayn's, speaking homeopathically, wants to ward off threat, if any, by having Egypt follow in Europe's path, now more than ever; al-Tūnisi's, however, and this is quite interesting, seeks to ward off threat which would hover over Egypt if it fails to follow in Europe's path.

Do Husayn and al-Tūnisi say the same thing? Pretty much, I think. In any event, one thing is about to become clear: their invocations and urgencies begin to look like leaves in the wind. I mean the halcyon days of what appears an East-West rapprochement seems to be on the wane. Ominous clouds are drifting in, turning that half-century long intellectual brilliance into fanatic night. If to Lutfī al-Sayyid and his disciples Europe stands for political supremacy; if to Isma'īl Madhhar it signifies scientific progress; and if to Husayn it embodies the ideals of education and cultural development—well, it will be this, that, or the other no longer. For an opposite portrait, an opposite view of the West looms up out of darkness and renames the West as evil, politically, culturally, morally. And yet, from the two opposites, to use the Hegelian thesis-antithesis formula, a synthesis will follow and will have a different character, too.

165

But first allow me to outline this dark view. For that, I return briefly to al-Afghāni, Abduh, and Rida. Their reformist ideas, as you saw, are bright and original; so are al-Tūnisi, Madhhar, and Husayn's, among others. And you'd think, given this double wham of brightness, East-West rapprochement would be a cakewalk to achieve at last. But it isn't. All such ideas get blighted after 1938, and this by no specific conscious agency either. It may be historically proper to say that they generate their own suppression or demission. Yet putting it that way still violates historical unfolding. You see, when two events occur successively or even simultaneously, it hardly means the first causes the second. But it does mean one event is inscribed in a chain or in a system within which it refers to the other, to the other event, without any specific agent, subject, or a consciousness directing it.[389] What I'm suggesting is that all ideas from al-Afghāni to Husayn don't directly cause the negative reaction that now circle around the West

So when al-Afghāni, Abduh, and Rida invoke, for example, the idea of return to the origins—to the self, to Arab-Muslim self, its early history, its early traditions before the decline, even before the four schools of Jurisprudence—something happens. And this invocation hardly signifies negative feelings against the West; they simply desire Arab-Muslims to be in touch with their traditions. Nevertheless, that something happens certainly disrupts things: it sets in motion ideas untapped before, creating lots of rumblings in the community. Meanwhile these rumblings get louder and deeper as angry emotions flood the scene. Europe, it's now felt, fails miserably to seek understanding of the destitute conditions of the colonized peoples or to reach out to address their causes. In effect, the gates open wide to let the floods of resentments and dissatisfaction sweep through the Arab-Muslim community almost from end to end: Mid-East, India, Persia, and Turkey. The end result is a terrible blow to East-West positive portrait as drawn by the scholars just mentioned. The tremendous efforts hitherto exerted to bridge differences now dwindle to a tiny, vehement cry. A cry that pulls these two spheres into polar opposites. And this polarization isn't simply confined within the orb of politics, as Arslan has already hinted.[390]

166

The new portrait consists with the view that the European or Western way is a blind alley leading nowhere; worse, it leads Arab-Muslims only to confusion and immorality. Islam, therefore, must turn in on itself if it's to re-capture its glory. The Algeria Malek Ibn Nabī, you recall, already adumbrates that thought: the cycle of the West is now nearing its end, he says, so the Qur'ān shall fill the cultural vacuum at the level of humanity as a whole.[391] This procedure becomes

---

[389] I've discussed this issue earlier in a different context, but with the same results concerning the operation of historical evolution of ideas. See above, pp. 60-61

[390] See above, pp. 158-162.

[391] See above, pp. 168-172.

218

the yeast of revolutionary fundamentalism which views the West and itself in a state of struggle without recourse. The West has designs on Islam, and this is not just at present. It goes back to the Crusades period, though still on-going today under the deceptive guises of freedom, equality, justice. So the binary structure—Europe versus Islam or East versus West—returns with a vengeance, as if from the dead. In fact, reams of printed material on the subject fill the place. The phenomenon then spreads into the West itself, especially during the peak of imperialist period. It so colors Islamic thought in all of its aspects that it eventually ossifies into the bleached dogma of Muslim Brethren.

This phenomenon issues from the pens of Abu al-'A'lā al-Mawdūdi of Pakistan, Ali al-Husni al-Nadawi of India, and Hasan al-Shirazi of Persia. Unfortunately, consideration of these scholars falls outside the purview of my project here. So I must refer you to Arabic translations of their respective works for a comprehensive exposition of their thought.[392]

However, the phenomenon takes hold among Arab-Muslims scholars—for example Nejīb al-Kaylāni who sees the struggle between Islam and the West as one between spirit and matter or light and darkness. Islam is a comprehensively spiritual philosophy covering all aspects of life—politically, economically, socially, or scientifically, including law, international relations and even military associations, artistic and literary innovations. It has a two-fold enemy: Western thought for whose sake the most devastating weapons have been enlisted; Arab-Muslims who succumb to this thought in an attempt to justify its precedence in matters of scientific and technological progress. But this is superficial progress at best. Why? Because these sciences study man only in so far as the eye can see, even under microscopes. As such it fails to see man's interior or grasp his conscience, spirit, desires, disposition and instinct. Consequently, modern Western civilization, which diverges from this concern, relinquishes the straight

---

[392] Abu 'Ali al-Mawdūdi, *Nahnu wa-l Hadāra al-Gharbiyya* (Beirut: Mu'assasat al-Risala, no date); Abu-l Hasan 'Ali al-Husni al-Nadawi, *Mādha Khasira al-'Ālam bi-Inhitāt al-Muslimīn* (Beirut: Dar al-Kitab al-'Arabi, 1965; Hasan Shirazi, *Kalimat al-Islam* (Beirut, 1964).

path. And the living being that's nourished by this civilization turns out badly: an incomplete being tossed between the claws of anxiety, rupture, fear, boredom, excess, and deviance.[393]

167

Muhammad Qutb is another formidable scholar most of whose work is known in the West through translation—except for one book which, so far as I know, remains untranslated; it scathingly criticizes the West in general and Freudianism in particular. Of the latter criticism, itself being quite long and well-informed, only short excerpts, and only in summary, may be presented here. He deems Freudianism the cause of many ills in the West: for example, egoism intensifies the individual's hatred of society, so that whenever she or he mentions the word, thoughts of oppression, arbitrariness, disparagement follow on its heels. This is exactly what has gradually cankered both European and American societies to the point of destruction. What's more, existentialism itself, so widespread in France, is no more than an extension of the suggestive power of Freudianism; after all, it calls for the destruction of every single obstacle in the way of the individual's self-fulfillment.[394]

But experimentalism dominates the modern age, though no one can deny its many brilliant scientific achievements. Still, experimentalists believe in the senses and nothing else besides, which, needless to say, excludes other matters associated with them. That is, their belief compels them, as a matter of course, to reject, deny, or contradict what other important scientists, philosophers, and spiritualists have to say about the spirit. Consequently, bodily movement, or any movement for that matter, is physiologically, chemically, or electrically conditioned. To this extent, everything pertaining to the spirit is occulted or has no existence. As a corollary, society, religion, ethics—all are chimeras, even family discipline is something fabricated. As to the sublime ideals, this is mere superstition and ludicrous. They thus undermine ethical responsibility. The

---

[393] Nejīb Kaylāni, 'Adā' al-Islāmiyya (Beirut: Mu'assasat al-Risāla, 1981), p. 29.

[394] Muhammad Qutb, al-Insān bayna al-Mādiyya wa-l Islām (Beirut: Dār al-Shurūq, 1978), p. 45.

communists, on the other hand, believe only in the material dimension of life, so that morals have no solid, objective foundation; everything, including human association, originates in relations of production, while religion, a concoction of feudalism and capitalism, is opium for the people. Economics is be-all and end-all of existence. It follows that the greatest calamity for mankind here is limiting human needs for no more than food, clothing, and sexual satisfaction. Everything else, such as faith, is secondary.

These, to sum up, are the currents dominating the West: history as record of relations of production, feelings as physiological and chemical movements, behavior as the outcome of sexual desire. Qutb understands all this to be ultimately the effect of rigid, austere Puritanism from which the West is still trying to liberate itself. Well and good. But there's a price to pay. Such a liberation—which, consciously or not, restricts the domains of self, life, and history to a puny thing called materialism—comes to shake the very foundation of humanity. And Qutb thinks those scientists and scholars who've accomplished their mission finish by sullying humanity.[395] The hateful injuries perpetrated by Freud and adopted by experimentalists and materialists hurl mankind to the lowest depths of degradation, where all sublime ideals become superstitions among Westerners. Finally, those who view the West with admiration are either blind or deliberately ignore how America treats Arab-Muslims in Mid-East, how the French treat Arab-Muslims in North Africa, and how Godless Russians join the West in setting up Israel and use religion as cause against Arab-Muslims in the Mid-East. And if the West possesses the power and control on whose basis it erects its philosophy, then the bitter fruit of this philosophy is but war that destroys in a moment what humans have built in centuries. [396]

168

'Abd al-Mun'im al-Nimr, another notable Arab-Muslim scholar, follows in Qutb's steps. Some aspects of his work are fairly known in the West,

---

[395] *Ibid*, pp. 178-180.

[396] *Ibid*, p. 219.

excepting a work which, again, in so far as I know, remains untranslated. Here he augments Qutb's argument by including the Russians. We Arab-Muslims, he says in effect, incline neither easterly nor westerly. If you hear anyone or if you hear an interior voice (inside you) summoning you to adapt to or learn from Western civilization or from Eastern Marxist civilization, this is but a satanic voice calling you to your doom. Opposite that, my friend, you have Islam: here's a total, subliminal personality deriving from its sublime founder, from its just laws, its systems of rule and ethics for all time and place as wrought by God almighty. Naturally, such a religion differs from everything known as positivist philosophy, Western or Marxist.[397]

Nevertheless, al-Nimr is quite careful not to overshoot the mark. Though admiting *Sharī'a* to be of divine provenance and Islam for all time and place, he places Islamic system of rule in a grid of historical unfolding the better to defend its legitimacy. Even if his backward look takes on the aspect of a traditionalist haven. For example, he considers the period of Islamic conquests when Arab-Muslims gain power over certain dominions of Eastern Roman Empire. Since then, and after taking hold of more dominions, Islam not only emerges as a threat to the Christian world; it gradually acquires the status of a resentful, rancorous, malicious object. And so waylaying it, containing it becomes the order of the day. But who, he asks, is really behind this resentment and hatred? Not the people, of course, but the clergy and feudal kings. The Crusades, then, naturally eventuate from such hatred which itself increases after the withdrawal of Europeans from Mid-East land.

Then geographical discoveries follow. But, he asks again, do these discoveries discover land originally unknown or are they a mere pretext to colonize the East? These lands, claimed to have been discovered, actually have their own laws and systems of rule. Portugal, for example, a leader in such missions, claims to be no more than making a discovery of Africa; but then it

---

[397] 'Abd al-Mun'im al-Nimr, *al-Islām wa-l Gharb Wajhan Liwajh* (Beirut: al-Mu'assasa al-Jāmi'yya li-l Dirāsāt, 1982), pp. 37-8.

turns around and fulfils its hidden goal by expropriating Islamic lands in the East. Consider America. Isn't the original thrust a bluff calculated to reach India because it's governed by an Islamic state at the time? After Portugal and Spain, we have England, France, and Holland—all driven by ravenous, voracious greed for Islamic land? In the final analysis, let me say this: forgiveness and good will shown by Islam toward the world is countered by a fanatic, ravenous West. Consequently, the Crusades continue unconfined: if the first Crusade occurs in 1099, today, and since 1948, we now live through the tenth Crusade. Indeed, the establishment of Israel in the Mid-East replicates that of the Crusaders' petty states in the region.[398]

169

Yusuf Qurdāwi, a contemporary, echoes al-Nimr but contributes his own, perhaps prophetic, insight. If this is Europe or the West truly, he says in effect, then whatever solutions it proffers to us by way of modernization are intrinsically suspect, vicious, and, therefore, fundamentally foreign to us. Now these solutions may be limited to Islamic solution, democratic liberal solution, and socialist-communist solution. These, in turn, may be classified into only two kinds: the first, the Islamic, is the natural one; the other, the democratic liberal or socialist communist is an importation from a land not ours and by a people other than us. What's more, they wouldn't have come up in the first place if it weren't for the abject decline that afflicts every domain of life in the Arab-Muslim world— which, let me quickly add, is itself the result of Arab-Muslim's estrangement from authentic Islam. Finally, experience shows that every imported thought, though at first may seem glittering and bright, soon loses its luster. And the next phase isn't to be inaugurated by the left or the right, but rather by the logical solution that's the Islamic solution par excellence.[399]

170

---

[398] *Ibid,* pp. 30-34.

[399] Yusuf Qurdāwi, *al-Hulūl al-Mustawrada wa Kayfa Janat 'ala Umatina* (Beirut: Mu'assasat al-Risāla, 1980, p. 7.

Qurdawi's solution must then be irrevocably ratified. And what could be surer for the purpose than giving it some historical perspective. That's easily done by reviewing, in order to refute or reject them, a whole century's worth of crackpot heads. Those who at one time or another marvel at Western science and philosophy, circulating their ideas among Arab-Muslims, like a merry-go-round. And what, pray, are they but patrons of the West in its very hostility to Islam. Muhammad Muhammad Husayn puts his own edge on his contemporary Muhammad al-Bahī and then, like two knives, they sacrifice those so-called patrons with their reflections and observations. (You already met those scholars, among others, before. I think you'll recognize them as soon as you hear their names.[400])

Alienation (in the sense of westernization), Husayn begins, starts off with al-Tahtāwi and al-Tūnisī. Their patronage of the West paves the way for the penetration of Western ideas into Arab-Muslim cozy environment. Alienation, oh my fellow countrymen, serves a two-fold purpose: to protect or safeguard imperialist interests by reducing the gap separating East and West, and to loosen the knotty religious ties that bond all Arab-Muslims together into *Ummah Muslima*.[401] On this plank of Arab-Muslim platform Husayn will next assess al-Afghāni's attitudes and his personality along with those of his friend Abduh. First of all, al-Afghāni is certainly a strange character. He forms secret societies which include Jews, and detaches himself by means of his uncanny thought from authentic Islam; he even attacks the English in favor of the French; in short, everything he says and does—not to speak of his secret societies, his sanctioning assassination as a means to reach his goals, and his exalting freedom from the bonds of religion, its heritage and traditions—indeed, all this and more stirs up doubt and suspicion around him.[402]

---

[400] See above, pp. 122-134.

[401] Muhammad Muhammad Husayn, *al-Islām wa-l Hadāra al-Gharbiyya* (Beirut: al-Maktab al-Islāmi, 1979), p. 45.

[402] *Ibid*, p. 76.

224

What about his friend Abduh? He's as worse: imperialism certainly spurs him to open up the door of *Ijtihad*, so that he may bring Islam closer and closer to Western civilization. What a daredevil turning his role and that of al-Afghānī into something like Luther's or Calvin's, those Protestant leaders who want to set up a different kind of Christianity; they, too, want to set up a new Islam. They've failed miserably, however, shrinking at last to a mere tool in the hands of atheism camouflaged as modernization, advancement, or what not.[403] So the struggle of old and new goes back to the beginnings of alienation. The most prominent proponent of modernization, and its concomitant alienation, is, of course, Taha Husayn. After all, hasn't he categorically, unwaveringly insisted on Egypt's becoming a Western province? More than that. Hasn't he summoned Egypt to erect its system of rule upon a civil basis completely free of religion? And called for Arabic language to be subjected to the law of historical evolution? As a result of these aberrations, among others, corruption and turmoil now descend not only upon Egypt but upon the entire Arab-Muslim world as well. Even Arabic literature is hardly spared this corrupt deviationism: indeed, the novel has become nothing but a dangerous influential tool for disseminating more corruption.[404]

171

Muhammad al-Bahī, the other knife, treats of the same subject as does Muhammad Muhammad Husayn: that is, alienation-westernization trends in Arab-Muslim thought. His main contribution centers around two historical trends: the first starts with the Indian scholar Ahmad Khan in the second half of the nineteenth century who's utterly taken by Western natural science and civilization, as some thinkers today show wonderment at what's called "science" and the technological achievements based on it.[405] The second trend is exemplified by al-Afghānī and his advocates of religious reform. But what does

---

[403] *Ibid*, p. 175.

[404] Muhammad Muhammad Husayn, *al-Itijāhāt al-Wataniyya fi-l Adab al-Mu'āsir* (Beirut: Mu'assasat al-Risala, 1980), p. 229.

[405] Muhammad al-Bahī, *al-Fikr al-Islāmi al-Hadīth wa Siātuhu bi-l Isti'mār al-Gharbi* (Beirut: Dār al-Fikr, 1973, p. 44.

all that yield? After al-Afghani, the reformists represent a movement of sponsorship and salvation, while the advocates of modernization, following Ahmad Khan, symbolically, as it were, re-enact the invasion by Western Crusades of Arab-Muslim foundations. This modernist predilection for the West or, what amounts to the same, westernized Islamic thought is but the adoption of everything from the West blindly and without caution. It's also the trend that argues that the Qur'ān is a human creation—as Taha Husayn has said, for example; or that Islam is a religion and not a state—as 'Ali 'Abd al-Razzāq has said; or, finally, that Islam is a superstitious metaphysical religion—as the academy's professors of philosophy have said.

Worse still, and most cunning is the Marxist claim that religion is opium for the people. Several Marxists, such as Khāled Muhammad Khāled and Mustafa Mahmūd, have tried to disseminate their ideas in volumes cloaked in religious garbs. What's outrageous is that they've added not only some Qur'anic Surahs to their communist propaganda speech, but also a few of the Hadīths (prophetic tradition) attributed to the Prophet Muhammad. In the final analysis, al-Bahī thinks that Marxism, far from being a call for the advancement of humanity, is convocation to retrogression, to deterioration, the return of man to slavery and of thought and faith to coercion. For this reason Marxism and the Arab-Muslim world can't be compatible bed fellows, to say the least; the former has no place in the latter.[406]

Toward the end of his book, al-Bahī reiterates his position loud and clear: the advocates of modernism in Arab-Muslim thought, he says in effect, are no more than superficial imitators or conformists, and because of them Arabic literature today suffers from a crisis of separatism in its portrayal of contemporary life. These modernists merely live in the shadow of others and off the residues or surplus that has lost its significance and dignity in the contemporary currents of humanity.[407] What's more, Islam since the nineteenth century has confronted

---

[406] *Ibid*, pp. 376-391.

[407] *Ibid*, p. 417

Western Crusades motivated as they are by a spirit of revenge. And the outcome of this confrontation is two-fold: on the one hand, the advocates of westernization have succeeded in substituting tribalism for Islamic bonding, as in Turkey, for example, and so caused a vacuum in contemporary Islamic thought; on the other hand, Islam, ironically enough, has benefited from this confrontation which has reawakened Islamic consciousness and made possible the emergence of reformist tendency. Above all, the confrontation demonstrates that Islam is for all time and place, better still, above time and place.[408]

Part Three

172

In the history of nations, you search in vain for a comparable intellectual debate at the center of Arab-Muslim world. True, everywhere in the West, you find controversies: secular science versus creation science; metaphysical naturalism versus methodological naturalism; preformationism versus natural selection; Christian fundamentalism pandering to state politics for influence; Protestants versus Catholics. Even in the Soviet Union, before the fall of the Berlin Wall, you find heated controversies over whether or not to go the democratic way and open the country to market economy. But none of these controversies (there are many others) comes close to what has been transpiring in the Arab-Muslim world since the eighteenth century. Let me put it this way: the debate still on-going is whether or not to westernize and, as a significant corollary, whether or not to separate religion from the state. This last controversy characterizes the uniqueness of Arab-Muslim debate.[409]

And so the sequence of Arab-Muslim view of the West comprises two tenors: the first sings the praises of the West as emblem of power and freedom, the second reduces it to a threat to Islam and Man. These two agonistic versions

---

[408] *Ibid*, pp. 499-502.

[409] It's quite ironic that the results of the January 2005 elections in Iraq underscore the religious domination. What that means isn't difficult to predict.

of the argument plumb the depth of anxiety and crisis facing Arab-Muslims today as they attempt to assess the nature and quality of development they desire for themselves. Actually, this entire question of development (or lack thereof) is but a dimension of the portrait of the West they've been painting for three centuries. Only a whole century goes by before certain Arab-Muslims and Muslims (India, Turkey, Africa) realize that what has come to light in one spot of the world imposes itself, willy-nilly, on other spots. Which fact makes it inevitable for nations to accept and follow. If some don't, however, if they reject the enlightenment, then they must not only have effective means or alternatives to counteract or counterbalance it, but to compel respect of and cooperation by the West as well.

173

Truth to tell, at no time does outright rejection of West enlightenment appear totally fulfilled. For example, even Sayyid Qutb (not to be confused with Muhammad Qutb)—the most vehement, most thoroughgoing Arab-Muslim fundamentalist, who equates the West with the state of "ignorance" characterizing pre-Islamic age—is still not closed to it. In his voluminous thought, theirs is one aperture at least, and through it Arab-Muslims can see the glimmer of a conciliatory ideology or, if you will, pedagogy. Islam, he says in effect, allows a Muslim to receive instruction in sciences and arts (organic chemistry, physical chemistry, astrology, medicine, agriculture, administration, insurance, and so on) from a non-Muslim. But it doesn't allow a Muslim to receive instruction in the principles of dogma, the elements of his conceptual thought, the course of history, his system of rule, interpretation of his spirit and vitality, and social ideology from non-Muslim sources. You see, Qutb here defines the parameters specifying that no idea purporting to accommodate two different authorities—Islam, on the one hand, and that of the other, on the other hand—is to be admitted.[410]

But the question of assessing intercourse with the other (by which the West is meant here) isn't as simple as it looks. Consider Sheikh Abduh, for

---

[410] Sayyid Qutb, *Ma'ālim fi-l Tarīq* (Damascus: Dar Dimashq, 1965), p. 173-5.

instance. He's twice a pioneer: once he summons Arab-Muslims to return to the sources of early Islam for inspiration, and again he initiates the movement of religious reform. In both instances, he's lionized by the majority of Arab-Muslims as innovator in teaching and calling for harmony with the modern world. And yet a scholar like Muhammad Muhammad Husayn, as you just saw, raises suspicion about him and about the veracity of his faith. Even as his friend al-Afghāni and his student Rida hardly escape that fate. Accordingly, the upright, faithful Abduh is converted into I-know-from-nothing; worse, he becomes an agent of England and a pioneer in westernizing thought.

The case of Abduh is certainly symptomatic of a profound anxiety. But it's also symptomatic of a healthy ambience. True, Egypt, and beyond it the Arab-Muslim world, finds itself in the grip of two opposed viewpoints which arise from the tenor of Abduh's view of Europe (and the West). However, his thought is neither a sell-out to the West nor an advocacy of isolationism. Which fact prompts a third viewpoint surrounding his personality. One exonerating him from Husayn's suspicious attitude—and showing that things aren't made of black and white. In the eyes of Muhammad 'Ammāra, for example, Abduh is the first to harmonize two contradictory authorities or systems of thought. Abduh, he says in effect, is no dreaming advocate of the return to a bygone age, first half century or centuries of decline, for the purpose of molding contemporary society, nor is he trying to coerce Arab-Muslim community, with its distinct culture, to put on the cloak of western civilization. After all, Abduh himself admits that he certainly diverges from the opinion of the two opposed groups—the students of religion and their followers, and the students of modernization and their followers—that make up the body of Arab-Muslim community.[411]

This third viewpoint is actually evaluative, steering, as it were in mid course. Another contemporary scholar who endorses it says that the conciliatory movement initiated by al-Afghāni and Abduh represents another liberal dimension of Islamic tradition for confronting challenge, Western or otherwise.

---

[411] Muhammad 'Ammāra, al-'Arab wal-Tahadi (Quweit: Sulsilat 'Ālam al-Ma'arra, 1980),p. 304.

For it's now clear, particularly after al-Afghāni and Abduh, that the essence of confrontation is cultural and not military, religious, or political. Conciliation is the Islamic response which proves fruitful as well as in matters of such cultural confrontation.[412] Something Arab-Muslims ought to investigate since it's in their own backyard.

174

Even though Europe's portrait splits into two sharply opposed currents in Arab-Muslim mind, there's still room in it for syncretist thought. Which, as the cultural theorist Muhammad al-Jābiri puts it (you'll hear of him again later), amounts to integrating something from Islam with something from the West, that is, uniting the best in each—the best from the one and the best from the other.[413] And the scholar Muhammad al-Ansāri echoes that constructive idea by identifying two events: first, the failure of both Western liberalism and the rigid movement of return to early Islam; secondly, the positive gesture, despite some disappointment with the West, advanced by al-Afghāni and Abduh toward the West. Consequently, syncretism triumphs over such odds and now becomes a certainty after four decades, especially with the advent of Marxism and Fascism.

It's worth pursuing this thought a bit more here. After al-Afghāni and Abduh, several Arab-Muslim scholars underscore syncretism as the only open road to Arab-Muslim renaissance. To begin with, Mansour Fahmi, a critic of Taha Husayn's extreme position regarding Egypt set down in his 1938 book,[414] declares with caution that Egypt isn't and shouldn't be thought of as a Western province and that imitation of the West, while advantageous to the country, has limits. Ahmad al-Zayyāt dedicates a special volume of his magazine *Majalat al-Risāla* to the spirit of harmony between East and West in which he expresses urgency to find the missing link. The missing link is further articulated by

---

[412] Muhammad Jābir al-Ansāri, *Tahawulāt al-Fikr wa-l Siyāsa fi-l Sharq al-'Arabī* (Quweit: Sulsilat 'Ālam al-Ma'rifa, 1980), p. 9.

[413] Muhammad 'Abid al-Jābiri, *al-Khitāb al-'Arabi al-Mu'āsir: Dirāsa Tahlīliyya* Naqdiyya (Beirut: Dar al-Tali'a, 1982), p. 53.

[414] See note 212 above.

Ahmad Amīn. In Eygypt, he says in effect, there's a missing link of whose existence in the scientific and philosophical circles Arab-Muslims seem barely aware; it's actually one of the major cornerstones which ought to be put in place, so that they can build upon it their renaissance. This link is the bevy of scientists and thinkers who attempt to bring together Islamic culture and Western civilization. Arab-Muslims are in dire need of more of these savants, for no genuine renaissance can begin to name itself as such except with them.[415] The same sentiment resounds from the pen of another scholar who, after undergoing a crisis of conscience, declares that he still shares with his colleagues the thought of Arab-Muslims' need for embracing a bit of enlightenment from the West, but that he disagrees with them concerning the matter of spiritual life. Such a life, he argues, is indigenous to Islam and therefore can't be imported from the West. The West has its own indigenous spiritual life of which Arab-Muslims can't partake: after all, it's different and foreign to Islam. Arab-Muslim have only one source to dip into: they must appeal to, must search their own history, their own education, their own heart for this life.[416]

175

Obviously, the act or thought of incorporating a bit of Western enlightenment into Arab-Muslim self, of inoculating Islamic education with a dosage of Western thought seems to be the way to Arab-Muslim renaissance. Once this is secures, then the next step to bridging the gap between the material West and the spiritual East becomes possible. Albeit the pineal gland which stimulates color change in both sides is yet to be found, the thought of syncretism is alive and well. Mustafa Mahmūd lucidly expresses this thought as follows: after a long journey of doubt, he arrives at the conclusion that spiritual Islam can coexist with material West; in point of fact, it proffers the latter the only way out of its clogging materialism, the only salvation, the only solution. What's more, it offers the West spiritual heritage without commanding or coercing it to give up

---

[415] See al-Ansāri, p. 94.

[416] *Ibid,* pp. 69-70.

anything of its progressive accomplishments or even its material supremacy. All what Islam wants is to effect the marriage between matter and spirit, so that a new culture may constructed, a culture of power and mercy. Mahmūd, who subjects the Qur'ān to electronic analysis in order to affirm its divine origin, strongly disagrees with his colleague Khaled Muh'i al-Dīn with the respect to the possibility of harmonizing Islam and Marxism. How could that ever transpires, he asks? Do you really think this god forsaken, materialist Marxism accords with pure pristine Islam when each ideology logically, categorically rejects the other?[417]

And yet al-Ansāri, who reports this quarrel, counters Mahmūd's remark and agrees to al-Dīn's idea. He holds that Islam is naturally, inwardly, or intrinsically conciliatory. Accordingly, he contrasts modern syncretism with esoteric syncretism. For he argues that the former is an evolutionary encounter between Mid-East and Western mind rooted in Greek soil. Therefore, it can more easily interact with Western mind than that esoteric syncretism which finds in modern mind a refutation of both its epistemological foundation and veiled doctrinal infallibility. It penetrates into the essence of historical development, societal and cultural, and renders the nature of Arab-Muslim mind, ancient and modern, better committed to it. It follows that if the modern will to return to early Islam, intransigent as it is, is itself undertaken in reaction to the view of the West in the second half of the nineteenth century, then its counterpart, modern syncretism, is no more than a response to Western globally irresistible influence. So much so that to think and speak of spiritual East and stop there—well, wouldn't that itself be an effect of Western influence, too?

176

Zaki Nejīb Mahmūd (another important Arab-Muslim scholar not to be confused with Mustafa Mahmūd) assumes a position representing the highest point syncretism of West and Islam reaches in the domains of education and thought. If freedom, he says in effect, is what distinguishes the West, let's then

---

[417] *Ibid*, pp. 10-12, and 225-227.

search for it in our heritage; and again, if rationalism is the commodity most brisk in the West, let's then set out in quest of it in our classical Islamic thought. And let's perhaps begin with those individuals who call themselves al-Mu'tazila.[418] Mahmūd arrives at this position after long-drawn personal agony, for he declares openly at the start of his book that despair has struck often times in his search for a way out. That is, a way out, leading Arab-Muslims to be what they are and what they want to be—in short, to the educational commingling of East and West in which originality abides and where it keeps abreast with contemporary life.[419]

More inspiration comes to him, he continues, from one of the seminal thoughts of Herbert Reed's whose gist is this: there's something called heritage; its values resides in the fact that it's a cluster of technical means which can be useful as a tool for analyzing what's going on today, knowing already how secure we are in whatever fresh endeavor undertaken by us for enhancing our life. And so Mahmūd begins his search for those elements of the heritage that are beneficial to the modern age: one such element is al-Ghazāli's doubt, another the sensuality of al-Tawhīdi, a third the rationalism of al-Mu'tazila, and so on.[420] At this juncture he suggests a new kind of philosophy to be founded in a duality of heaven and earth and of one program and another. That way, he says, we'll march on the straight path before us if we make room for a program consisting of natural sciences, on the one hand, and another based in absolute truth. The first derives from observation, experimentations, and soundness of application; the other, such as ethics, differs in that it doesn't so much depend on the senses or experimentation as on keenness of perception, on direction of inspiration, to what transpires or circulates among people in terms of customs and traditions.[421]

---

[418] For further information on Mu'tazila, see Fatema Mernissi, pp. 32-40; see also F.E. Peters, pp. 136-46 and 147-53.

[419] Zaki Nejīb Mahmūd, *Tajdīd al-Fikr al-'Arabi* (Beirut: Dār al-Shurūq, 1982), p. 15.

[420] Al-Ghazāli, a historical realist of the thirteenth century, see F.E. Peters, pp. 188-93 and 228-32; al-Tawhīdi is a literary figure of late tenth and early eleventh centuries, see William al-Khāzen, p. 20, p. 33, and p. 165; and Mu'tazila, see Mernissi and F.E. Peters.

[421] Zaki Mahmūd,, pp. 282-3.

And so Mahmūd jubilates over finding the missing link he's searched for and which combines the rigorous demands of science with the subtle fundamentals of man. Actually, his approach hardly differs from that of Muhammad Abduh, Taha Husayn, al'Aqād and al-Hakīm on whom he depends for his findings.[422] For he says: when Abduh attempts to set Islamic heritage in the light of modern age, he is probing his way toward syncretism; when al'Aqād tries to defend Islam by refuting those who speak against it, using for the purpose his Western and Arabic forms of education united in one structure, he wants to syncretize between the two or combine them in a common domain; when Husayn critiques pre-Islamic literature in light of modern thought, he too wants to accomplish the same end; and, finally, when al-Hakīm writes so many dramas attempting to fuse matter and spirit, the eternal and the ephemeral, he, too, desires to reach the same end. So we can, obviously, trail these pioneers' steps in our modern history and thought today. There we find how each works so painstakingly to weave together Western thought and Eastern thought into one continuous braid.[423]

177

You may ask what, if anything, Mahmūd's philosophy yields You see, for the first time in the history of Arab-Muslim thought—and, I think, it's a unique moment—two systems of thought or two research procedures articulate a grid of interdisciplinary approach to the comprehension of society, politics, and behavior. Of course, let me quickly add, these systems or procedures each might very well be construed as mental compartments isolated one from the other; what's more, they each, in turn, might lead to the development of two separate languages: language of experimentation and language of imagination or inspiration. That the second alternative is, to say it again, possible, it really depends on the Arab-Muslim will to integrate or reluctance to integrate the two systems. In a word, it's

---

[422] 'Abas Mahmūd al'Aqād is a formidable twentieth century Arab-Muslim historian. See William al-Khazen, pp. 52, 95, 105, 115, 117-19, 121, 123-4, 127-30, 133, 135, 138. Tawfīq al-Hakīm is a twentieth century Egyptian dramatist.

[423] Zaki Mahmūd, pp. 272-73.

a choice. After all, Mahmūd relies on a truth that has defined Arab-Muslim understanding of the world as follows: Arab-Muslims, in their daily-imbibed religious passions, still approach things magically, which treats or tackles them through methods other than those of their natural causes. Speaking for the entire Arab-Muslim world, he says that "without Western Enlightenment, its scientists, its educational know-how, our life here would appear barely different from that of primitive man in its earlier stages."[424]

All in all, Mahmūd's philosophy signifies both a future to come (if it's permitted to come at all) and resolve to address existing state of affairs. From this perspecdtive, you see, it's not an ideology in quest of a median point or space between the West and Islam; rather, it's an amalgam, an interdisciplinary methodology whose history goes back to al-Tahtāwi, Mubārak, and al-Tūnisī of the first half of the nineteenth century. Syncretism, then, for that's what it is, will succeed better practically at the level of government than merely adopting and adapting to Western liberalism alone or returning to early Islam alone. This is so because, given the disciplinary approach, it possesses the capacity to satisfy the various tendencies of the populace, even if it prolongs a period of crisis and expectation.

Speaking of the populace, and from what I'm able to glean from Mahmūd's philosophy, I can say this: Arab-Muslims in general are pious, very devoted religious people. To that extent, they constitute an objective force that any system of thought other than that of theology must contend with. Mahmūd's philosophy of syncretism, I think, easily, though painstakingly, adapts itself to that requirement. Again, Arab-Muslims are pious, but they're interested in upgrading their psycho-social and political life; they're also interested in social progress. Accordingly, syncretism, since it's a form of interdisciplinary research, is capable of interpreting faith in such a way as to justify people's interest in their own social progress. Science may be used to confirm the truth of the holy book,

---

[424] *Ibid*, p. 61.

as Mustafa Mahmūd shows.[425]   Or faith may inoculate science with ethics the better to serve mankind, as Muhammad Iqbāl shows.[426]   More than that, it helps persuade the pious that religious belief isn't necessarily something that can be embodied or made incarnate in socio-political operation and practice. Faith can participate in all sorts of political campaigns, holds important discussions on what's good for the country. But as soon as this operation comes to an end, so would faith's role in its socio-political deliberation. After all, faith's proper role is to instruct people in ethical and moral issues that are as much vital for the success of political process as any non-religious political system of representation designed for the advancement of Arab-Muslims.

---

[425] See above page 202.

[426] See Muhammad Iqbāl, p. 14.

Chapter Four

Toward a Critical View

Part One

178

Mirsepassi and Plato—what a couple! Persia and Greece, East and West together at it again, after 2500 years! But this time for peace, not war. And what do they talk about? Muslims and Arab-Muslims today? Yes, they do, though Plato doesn't know or doesn't know of them. At any rate, they talk and think the same thing but in different ways and, of course, different languages. Mirsepassi advises them "to face the West, walk through it, get to know it, then look back"; Plato, in his *Alcibiades*, speaks to them about ontological knowledge of self, or knowledge of self through the other. And he thinks they understand him. And frankly, it isn't a big deal either. After all, they've translated him or some of his works, though not *Alcibiades*. Or perhaps they have, who knows?

Well, because it's ontology of self, not a psychology of self. It derives from or takes shape as contemplation of the soul by itself in terms of the metaphor of the eye. Plato asks: how can the eye see itself? The answer is that it can't, pure and simple; one can't look at oneself in a mirror. One has to look into another eye, that is, an eye in oneself, though in oneself in the shape of the eye of the other. And there, in the other eye, one sees oneself: the eye serves as a mirror. So when the soul contemplates itself in another soul, which is like its eye, it will then recognize itself (and its divine element). In short, to acquire self-knowledge, to try to grasp the mode of being of oneself, one asks oneself what one's done, what one's thinking, what the movements of one's ideas or one's representations are, to what one's attached.[427] In so doing, one becomes what one is, or, to put it in another way, one is what one becomes. And one is and becomes and becomes what one is each time. Isn't that what Mirsepassi in his way talks about, too?

179

Still, you may ask: how does Plato's metaphor of the eye translate into Arab-Muslim experience? Well, since the ninth century, many savants (historians, geographers, travelers, diplomats, educationalists, reformers, philosophers, scientists, poets, and cultural theorists) might have discovered that life, after all, is nothing but an experiment of knowers—not a duty, not a calamity, not trickery. Or life as a precious means to knowledge. They don't say so in the open, of course; they each act it out in their own way. Besides, the West (or Europe) happens to be contiguous, a next door neighbor, so to speak, in the geographical sense. So why not find out who and what it's like? Such a question might have occurred to our savants out of curiosity—curiosity as unconscious virtue or, if you like, as instinctive morality. Certainly, it couldn't have been fostered by orthodoxy which is known for its dozing passions, also for having no respect for reason and intellectual conscience. Rather, Arab-Muslims' exposure to various peoples and cultures, as you saw, including translation of Greek science and philosophy is, I wager, the matrix of that question.

Accordingly, life, as far as they can judge assumes the form of the West or other in relation to them, or that they find the West in life to be an experiment. In short, a means to knowledge, to self-understanding as Arab-Muslims, probing for potentialities they know they're there but remain untapped, deferred, delayed. In Plato's ontological language, life, West, other or simply the eye of the other acquires the status of mirror wherein Arab-Muslim savants contemplate themselves, reflect on who they are and how they can develop integrative mechanisms linking past and future history, social ideal and social reality. In a word, how to become interpreters of a culture in progress.

---

[427] See Plato, Alcibiades. See also M. Foucault, "On the Genealogy of Ethics: An Overview of Work in Progress, *The Foucault Reader*, ed. Paul Rabinow (New York: Pantheon Books, 1984), pp. 366-372. Foucault's discussion is seminal to my work here.

You see, in postmodern era, you can no longer separate self from the other, or, what amounts to the same thing, the constitution of self from the constitution of the other. Now if you drop or discount Plato's metaphor altogether, you may reach this conclusion: it's downright self-contradiction to insist that one causes one's own knowledge of oneself, that one can bear the entire and ultimate responsibility for one's actions and thoughts oneself, and absolve chance, ancestors, society, the world, the West, or God—in a word, the other. Put otherwise, one could no more pull oneself up into existence by the hair, as it were, out of the swamp of nonbeing than one could turn lead into gold. If one could, if Arab-Muslims, past and present, could, they wouldn't have bothered to learn about the West and themselves as they have in the first place. Rather, and this is the contradiction of contradiction, they've accomplished their mission precisely by contemplating themselves in the eye of the West. The same holds for the West as well. Exchange, now more than ever, and for ever, is the name of the game.

180

Allow me to interject a brief remark at this point. Today's Islamists, given the tunnel vision of many politico-religious parties into which they organize themselves, seem to be incapable of comprehending how these ancestors, that is, their ancestors, have accomplished their heroic feat. They veil such incomprehension with the cloak of the well-worn heading of *Ummah* by setting off bombs, by killing their own fellow countrymen and women (and not only countrymen and women) and, to top it all, by erecting discourses of right which they claim impose limits on so-called abuses of power both internally and externally. This unwieldy situation, unwieldy perhaps for being tragically ironic, is but symptomatic of Islam having lost much if not all of its ethico-religious status, and, consequently, become an ideology of and for the masses. It no longer raises *Jihad* both as self-overcoming and as a rallying point for preserving the common heritage and safeguarding the threatened historical existence of Arab-Muslim peoples; it's now no more than a tool for political manipulation, pure and simple, a kind of bogeyman conjured up by turns against the West and Mid-Eastern local governments.

And here I'd like to speak in behalf of Islamists for a change. I mean to articulate their unconscious weakness. Suppose they comprehend the significance of the dialectical relationship of self and other, they nonetheless tend to suppress or ignore it; and in so doing, deem their behavior an effective bulwark against the collapse of their autonomy and political unity. In other words, they refuse to embrace that relationship because they seem to be unaware that their much touted autonomy and unity, which they think viable, have no legs to stand on. That's why these words ring false—a ruse to gain time, a fiction without form. Once again, they don't know that, and because they don't, they suffer an identity crisis camouflaged as it is by their feeble, though deadly, defensive tactics. And to complicate things still more, their sense of dignity, rooted in tradition and memory, leaps into play: they want to struggle for the survival of Islam which, ironically, has never been threatened as a faith. As a corollary, they assume a unified will that makes of their deed and substantial ego causal antecedent to ideological thought. They unwittingly belittle or reduce themselves to a huge group of ideologues defending an amorphous political order. But this is exactly where they get things wrong.

181

To put it otherwise, Islamists desire to lift themselves up by their own bootstraps. Well and good. But that entails assuming they know who they are, which isn't the case; and what exactly they want, which isn't the case either; above all, it entails knowing their self to be as much unified as undivided, and, therefore, existing apart from the other, which is a fiction since Islam and the West can't be thought apart from each other historically. In a word, Islamists confer fictitious value upon themselves by devaluing difference. I mean they interpret and misinterpret themselves as valuable through negating the other's difference and value. Hence they fetishize themselves, become a valuable thing-in-itself precisely by suppressing the dialectical relationship of self and other, without which, needless to say, no self exists and no other either. Arab-Muslim intellectuals, on the other hand, want to become what they are—human beings who are new, unique, incomparable, who give themselves laws, who create themselves and take intellectual control of their own aspirations. Rather than negating the other's difference, they seek their honor, their value through that difference, and affirm themselves. The position from which they can do so isn't the position of the so-called period of decline which is a prelude to death. Rather, it's the position of the other—the other as mirror, as means to this self-affirmation as viable force in interpreting a culture in progress.

Islamists and Arab-Muslim—could they be compared? Surely. The other, the West, is definitely that which both groups have certain views about in common. But then they part ways in their approach to it. The former select or extract only a few effects or characteristics from a continuum of possibilities and deny the other; the latter allow for the discovery of this very continuum and the fact that the other's difference can be mastered.[428] This double discovery gives our savants, the modern more than the medieval ones, to realize that learning and understanding is what actually matters, and matters both because it's an on-going process and because self-invention has no end point

Part Two

182

Let's conclude our narrative. The tide of knowledge of self and the West continues to flow in the second half of the twentieth century. Its course, no doubt steered both by Western culture and traditional Arab-Muslim culture, eventually

---

[428] The West thinks the reverse is true—which is false. The West has fabricated orientalism (which in turn fabricates the Orient) with which it wants to associate itself. It has done so only by looking to the past and conferring a privileged status dogmatically upon classical Greco-roman civilization and implicitly upon contemporary western society, as if the West knows the past fully and the present fully, which is false as well. Difference doesn't ever occur to it or compel its respect. E. Said's book, *Orientalism*, can perhaps be understood and appreciated only from this perspective.

curves around the corner to take on a different coloring: it becomes criticism directed at once at the self and the West.

But before we come to this turning point, let's recall two features which, as you saw, could scarcely be distinguished from each other. The first is the liberal secularism of early nineteenth century, which Arab-Muslim and Ottoman-Muslim savants approve of, assimilate, or both. It calls for separation of state and religion, the better to ensure the prosperity of both. What' more, the welfare of society, it claims, may best be guaranteed by the state's number one concern—individual freedom. I mean freedom of the individual to fulfill him- or herself so as to contribute to the intellectual and spiritual enhancement of culture—what I referred to a moment ago as interpreters of a culture in progress.[429] The second feature is reformism. It stands for revival of Islamic tradition and reassertion of Islam's unique and perfect truth. But the truth of the matter is that this reformism occurs under the stimulus of Western liberal thought, and leads to a gradual reinterpretation of Islamic concepts in order to make them comport with the guiding principles of Western thought of the time.

Non the less, these two features-in-one soon split into what looks like irreconcilable parts. On the one side, you have Arab-Muslim intellectuals so profoundly impressed by Western liberalism that they divest it of all negative qualities. They are the organic intellectuals who not only refuse to politicize their intellect; they want to get on with the double task of culture building and bridge-building between East and West. In short, they consider themselves and Westerners as equal partners in culture. On the other side, you have traditional intellectuals who intellectualize politics. Now given how history operates without conscious intervention by a subject, the very tendency to revive Islamic tradition under the stimulus of Western liberal thought compels these traditional

---

[429] Having said that, there's perhaps the unstoppable irony of how the individual is taught to sacrifice him or herself, his or her own advantage, development, promotion, elevation, and reason for the good and benefit of society. In other words, the unreason of society, while encouraging the individual to seek knowledge, teaches him or her to allow him- or herself to be transformed into a mere function of the whole, even at the expense of death. Obviously, the contradiction between motive and principle is staggering. However, some Arab-Muslim savants, as we shall se, probe this matter, though not sufficiently, with the aim of raising Arab-Muslim awareness of it.

intellectuals to reject the West based on ethical or moral grounds. For a while this rejection seems definitive because it presupposes a prior rejection of everything Western or even Eastern that's not compatible with Islam as a faith and as a way of life.

183

Such rejection or, if you will, incompatibility, though ill considered, has a historical provenance. For a long time, actually since late fourteenth century, Islam becomes vulnerable; it loses its center of gravity almost totally, and breaks up into disparate socio-historical and political entities. The roots of this break up, in turn, go back to mid eighth century when the old family rivalry resurfaces or comes to a head. A long story.[430] In any event, then from the fifteenth century on the rise of Europe (West), its insatiable curiosity and greed stifle certain Arab-Muslim countries, such as Egypt, Algiers, and Tunisia. Though Europe has no intention of doping so, the effect is devastating: a slowdown of communications on almost every level and dissolution of all bonds linking Islamic and Arab-Muslim communities. More than that, Arab-Muslims turn in on themselves and derive intellectual sustenance (if you can call it that) from twelfth-century mysticism or belief in occult forces and fantasies that creep into the popular mind like leeches, rendering it incapable of thought and afflicting it with moral paralysis.[431]

Finally, to add insult to injury, the French occupy Egypt in late eighteenth century and spread all over North Africa. This is the beginning of

---

[430] See my brief reference to this issue above, pp. 87-88. See also Reza Aslan, pp. 24-26. In these pages Aslan discusses the same matter but leaves out of count Qussay's descendents—Abbās and Umayya—who, to cut corners, soon split over the practice of who should provide bread and water to the pilgrims flocking to Mecca each year. Above all, the split eventually mushrooms into a bloody conflict between the descendants, the Ummayad and Abbasid dynasties, which eventually rings Islam's knell.

[431] There are several sources to consult for further information on this complex history. Albert Hourani, *Arabic Thought in the Liberal Age*; Hichem Djait, *Europe and Islam*; Maxime Rodinson, *Europe and the Mystique of Islam*, trans. Roger Veinus (Seattle: University of Washington Press, 1987). Though these sources may provide some insight, the history of moral paralysis per se hasn't been written yet.

love-hate relationship between Westerners and Arab-Muslims. The relationship itself embodies a paradox. On the one hand, it enables a majority of Arab-Muslims to escape from their decadence and torpor, by breaking up their rigid social order and freeing them from isolation and superstition. In a word, it sharpens their disparity. Djait puts it well, "the shock of the encounter with Europe opened their eyes to an evident and utterly unheard of disparity in power."[432] On the other hand, it fulfills a vision begun in the fourteenth century: the establishment of an Arabic Chair, among others, in European capitals.[433] And this not only for study of the Mid-East, but also for teaching Arab-Muslims about things they don't know or have—human sciences. The French, says the Egyptian historian Jabarti in effect, make great efforts to learn Arabic language and the colloquial. In this they strive day and night. And they have books especially devoted to all types of languages, their declensions and conjugations as well as their etymologies. These works make it easy for them to translate whatever they wish from any language into their own language very quickly.[434]

184

I think the point I'm trying to reach here is this: whether it's a mater of rejecting the West or accepting it, the end result is ultimately the same. Since the eighth century, or better, since the break-up of Islam into disparate, isolated socio-historical or socio-political entities, Arab-Muslim identity is no longer defined or experienced within the Islamic space called *Dar al-Islam*. Now that the encounter with the West has taken place, Arab-Muslim identity lives as or occupies a position in universal history comprised of both East and West. As Islamic faith persists in losing ground within the limits of society, its practice, if at all, will become more like belonging to one spiritual family among others in a pluralistic context. I mean the more Arab-Muslims get farther and further way from the periods of decline and of colonialism, the more they look, inevitably, to outside

---

[432] See Djait, p. 127.

[433] See E. Said, *Orientalism*, pp. 49-51.

[434] See B. Lewis, pp. 295-6.

cultural models as tools for restructuring their life. Already, you see, Arab-Muslims, whether they realize it or not, bridge the gap between East and West. But exactly the same may be said of the West. It, too, can hardly define itself outside Islam. In fact, Islam and Europe, to say it again, belong to the same stage of history that founds the modern world.[435]

185

And so the age of criticism takes off in the second half of the twentieth century precisely in that context. The leading signifier here is orientalism, naturally, just a couple of decades before E. Said's groundbreaking work. The subject is of great significance and relevance today, whose philosophy (if it has one) constitutes a major feature of Arab-Muslim view of the West. Eventually, however, the subject is bracketed to give right of place to another kind of criticism that's focused, as you'll see, more on objective (if that's the right word) cultural critiques of both East and West than on an exclusively subjective view of the West.

Anyhow, it all starts in the twenties with the Lebanese scholar familiar to us from last chapter. He's Shakīb Arslān who at one point in his life sojourns in Europe for a while, in Switzerland in particular.[436] There he has occasion to get acquainted with a number of publications by European missionary societies. Being both reformist and nationalist, spending his formative years under the tutelage of Abduh's the school of thought, he gradually waxes suspicious with respect to the Christian missionaries who attempt to convert African Congo to Christianity. It's not too long before he realizes the political stratagems underneath it all: the borderline between missionary activities and orientalizing work, now that both target the Mid-East as well, blend without any noticeable distinctions. For him, what Mustafa Kamāl, for example, has done in Turkey—separating state and religion—is simply outrageous. Why? Because he thinks

---

[435] See Djait, pp. 105-113. And for further information on the same subject, see Thierry Hentsche, *Imagining the Middle East.*

[436] See A. Hourani, p. 306-7.

Islamic *Sharī'a* is flexible enough to adapt itself to the modern age. More than that, his outrage stems from Kamāl's adoption and use of Swiss civil law which embodies principles and formulas reaching back to Roman legislation and which is much more ancient than Islamic jurisprudence. And this, therefore, is the straw that breaks the camels back: Kamāl's justification for abolishing *Sharī'a* isn't just baseless; it's a downright unadulterated lie no less.[437]

186

It's worth mentioning that Arslān isn't the first to contest, rebut, or fulminate against orientalists' claims. The contestation reaches back to the nineteenth century when al-Afghāni and Abduh, motivated by religious considerations, inaugurate the career of their backward-looking or return-to-the-sources school (a.k.a. *salafiyya*).[438] (Recall that this backward-looking gesture or *salafiyya* is a precursor and, as it were, precocious firstling instance of an idea underlying mid-twentieth-century slump in East-West relations or in Arab-Muslim view of the West.) In any event, in the second half of twentieth century, as Arab-Muslims recognize how the purposes of missionaries intersect with those of orientalism, the scholar Muhammad al-Bahī, whom you met before, has this to say about the subject: if orientalism is on the surface nothing but a type of missionary work, then the study of the nature and quality of this work might lead to a more objective study of the real purposes of orientalism.[439]

Bahī's remark confirms what Arslān has always suspected: missionary work and orientalism (or imperialism) go hand in hand. In point of fact, soon enough Europe, in the name of missionary activity, comes to occupy the entire Mid-East, including parts of the Ottomam Empire which, too, get swallowed up by 1918. The principal colonial powers are England and France, though Russia

---

[437] See Shakīb Arslan, *Hādir al-'Ālam al-Islāmi* (Beirut: Dār al-Fikr, 1973), 3rd volume, p. 345.

[438] See Hourani, pp. 37, 149, 230-31.

[439] See Muhammad Bahī, p. 525.

and Germany play some role as well.[440] But the question is this: how do these powers come to colonize the region? Well, you have to trace the various activities carried out by missionaries in the fields of politics and education. In this way a clear picture begins to form concerning the manner in which these powers have managed to dominate.[441]

For example, as E. Saīd puts it, to colonize means at first the identification—indeed, the creation—of interests. These could be commercial, communicational, religious, military, cultural. And here he gives the example of Britain. Britain feels that it has legitimate interests as a Christian power to safeguard Islam. So it develops a whole complex apparatus for tending these interests. Such early organizations as the Society for Promoting Christian Knowledge and the Society for the Propagation of the Gospel in Foreign Parts are succeeded and later abetted by the Baptist Missionary Society, the Church Missionary Society, the British and Foreign Bible Society, the London Society for Promoting Christianity among the Jews. These missions, Saīd quotes Abdul Latīf Tībāwī whom I consider next, openly join the expansion of Europe.[442] Add to these the trading societies, learned societies, geographical exploration funds, translation funds, the implantation in the Orient of schools, missions, consular offices, factories, and sometimes large European communities, and the notion of interest will acquire a great deal of sense. Thereafter, interests are defended with much zeal and expense.[443]

187

---

[440] See Derek Hapwood, *The Russian Presence in Syria and Palestine, 1843-1943: Church and Politics in the Near East* (Oxford: Clarendon Press, 1969).

[441] Chinua Achebe's novel *Things Fall Apart* (London: Heinemann, 1958) depicts, paradoxically speaking, not only the tragedy of Christian missionary work but the political manipulations underlying it.

[442] See A.L. Tībāwī, *British Interests in Palestine, 1800-1901* (London: Oxford University Press, 1961), p. 5.

[443] E. Said, pp. 99-100.

Tībāwi, whose translated work Saīd quotes, pioneers another study (in so far as I know, not available in translation) in which he reconstitutes the foundations of orientalism since the Byzantine-Islamic wars preceding the Crusades. Too extensive to sum up here, I shall merely describe schematically some of its highlights. Francis of Assisi initiates a quest for means to convert Muslim infidels to Christianity; and Raymond Lull, with a psychological scalpel of sorts in hand, wants to explore the innermost gizzards of Islam so as to expose its shortcomings.[444] At last, this kind of push things Arabic and Islamic culminates in the establishment of a Chair at Cambridge in 1636. The purpose is to serve the king, promote commerce with Mid-Eastern provinces, and, of course, glorify God by expanding the Church's possessions in the region. As a result, Europe's ambitions mount, and before long, it gobbles up huge chunks of land. Once there, all sorts of evangelists flock in to lay their little square bricks to the Christian Edifice, purporting to influence the course of learning and teaching in all Arab-Muslim lands.[445] Besides, a great number of specialists in Arabic, Persian, and Turkish languages become tools to be manipulated by orientalists.[446]

If the purpose of orientalism is to enlighten Arab-Muslims or simply to bring them to the Gospel, the purpose of Tībāwi's study, it seems to me, is to disabuse them of that charming illusion. I mean Christianity wants, through its orientalist avatars, to lead Arab-Muslims into the realm of angels and seraphim that has no connection with reality. But isn't that precisely a violation of Arab-Muslim ethos? After all, "the righteous shall dwell in bliss, rejoicing in what their Lord will give them." What does the Lord give them? Not only will they "eat

---

[444] Lull, thirteen to fourteen century savant, advocates the study of Arabic, founds a college for Arabic study in Mallorca in 1276, and undertakes a number of missionary crusades for the conversion of the Muslims. His most important work is *Ars Magna*, a defense of Christianity against the teachings of Averroes.

[445] This history continues even today: Aslan reminds me that after 9/11 a series of articles encourage Western counties to invade Muslim countries, kill their leaders, and convert them to Christianity. See Aslan, "Prologue," p. 15.

[446] Abdul Latīf Tībāwi, *al-Mustashriqūn al-Nātiqūn bi-l Inglīiziyya*, ed. Muhammad Bahī (Beirut, 1963), p. 585.

and drink to their hearts' content, they shall recline on couches ranged in rows. To dark eyed houris We shall wed them."[447] Would the Christian God in his angelic realm wed his righteous to fair or blond women? I doubt it. I bring up these things here because al-Tibāwi (like thousands of Arab-Muslims) doesn't confuse matters: his critical thought doesn't interfere with his religious sentiments; in him the thinker and critic doesn't stifle the man of religion, and the other way round, too. He makes distinctions; he also makes allowances for imagination and inspiration. All in all, Tībāwi's study may be simply dubbed critical objectivity or, if not that, at least it paves the way for the latter's advent.

188

Here's a tiny taste of his critical stance. He confines his remarks within the orbit of English orientalism. This orientalism takes off by force of those commissioned to carry on missionary service or military service in an Arab-Muslim city or country. There are others who volunteer for either service. At any rate, the first obstacle in the way signals a distorted, hostile attitude on the part of both groups. If, for example, a believer believes Muhammad to be the last of the prophets, and has received revelation from God, these orientalists counter by insisting on the Qur'ān's being a creation of Muhammad. In this sense, "a believer and an orientalist," says al-Tibāwi, "are like two magnetic poles repulsing each other when it comes to Islam's principles. Some orientalists, in addition, say, in the same breath, that Muhammad's religion may be distinct, yet not all of it of divine provenance. Such a dualism implies contradiction because it neither denies the religion nor affirms its divinity. Thus, "instead of bridging differences, orientalists and Islam remain at loggerheads."[448]

Consequently, even a comparison of Christianity and Judaism leads to no new understanding at all—at least not in the fashion in which orientalists present the case. Truth to tell, it breeds and has bred ever new hostilities, and orientalists have had the lion's share in perpetrating this sad situation. At this juncture,

---

[447] The *Koran*, 52:6-8.

[448] *Ibid.* p. 598.

Tībāwi observes that Christians alone are the ones who, for centuries long, try to understand Islam, or better, to misunderstand it through the prism of Christian idioms and expressions—never in its own right.   Meanwhile Arab-Muslim lookout remains the same, never deviating from its unconditional faith in divine inspiration.   On the other hand, no Arab-Muslim has ever attempted to insert or inscribe Christianity, respecting its principles, into any framework other than its own. Besides, the Christian hardly encounters in his sacred books any explicit restrictions barring him from accepting an Arab-Muslim viewpoint of Islam. And yet he rejects not only the latter's opinion of Christianity, but also his own opinion of Islam itself. The Christian, being no votary of knowledge but like someone perceiving something striking in this Arab-Muslim (or Islam), turns on his heels, as it were, and, instead of looking and listening more keenly, runs away from the striking thing, saying to himself, "I failed to change this man's two opinions."[449]

189

That means orientalists in general, continues Tībāwi, wish neither to hear out nor heed Arab-Muslim views that reject such Christian contradictions. A contemporary orientalist, desiring to sound or be thought of as objective, winds up his inquiry, saying, "The world soon shall see what happens when the living Gospel of Jesus brandishes its true image worthy the Millions of Muslims." A strange bird, to be sure. Another facet of this so-called orientalist objectivity has it that Islam, according to Protestants, needs drastic reform.   But this is propaganda designed to shake Arab-Muslims' valuation of Islam. What's more, it betrays another kind of contradiction. For example, it says Islam is rigid and spurns systemic change, yet when change occurs it says change leads to Islam's destruction. This propaganda blows hot and cold at the same time. Tibāwi finishes by pointing out this irony: the enthusiasm of orientalists rooting for

---

[449] *Ibid.* p. 602.

reformists has resulted in the latter's diminished influence in their own very environment.[450]

To sum up, Tibāwi's is the first critical voice in the second half of twentieth century. A sort of double-edged sword if you will: it corrects Western spurious knowledge of Islam and criticizes slothful Arab-Muslims. He advises the latter to let change, if they want it, well up from the community's own heart. And this begins the moment the community sees to it that it secures soberly, and he means soberly, its independence and freedom from any foreign coercion or control. In addition, religious consciousness, he wants them to know, is a matter of spiritual and intuitive experience which no analytical or empirical system can capture. Those living outside its orbit can't even begin to grasp its intrinsic signs. Regarding orientalists, Tībāwi doesn't hate them, but loves Arab-Muslims more: though the former try to understand, they fail for lack of earnestness and candor toward the latter's faith. He rejects the orientalist image of Islam because he thinks an independent Arab-Muslim will always make up his own mind about his own affairs. And he wants to tell them that face to face

190

Tībāwi's other critical voice pivots round the question of religious dogma. It demonstrates the forced, unwholesome incongruity of Christianity and Islam. Not that the two systems, including Judaism, aren't amicable bed fellows—they're all, as you saw, born in the same bed by the same father—but that orientalism's interpretive and misinterpretive horses run so wild they trample on Islam's ethics and spirituality, driven, as they're, more by superior or supercilious desire to scuttle the ship of faith than by genuine willingness to understand or appreciate it. Naturally, Tībāwi has no other recourse but to defend Islam, and defend it not so much by denouncing the other as by simply referring to the portrait orientalism draws up of Islam as—unacceptable. "Unacceptable," this is precisely the word he uses, and nothing else besides. An independent Arab-Muslim can and must put his own house in order first, without obsequiously,

---

[450] Ibid. p. 603.

again, without obsequiously, depending on the West for his intellectual weapons. It's one of the most polite responses an Arab-Muslim cultural theorist makes to orientalism's unruly passion, not to speak of unruly reason.

191

Abul-lah al-'Urwī is another cultural theorist with particular focus on the orientalism's failure in the domain of history. He's a colleague of Tībāwi whom he respects immensely. More than that, they share the critical distance and thoughtful reflection so vital, so necessary for bridge-building between East and West, though they differ in their interpretive methodologies. But first, let me briefly tease out certain of his remarks on orientalism within their general context so as to use them as a stepping stone toward his critical insights into East-West relations. His critique of orientalism begins with his first book *al-Idolojiyya al'Arabiyya al-Mu'āsira,* and continues into a second book *al-'Arab wa-l Fikr al-Tārikhi* in which East and West are juxtaposed the better to carry out an objective assessment of both. The two books appear in 1979 and 1980 respectively, the same year E. Sa'īd's publishes his *Orientalism.* Neither author knows of the other—and that, incidentally, is quite interesting.

In any event, in his first book, al-'Urwī devotes a whole excursus to examining the aftermath of orientalist historiography. Through its orientalists, he says in effect, the West casts doubt on Arab-Muslim historical studies. They (it) accuse(s) such studies of being ideologically based and biased. Well, what of orientalist studies themselves? Aren't they similarly skewed? Boasting of its historical objectivity, it seems to brand itself unwittingly by the same accusation. Here al-'Urwi cites several authors.

These writers reveal, to the attentive reader, how their ideology, ostensibly claiming scientific rigor, actually betrays a priori suppositions lacking empirical support yet treats them like foregone conclusions. As to Goldziher's school, it hardly resists casting aspersions on certain truths in Arab-Muslim history—for example, the case of the battle of Badr.[451] Despite thorough examination, it all but denies the battle having occurred. This negative propensity on the part of orientalism is the (il)logical outcome in almost every critical analysis when it doesn't admit either of overshooting the mark or of exceeding the proper bounds of a field it remains unqualified to handle in the first place. In a word, orientalism's ingrained habit is such that it valorizes the science of classical history when compared with contemporary historiography and devalues it when compared with the Greek model of historiography.[452]

192

It's worth mentioning, continues al-'Urwī, that classical Arab-Muslim historiography hasn't been properly or disinterestedly carried out either. No wonder if orientalism, which rejects classical historical analysis, doesn't consider this historiography as grounded in objective knowledge. Yet orientalism itself isn't exempt from short-sidedness when it behaves as if critical analysis of history is devoid of ideological prejudice. To prove his point, al-'Urwī tries to develop Tībāwi's critique of orientalism of the English type. And here he demonstrates his critical acumen that cuts both ways.

He cites Gibb's remark with respect to the future of Islam which, as in the past, hinges on the theologians' depth of insight and their ability to resolve the new, knotty issues confronting them. Now Tībāwi interprets the remark as a sympathetic view of Arab-Muslim position; al-'Urwī, however, sees it as a call to return to the sheikhly perception or consciousness of old which Arab-Muslim history has actually already transcended. Accordingly, he asks, referring to the English school of orientalism: could this heedless, unfelicitous stance (Gibb's) be no more than lipsalve or deceptively kowtowing to religious beliefs for some

---

[451] Sa'īd corroborates that negativity, though not in reference to the battle: "Ignaz Goldziher's appreciation of Islam's tolerance towards other religions was undercut by his dislike of Mohammad's anthropomorphisms and Islam's too-exterior theology and jurisprudence." In other words, without knowing al-'Urwi, Sa'īd affirms his reference to negativity in Goldziher's thought about Islam. See *Orientalism*, p. 209.

[452] Abdul-lah al-'Urwī, *al-Idolojiyya al-'Arabiyya al-Mu'āsira* (Beirut: Dār al-Haqīqa, 1980), 3rd edition, p. 104.

political gain?[453] You see, both thinkers agree that English orientalism desires to infix or wedge Islam into two positions without recourse: either Arab-Muslims remain loyal to Islam as it is, in which case no progress from would ever be hoped for, or else they march in step with progress and modernity, in which case Islam would then disappear from the face of the earth. But they differ on the issue of religion. Al-Urwi accepts historical bias, for it's a human, all too human reality; however, he still advocates the use not of religion, but of reason and intellectual conscience in matters of historiography.

193

Al-'Urwī winds up his first book with this scathing view of orientalism: orientalism betrays a deliberate carelessness when it comes to grasping Mid-East's transition from one historical stage or era to another. Such transition consists in formation, break-up, and transformation as well as their side shoots. Orientalists, failing to bear in mind the immensity of time spanning each era (how could they if they don't peruse their own history?), not only express naïve surprise at Arab-Muslims confronting huge difficulties in securing stability for themselves; they scoff at or persist in harping on the negative aspects of the experience as well. Hence al-'Urwī believes that a critique of orientalism must lead to critique of the West. Which, in turn, paves the way, hopefully, for a new invention: in place of orientalism, to use T. Hentsche's words, "stubbornly, abusively constituting its object, isolating that object, and even creating its own Orient,"[454] let's have debate and discussion; let's beat down all crafty, manipulative politics, but let's also admit to our "ethnocentrism as the very prism of our perception instead of imagining it can be discarded";[455] finally, let's have

---

[453] *Ibid.*, p. 109.

[454] See Thierry Hentsch, pp. 190-205.

[455] Ibid., p. 192.

truth judge between East and West. That way, we may better define our ethos each, the better to bridge our differences.[456]

Al-'Urwi himself, in fact, inaugurates such a move. He debates Gustav Von Grunebaum, for his "method" reflects orientalism's so-called "scientific" approach to the Orient. Briefly, Grunebaum first discounts Arab-Muslim sciences, despite their varied achievements. Why discount them? Because they aren't guided by modern scientific findings. Yet he fails to consider how seventeenth-century European scientists themselves, for example, depend on theories or formulas quite different from contemporary ones. Secondly, he disregards the actual causes of Arab-Muslim decline. If he takes it up at all, he ascribes it to such hackneyed concepts as dependence, isolation, and personal piety. Finally, he fails to distinguish the four attributes underlying Arab-Muslim education: humanism, truth, tranquility, and sensuality. No wonder that such myopic "scientificity" not only blocks communications between cultures; it also underscores a priori negative judgments which reduce Arab-Muslim culture to a cold, statuesque, dead thing.

194

For al-'Urwī, critiquing orientalism and concomitantly the West isn't enough. The picture would remain lop-sided if no critique of the East is dovetailed to it. And that's precisely what he does. It's not that he observes critical protocol only; he also desires and aims for fairness if any form of East-West rapprochement is contemplated. What's also noble about this aim is for us to observe him critique his very critique of the East. I mean his attempt to redefine his objective as a critical appraiser of the conditions of knowledge, whether these have to do with the East or West. If anything, this critical attitude symbolizes his intellectual conscience in historical study, pure and simple.

In the two important books referred to earlier there runs a sequence of inquiries with respect to Arab-Muslim modern thought: who are we (Arab-

---

[456] I use some of Hentsch's apt words to help me capture more profoundly the essence of al-'Urwī's Arabic phrasing.

Muslims) vis-à-vis the West, he asks? And again, what is this Europe which, as an heir to the Crusades, calls itself Christian, and which today has become so powerful, so strong, so spread out around the globe? And now the critique of critique: in actuality, each time an Arab-Muslim thinker or writer presents his diagnosis of his society, a certain determinate image of the West inevitably gets incorporated into it. It's as if the East can't do or think without the West.[457] What Arab-Muslim thinkers ought to do is to take into account the fact that Europe itself, like the Mid-East, evolves and has evolved.

195

Accordingly, he continues, three aspects of Arab-Muslim present situation can be distinguished: the first relates to religion; the second to political system; and the third to science and technology. The man of religion or Salafi Sheikh ascribes the decline of Arab-Muslim world to alienation from ancestral faith. In that case, Europe's brain power, which has given it its scientific gifts, could be enlisted by us: after all, that power inheres in religious thought itself. The man of politics insists that the old bondage or backward-looking explains the current decline. The long rein of Ottomans in the region testifies to that. To remedy this defect, let collective rule replace individual rule through legal or constitutional elections. And to accomplish that, freedom of all individuals obviously must be guaranteed. Finally, the advocate of science, having Europe's and Japan's secret of progress in mind, calls on Arab-Muslims to adopt the same techniques that have led these nations to it. Here al-'Urwī comments: the Sheikh, the liberal politician, and the advocate of science—all respond differently to the same question: why Arab-Muslim world lags behind Europe? The first says religion, the second democracy, the third science and technology.[458]

As you can see, al-'Urwī is critical of all three Arab-Muslim scholars: for each wistfully, as it were, locates his answer in the past of the West itself. That is

---

[457] *Al-Idolojiyya al-'Arabiyya*, p. 30.

[458] Ibid., p. 42.

to say, the West looms so large in the consciousness of the one or the other as to overlay it completely. That's the reason why such consciousness, ostensibly a modern figure of guidance assumed to be infallible, is actually neither authentic nor truthful. If this insight points up anything, it surely signifies a basic rupture between Arab-Muslim society and its consciousness. As a corollary, you see no single Arab-Muslim thinker or layman, since the dawn of modern age, free of outside influences. In a word, and this is the point al-'Urwī is trying to reach, Arab-Muslims react to the other merely. They're thus reactive rather than proactive. Instead of looking into the other's eye that's already in themselves, but in themselves in the shape of the other's eye—in short, instead of contemplating themselves there, they take the back seat, as it were, and allow the other to initiate the question or manipulate them or both.[459]

196

In itself *Salafiyya* (the modern school calling for a return to the ancestors) is an interesting movement.[460] And in at least two ways: on the one hand, it's a sort of rebellion against conservative legal scholars (or Ulama). As such, it liberates, up to a point and in an epiphenomenal way, Arab-Muslim thought from the phantasmagoric, superstitious world of Sufism. On the other hand, *Salafiyya*, judged in light of exigencies of modern age, still partakes to some extent of Sufist mythologies—for example, proffering solutions of contemporary problems by looking to solutions of other problems raised in medieval times by other people. *Salafiyya*, though, accepts the fruits of modern science only on condition of adducing cogent testimony. But there's the rub. For such a position implies tacit acceptance of Arab-Muslim decline as a permanent reality. More than that, it sanctions the West and its sciences to depict Arab-Muslim societies not only as dubious in belief, but also petrified, backward, unamenable to rationalism. In

---

[459] *Al-'Arab wa-l Fikr al-Tarīkhī*, p. 53.

[460] What's fascinating about al-'Urwī's general critique is that he spares no one, European or Arab-Muslim, modern or medieval. This in my estimation is one of most pragmatic or, if you like, objective techniques bridge-building between East and West.

which case Arab-Muslims would have either to demand from the West decisive proofs or else preserve their distinct beliefs.

Let's be cautious, says al-'Urwī in effect. Let's not cavalierly think modern science affords complete or total explanations of every natural phenomenon. The truth of the matter is otherwise. I mean the concept of science originally develops precisely not on the basis of overarching or comprehensive causes of things, but rather on partial and temporary ones. And that's what Arab-Muslims should try to grasp, now more than ever. Arab-Muslims, like the optimists Husayn al-Jisr and Muhammad Ibn al-'Arāj, among others, pose questions that today's scientists may be unable or unprepared to answer.[461] In which case he would have the last word—and yet can't comprehend anything of positivist laws which enable man to benefit from nature. Consequently, this optimist continues in his gullibility to live among bootless, fantastic mythologies.[462]

197

Al-'Urwī finishes by underscoring this socio-cultural fact: Europe, and everything pertaining to that name in terms of enlightenment, has compelled he world into a tacit mode of inquiry of the type, where do I stand relative to that giant? The inquiry is certainly symptomatic of the inexorable march of Europeanization from China to Turkey, which hasn't stopped as yet and perhaps won't. As a corollary, whenever a nation-state appears and tries to hold onto its traditional ways, it fails, for the pull is such that it either goes under (remains isolated) or joins the march of progress and reform. In so far as Arab-Muslim societies are concerned, there exists a major drawback, the traditionalist groups called 'Ulama. Even if they opt in the march, they still feel threatened, and fear their interests are at stake. One way to get around this dilemma is to stipulate that reform, if it must be had at all, must be stripped of its foreign cultural,

---

[461] We already met Husayn al-Jisr. Muhammad Ibn al-'Arāj is a contemporary who blindly believes Western science is the panacea to all Arab-Muslim ills.

[462] Ibid., p. 31.

educational, and intellectual contents. Nevertheless, the question remains: does that stipulation change anything, really? Not at all. For European influence gets deeper and deeper everyday, so that a nation-state, for blindly following in Western footsteps, willy-nilly or sadly ironically, turns into a garrison protecting Western interests merely.[463]

The irony doesn't stop there. In such circumstances a new specimen of intellect comes into being. This is the educator who blows things out of proportion: he labors diligently to prepare Arab-Muslim minds to accept Western values and ways lock, stock, and barrel, and who seems utterly convinced of the efficacy of European liberal principles and goals. But this so-called liberal intellectual wrecks things: he becomes, in turn, an easy target of suspicion by his own fellow countrymen. In their eyes, he isn't only a tout of things Western, he's a traitor as well. In the end, he has no recourse but to relapse into traditionalism once more and, in so doing, opens up a space for other ills, namely Marxist ideologies infiltrate the Mid-East on the pretext of blocking Western influences. And the wheel of fortunes keeps on turning.

198

Then the wheel turns toward the West. It shows that while the West has changed the world, it now itself undergoes change. Constant pressure of query by Arab-Muslims forces it in that direction. And so, to maintain this pressure of relativisation of Western culture (for that's what it is), al-'Urwī suggests continued questioning (Roshdi Rashed would continue to do so at the turn of the twenty-first century). The purpose is to render it less haughty, less too free-wheeling, says al-'Urwī, the better and faster for it to realize that its identity can only be shaped by encountering the other, in this case the Arab-Muslim world. But so far, other than circumstantial writings, no thinker outside the West (which is far more important than from inside it) has carried out radical criticism and assessment of the essence of Western ideology. True, rationalism applies everywhere—in nature, in man, in history. But the truth of truth remains this:

---

[463] *Al-Idolojiyya al-'Arabiyya*, pp. 128-138.

face-to-face dialogue between Europe and non-European world must be upheld always. Would such dialogue ultimately lead to a radical, relativizing critique? Should that happen, one can at least say both Westerners and Easterners share the good burden equally.[464]

The upshot of these thoughts is this: any attempt in the way of reconciling Western and non-Western worlds, al-'Urwī believes, must go through a dual, in tandem critical performative: one from inside Europe, the other from outside. Some philosophy—existentialism, humanism, liberalism, Islamic ethics, the Qur'ān, or even socialism—might pave the way for such a performative and open up a healthy face-to-face dialogue. While this persists merely as an expectation, however, not only misunderstanding and subsequent conflict between East and Wes deadlocks; that other conflict, more deadly, between critical thought and ideological thought would continue as well.

199

As you can see, al-'Urwī's views (I hope I presented them clearly enough even in brief) constitute a sustained analysis of the problems of Arab-Muslim societies and governments based on mature knowledge and understanding of Western liberal thought. This analysis, and the objective stance that sustains it, has furnished the basis for more thought and more analyses, that is, more sundry, wholesome, forward-looking reactions from diverse cultural theorists of the last century's final two decades. Unfortunately, however, there's hardly space in this work to include all or even half of them. But three important cultural theorists, Muhammad 'Ābid al-Jābiri (whose work is unknown in the West[465]), Hichem Djait, the first more directly than the second, and Roshdi Rāshed epitomize those reactions. A breath of fresh air seems to blow from the pages of their work, and suffuses mine here with the scent of conclusion.

---

[464] "Oropa wa ghayr Oropa" *Majallāt Qadāya 'Arabiyya*, volume 4, 1974, p. 36.

[465] See Mirnissi, pp. 36-8.

Al-'Urwī, says al-Jābiri, is definitely against fake or dubious syncretism, at least this is one's first impression. Except, however, for one dimension: he doesn't seek purity of origin in Arab-Muslim heritage alone or by itself; but rather—and that's the difference—he seeks it there in conjunction with modern European thought. Besides, the purity he seeks is that which incarnates Europe's authentic liberalism, while the modernism he desires is universal justice or socialism. In other words, al-'Urwī wants to syncretize, or will Arab-Muslim mind to syncretize, the past and future of the West, or liberalism and Marxism. Which, at a different level, means al-'Urwī's attempt belongs in the contemporary current of Arab-Muslim discourse which obeys one of two models: the European (or Western) or the classical Arab-Muslim. So when an Arab-Muslim contemplates modernity, he either has to adopt one of the two models or tries to harmonize between them. In either case, al-'Urwī, according to al-Jābiri, attempts not a syncretism of Islam's past and Europe's present, but only that of Europe's past and its future.[466]

At this point in the critique, al-Jābiri proffers his own alternative, namely Arab-Muslim self must give up both models described by al-'Urwī so as to be sufficiently independent to contemplate its soul and discover its authentic identity.

200

Let's try to understand what he means as exactly as possible if we want to appreciate his thought. Before doing so, though, a prefatory remark is in order. First, I'd say al-'Urwī and al-Jābiri are models of self-reflection that Arab-Muslims and Westerners will do well to mull over, sleep on, and ponder. Secondly, they have a meeting of minds, these thinkers, concerning the course of Arab-Muslim thought in the last hundred years: they feel that it urgently needs and calls for immediate critical assessment of its content. I return to this in a moment, since it's the burden of his book. Above all, despite differences in approach, both cultural theorists agree that critical confrontation in the form of

---

[466] Muhammad 'Ābid al-Jābiri, *al-Khitāb al-'Arabi al-Mu'āsir: Dirāsa Tahlīliyya Naqdiyya* (Beirut: Dar al-Tali'a, 1982), pp. 50-55.

discussion or debate with the West is for all intents and purposes of paramount importance as a cornerstone in the efforts of bridge-building between East and West.

Some highlights of al-Jābiri's thought may be classified as follows: at the beginning of modern age, roughly since the end of nineteenth century, Arab-Muslims find themselves facing a choice between two and only two models—either European or Western culture made accessible via colonization—and this is the source and spring of contradictory views and deadly tensions with respect to accepting this model, or else Islamic culture recognized and acknowledged through centuries-long decline which currently goes on amplifying with no end in sight. Consequently, three issues or limits in total define modern Arab-Muslim consciousness: Western culture, Islamic culture, and decline. All three have combined to fertilize several discourses.

201

First, the Salafi discourse. This discourse desires to recoup Arab-Muslim past glory and power. But this recovery can't be achieved without the collapse or destruction of what's considered to be its antithesis, namely Western culture. Put otherwise, Arab-Muslims' rise to glory has as its condition of possibility the fall of the West. Linking modernity to humanism, stressing the imminence of the decline of the West, extending Arab-Muslim downfall to cover the major portion of history, blaming external forces for the retreat and collapse of Arab-Muslim culture, transposing this collapse to the level of defeat and extinction—these are the major elements of modern discourse. An inevitable corollary of all this is the invocation of the lesson of history. That is, if the sweeping spread of Islam has been achieved after defeat of two great empires—Persian and Byzantine—then today's rise of Arab-Muslims to power can only be accomplished or founded upon the ruin of the West.

Secondly, the liberal discourse. This discourse proceeds along a different trajectory, though it has a few points of contact with the first. On the one hand, this discourse envisions Arab-Muslim modernity in place only if Arab-Muslims adopts the same principles and goals that have launched Western culture on its modern progressive path. In short, it looks to the West as a model to emulate in every endeavor: intellectual, philosophical, scientific. On the other hand, and this is perhaps the built-in contradiction, since Western culture has come into being without outside invader or tyrant, liberal thought wants to take hold of Western principles—with the proviso that the West itself vanishes from existence.

Obviously both types of discourse—the liberal and the Salafi—are naïve, impractical, and, therefore, untenable. In short, they're like two peas in the pod. Each advances or stipulates the same simplistic conditions for modern Arab-Muslim culture to become possible at all—the disappearance of the West. Now dissatisfaction with these discourses has given rise to a third—the syncretist discourse. This discourse simply blends the two, that is, it purports to combine what's best in each of the other two. That way, it keeps silent about what the Salafi discourse itself keeps silent about and what the liberal discourse, in turn, keeps silent about as well. And so the syncretist discourse, as you can see, finishes by embracing all the absurdity or the irrationality embedded in each of the other two.[467]

202

To sum up, Salafi discourse wishes to liberate Arab-Muslim thought by means of an old paradox of knowledge: it speaks of knowledge (science, technology, philosophy) but doesn't produce it; it wants reform but only through a bygone time or mentality. In a word, this discourse, and this is the absurdity of it all, wants the solution to a modern problem by looking to the solution of another problem raised at another time by another people. Liberal discourse, on the other hand, likes to bequeath to Arab-Muslims a history that's not theirs—and to do so through fabricating intellectual syntheses and disseminating them among the collectivity in miscellaneous forms having no affinities among them. Once again, Salafi discourse meets liberal discourse: both view modernity as a sort of leap over history, not the making of history. The first sees it as a way of returning to

---

[467] Ibid. pp. 27-31.

the sources (Qur'ān, Hadīth, Sunnah) before dissension, that is, before Islam splits up into warring sectarianisms; the second sees it as way of adopting Western models and principles before the era of colonization.[468]

This dualism of choice between Islam and the West reflects so many immense issues in the path of Arab-Muslim thought. All of which, and here he anticipates his own contribution, ultimately boil down to another dualism, this time between authenticity and modernity, on the one hand, and between these and whatever results from their syncretizm, on the other. After a lengthy exposition of those many issues (too extensive to include here), al-Jābiri draws the following conclusion: we Arab-Muslims, he says in effect, aren't yet able to grasp, realize, or practice authenticity and modernity, and we won't be able to do so, that is, renovate our thought or even erect a dream of modernity so long as we still kowtow to the authority of the model—*Salafiyya* or Westernization.

What ought to be done instead is this: let's seek self-knowledge, first of all, and let's fear no more to brave the action of growing solitary. That way, we can, for one thing, free our self from the manacles of that constraining model, that is, beat down our herd instinct that speaks out to us in one or the other choice; and we can, for another thing, deal profitably with all kinds of models in a sober, critical way. That, as far as I see it, would lead us to the true syncretism of authenticity and modernity.[469]

203

Hence the political discourse that he takes up next. Like the other discourses, al-Jābiri locates or frames this one within, so to speak, a similar but different dualism: should state and religion be separate or no? Once more, Arab-Muslims find themselves fatefully facing a choice. Liberal thinkers argue that the journey to attaining a flourishing modernity entails separation of state and religion; Salafi thinkers, however, counter by stressing that precisely separation of state and religion, or simply alienation from religion, accounts for the odious

---

[468] Ibid., p. 38.

[469] Ibid., pp. 56-7.

decline in which we Arab-Muslims live today. And the argument, of course, goes on intensifying endlessly daily, fanned this time by two ideological considerations: evolution development of the nation-state which places the issues of the relation of Islam and Arabism in the forefront, and the scrutiny of history.

And here, al-Jābiri points out, is how history gets to become the victim. The syncretist mercilessly cuts down history proper to fit his notion of a nation-state, something which hasn't really carried much weight as yet; the Salafi, however, ignores history altogether or, he merely relegates it to pre-Islamic era, demanding instead that God's kingdom be established on earth; while the liberal doesn't even care to respond to the issue of whether separation of state and religion actually makes for or leads to modernity, or whether the state in which he lives comprises both spiritual and secular authorities. And so one is left with the Salafi, the most outspoken voice there is.

This Salafi doesn't reject the liberal agenda (it's hard to know whether from a generous spirit or good conscience), but he certainly repudiates its frame of reference, that is, its European coloring, only to replace it with the idea of Islamic state. This latter he deems not only a project to be adopted and lived by, but also an experience promising plenteous dividends. In short, the Salafi knows that Islam has come into being on the basis of faith, but he isn't simply satisfied by acknowledging this historical fact. He wants to distill from it this moral-political lesson: what greatness and glory Arab-Muslim state has attained may be attributed only to its standing on the plinth of religion, and what decline and degeneration it has sustained is ascribed to the unfortunate practice of separating the order of religion and faith from that of the Caliphate.[470]

204

One of the many issues political thought puts forward is that of democracy. The Salafi understands democracy to be no more than *Shurah* (state council). Well and good. But such understanding has a negative property about

---

[470] Ibid., p. 95.

it: *Shurah* thrives by its opposition to sheer absolutism, not to a just tyrant. After all, al-Afghāni, the pioneer of *Salafiyya,* calls for such a tyrant as a means of rescuing Arab-Muslims from the dire and miserable conditions they live in.[471] Now if the Salafi is content with democracy-as-*Shurah,* the liberal as nationalist, but also as socialist would like to move from political democracy to social democracy within a nationalist framework, as has happened, for example, in the charter of the Nasirist experience—which has failed miserably.

But failure, of course, has incited the Arab-Muslim intellectual, when faced with such knotty situations, to raise new questions. And if he can't give an immediate answer, he puts off or tables the inquiry for a future review. As you can see, after this extensive exposition of the debate surrounding the issue of democracy, al-Jābiri devotes attention to analyzing the causes underlying Arab-Muslim failure to come to decisive conclusion. The upshot of the analysis is this: the very structure of modern Arab-Muslim discourse in all of its aspects contains that which prevents it from speaking for democracy both as a governing system and a social system.[472] If the Salafi calls for a just tyrant or a philosopher-prophet, then the nationalist, likewise, calls for a hero who joins unity to socialism in a centralized state. In both instances democracy has no place or no role to play. Indeed, the notion of a just tyrant is precisely what bars political discourse from speaking for democracy as a governing system. But what bars the same discourse from speaking for democracy as a social system is that democracy in a society comprised of many minority groups calls for a non-centralized system of government. And political discourse doesn't accept the logo non-centralization because it's governed by the ambiguity of nationalist discourse, that is, the ambiguity of unity and socialism.[473]

205

---

[471] For additional information on al-Afghani in this context, see Albert Hourani, pp. 103-129; see also Nikki R. Keddie, pp. 36-53.

[472] Al-Jābiri, p. 96.

[473] Ibid, p.143.

267

What about philosophical thought? Here al-Jābiri shows how the desire to establish the origins of the great legacy of medieval Arab-Muslim philosophy meets at the same time the European challenge head on. He gives the example of Mustafa Abdul Razzāq of whose method he approves, though with reservations. This thinker challenges those historians of philosophy and orientalists who consider that legacy to be no more than a copycat or distorted copy of Greek philosophy. To succeed in his efforts, he tries to steer a middle course between the austere Arab-Muslim legal scholars and orientalists: the purpose is to soften up or appease the one the better to reply cogently to the other. And so he returns to the sources and springs of Arab-Muslim thought, at the beginning of theoretical discourse and before the age of translation. However, al-Jābiri sees something that Abdul Razzāq himself doesn't see or hasn't seen.[474] In Abdul Razzaq's attempt to establish the origins of Arab-Muslim philosophy, he assumes that the initial germs of Arab-Muslim theoretical discourse (*Ijtihad, ra'y, fiqh* or jurisprudence) directly lead to Arab-Muslim philosophy in the technical sense of the word—such as the philosophy of al-Fārābi, al-Kindi, among others, though it does lead to a parallel line of thought, that of the jurists and spokesmen who remain unfriendly to philosophy.[475]

To demonstrate his point, al-Jābiri cites the instance of Abdul Razzāq's disciple 'Ali Sāmi al-Nashār. The latter notices his mentor's inadvertent shortcoming, and tries to correct it by following a different trajectory. Al-Nashār accepts the arguments of both the orientalists and those of the unfriendly jurists and theologians. In doing so, he deduces the special attributes of Arab-Muslim philosophical thought in two areas: scholastic theology which is the metaphysical aspect of that thought, and *fiqq* or jurisprudence which represents the scientific

---

[474] I agree with al-Jābiri. There's no direct line of influence issuing from *Ijtihad, ra'y,* and *fiqh* to philosophy in the technical sense. I refer to this matter briefly above in sections 65-66 where I point out that the different discourses appearing at the time, eighth and ninth centuries, constitute different aspects of a regulative idea: though this is an anachronism, the regulative idea is a sort of enlightenment rotating its light in different directions.

[475] Ibid., p. 146.

aspect of the same thought. Al-Nashār then concludes that Arab-Muslims have produced a new logical thought and invented the empirical method which later Europe takes over in order to structure the underpinnings of its modern civilization upon them.

206

You must admit, as I do, that al-Jābiri's an admirable thinker. His thought refracts as in a prism into a spectrum of critical insights into things Eastern and Western alike. And now having meandered through many lands, this thought returns for a final insight into *Salafiyya* and other intellectual matters, using Abdul Razzāq's and al-Nashār's thought to cast about for new philosophical possibilities. And I think he eventually leans more toward Abdul Razzāq's thought (as I would, too) than the latter's. Now al-Jābiri has the notion of self-sufficiency in mind, which I don't think he feels positively about.

He thinks (again it would be difficult to disagree) that al-Nashār's is a backdoor orientation leading to Salafi discourse; then, these, al-Nashar's and Salafi's discourses, coming together, steer their way toward the same target: self-sufficiency. But that's a suicidal impulse or act to corral the Arab-Muslim world back into the constraining enclosure of *Dar al-Islam*. "Yesterday we had no need of Greek philosophy," he says; "likewise, today we should have no need of it or its heirs."[476] Similarly, he sees Abdul Rahman Badawi's thought as meeting Salafi position and al-Nashār's half way, though the former takes the opposite path in which he denies all originality to Arab-Muslim philosophy; what Arab-Muslims have written is, according to Badawi (with whom al-Jābiri agrees to some extent), no more than Greek philosophy in Arabic letters.[477] As to Arabic Marxism (for example, the materialist trend incarnate in Husayn Murwa), it

---

[476] Ibid., p. 150.

[477] For further information, see William el-Khazen, pp. 54, 103, 105, 114-116, 118, 120, 125, 133, 136, 143, 148-9.

presents itself in the form of a naïve ideology which Salafi discourse describes as totally imported, piggy-backing Western ideology of the Marxist type.[478]

At this juncture, al-Jābiri proffers his own idea of a true modern Arab-Muslim philosophy. He points out three stages which, he thinks, might furnish a solid base for it: Badawi and existentialist thought, 'Uthmān Amīn and interiority, and Zaki al-Arsūzi and spiritualism.[479] Nevertheless, he discerns some built-in contradiction among these models: the contradiction between the rational character in aims and the irrational character in thought which, unfortunately, has marked the totality of contemporary Arab-Muslim philosophical discourse. For such discourse doesn't only ignore the rational trend in classical Arab-Muslim philosophy; it links itself to an irrational trend as well, and, in so doing, has recourse to the irrationalism in Western thought.

207

At bottom, al-Jābiri, given the state of things philosophical in the Arab-Muslim world, feels slightly disappointed. Especially so when it comes to a confrontation with Western thought. It seems to me that because of this feeling and the other (Western thought), he comes back full circle to the idea with which I began this chapter: Plato's ontology of self. I don't mean to say that this return and the conclusions he draws from it is effected through that ontology. He doesn't even mention Plato's name. It happens that he simply thinks in a manner similar to Plato's. That's all. But for us to appreciate this meeting of minds, we need to retrace our steps a bit.

Recall that al-Jābiri, quite insightfully, approaches philosophical issues, past and present, negatively. And this is not because he disbelieves in philosophy, but because it leaves much to be desired. For example, rationalism and critical sensibility, he contends, are two elements missing from the totality of modern Arab-Muslim thought. At the same time, though, this lack betrays Arab-

---

[478] Al-Jabiri, *al-Khitāb al-'Arab al-Mu'āsir*, p. 155.

[479] For the last two models, see 'Ali Zay'our, *al-Tahlīl al-Nafsī li-l Dhāt al-'Arabiyya* (Beirut: Dār al-Talī'a li-l Tibā'a wa-l Nashr, 1982), pp. 16-39. It's a condensed study of these philosophers and the role of language and consciousness in their thought.

Muslim self's own lack of autonomy. What deprives and has deprived this self of its autonomy is precisely the formula "we" versus "the other." The very pattern that pulls Arab-Muslim self, from the beginning of its modern awakening, back and forth between Arab-Muslim model and Western model. Now to liberate this self from the traditional bondage hardly means throwing the latter into the museums, but it does mean possessing it, examining it, and then transcending it.

As to unharness Arab-Muslims from the West, it's imperative that we deal with it in an intelligently critical fashion. That is, if we think this liberation signifies the condition of possibility of our advancement or renaissance, it mustn't be confused with the prevalent notion of the decline of the West, as modern Arab-Muslim thought would have it. But it does mean that the first thing this thought must do is to unhinge itself from this false frame of reference, that is, us and the West. It means instead confronting or looking in the eye of the West with critical contemplation: it means penetrating its culture through entering into a critical debate or dialogue with it; which also means, and this is most significant, studying it, its history, its categories, its relative conceptions, and, above all, understanding its principles and secrets of progress. Then from all this hard work, we take the seeds and plant them in our soil, the soil of Arab-Muslim thought and culture, to see how they flourish and to eat from their goodly fruit.[480]

208

In conclusion, what al-Jābiri recommends, if I read correctly between the lines, is a Platonic movement toward the other. If he, like al-'Urwī (despite some differences), sees no alternative than that of entering into a critical dialogue with the West, he's asking for a specific kind of knowledge—the acquired knowledge to be planted in the soil of Arab-Muslim thought and culture. This knowledge is none other than self-knowledge seen and reflected on in the mirror of the other—in a word, the self that's not pitted against the other, but, again, that which is complemented and contemplated in the other. But what's this self that he asks Arab-Muslims to know?

---

[480] Al-Jābiri, pp. 155-185.

Well, self is a reflexive pronoun, first of all, and has two meanings. Self means "the same." But it also conveys the idea of identity. In this case, the latter's meaning changes the question: from "what's this self?" to "Beyond this place or region, where shall I find my identity?" Al-Jābiri tries, underneath it all, to find the self in a dialectical movement: let's assume you are to take care of your self, but that doesn't mean you take care of your body; if you do, then you don't take care of the self. The self isn't clothing, tools, or possessions. Rather, it's to be found in the principles not of the body but of the soul. You have to worry about your soul. That's the principal activity of acquiring self-knowledge. The care of the self as self-knowledge is the care of the inventive activity performed on the self and not the care of the soul-as-substance.

One more question to end this exposition. How must we take care of this principle inventive activity, the soul? Of what does this care consist? One must know what the soul consists in (of). The soul can't know itself except by looking at itself in a similar element—a mirror. This mirror is the other. It, therefore, must contemplate itself in the other: that's to say, to know the other, as al-Jābiri recommends, to study the other, its history, its categories, its culture, and its concepts. In a word, to debate the other. In this knowledge and in this activity, the soul, the Arab-Muslim soul, will be able to discover rules to serve as a basis for just behavior and politically creative action. The effort of the soul to know itself is the principle on which this kind of political action can be founded, and Arab-Muslims will be good politicians in so far as they contemplate their soul in the other.

209

These ideas are taken up and developed even further by Hichem Djait whose thought I now turn to. Al-Jābiri, you recall, has called for on-going critical debates with the other (the West). This, he affirms, isn't only the strategic battle for Arab-Muslims' survival and progress, but also for their joining others as shareholders in the stock of global organization. Djait carries out that strategy brilliantly and almost point by point, even though he doesn't quote or refer to al-

Jabiri in his book.[481] After all, the ambience of Arab-Muslim world in the final
two decades of twentieth century is suffused with the deep urgency of this
strategy. That's why Djait's work epitomizes everything Arab-Muslims, who
care about the social, psychological, and political health of their country, could do
to become those shareowners.[482]

Djait's debate begins in the middle ages when Western Europe, now that
Byzantium has lost its political voice and power, suddenly realizes it has no
political value apart from its relationship to Islam. This awareness, of course,
upsets its equilibrium, as if to think—"Good heavens! Is my destiny now bound
up with this demented religion? Unheard of, unthinkable, absurd! Well,
naturally, such an attitude (and the attitude is incarnate today in America's
Christian fundamentalism) is going to, if not already does, blind it from ever
contemplating its soul in the eye of the other (this time Islam); it doesn't even
occur to it, now being in a froth over this awareness, to develop or perhaps
redefine its relationship cautiously, critically. Instead, Christian West labels
Islam and everything Muslim as avatars of evil and wickedness. In doing so, it
never grants itself the unprejudiced chance to get a reasonable view of Islam or
Arab-Muslims. Actually, on both popular front and scholastic front, it sees Islam
unreasonably; worse, it denies it as a religion and ethical system. Why so?
Because Islam threatens its sense of well-being, and forces it to develop a few
tricky prejudices up its sleeve. Above all, it's angry at Muhammad for having
blocked by his false prophecy humanity's evolution toward universal Christianity.
The rest of the story of Western view of and relationship with Arab-Muslim world
is a long footnote to this crucial and deadly, almost unshakeable prejudice.[483]

---

[481] Hichem Dajit, *Europe and Islam*.

[482] A point of clarification: needless to say, neither Dajit's debate nor anyone else's takes place
face to face; after all, Arab-Muslim cultural theorists are no politicians. Therefore, what they
write about is a fictional representation of the tenor and proceedings of what future East-West
debates should assume. In short, it's an invitation to both East and West to look each other in the
eye.

[483] What I'm attempting here is a contextualization of Djait's thought as it might have come to him
at the time of writing. See Djait, pp. 10-13.

Let's not forget, Djait quickly adds, that modern European rationalism—Goethe, Voltaire, Montesquieu—makes ample room for a new view or vision of Islam as an integral part of human life and happiness. Still, however, that's eighteenth-century view, something quite different from the view of the next age of imperialism and industrial revolution. "How much did the eighteenth century," Djait asks, "owe its generosity to the fact that it was not infected by a gangrenous will to domination?" A lot, I presume. [484]

However, that gangrenous will to dominate soon assumes the crushing force it has in the nineteenth and first half of twentieth century. Like E. Saīd, Djait shows how the burden of responsibility for this change falls on orientalism's marginal treatment of Islam. This marginalization eventually creates unconscionable distortions of the faith, thus constituting a link in a chain going back to the middle ages. And Djait, quite painstakingly, maps out some of those distortions which would be unnecessary to repeat here.[485] But he also makes a telling statement with a telic blossoming respecting the reason that permitted orientalism to flourish in the Arab-Muslim world. Although orientalism is gradually being discredited today, its origins and at least one hundred years of its history (1850-1950) are "conditioned by the Arab-Muslim world's incapacity for self-awareness"; what's more, "the very existence of orientalism symbolizes the era of inferiority and intellectual guardianship that the East has passed through."[486] The last statement suggests that the East, the Arab-Muslim world, is gradually becoming adept at modern methods of research. But certainly he wants to see more of such research afoot, so that that incapacity for self-awareness he speaks of may no longer be. What, then, must Arab-Muslims do?

---

[484] Ibid., p. 18.

[485] Ibid., pp. 42-73.

[486] Ibid., p. 58.

Allow me at this point to recap in a paragraph the headlines of a long, dense history. That way I can at once juxtapose the three brilliant cultural theorists we've encountered in the foregoing pages and sharpen a bit more their perspective contribution to the enhancement of Arab-Muslim life vis-à-vis the West. Eventually, I'll also include the fourth and equally brilliant Roshdi Rāshed whose writerly endeavors in science and mathematics seem to put Plato's ontology of self to effective use. A foursome, therefore, whose work taken as a whole construct a paradigm to be pondered, lived with, and applied in future East-West politico-cultural relations.

Orientalism intensifies during the span of one hundred years due both to Arab-Muslim's debility (in all the senses of the word) and their degenerate analytical tools. And yet the same period witnesses the blossoming of modern Arab-Muslim thought the substance of which, you recall, al-'Urwī describes as wretched ideology at best, and which al-Jābiri finds miserably or poorly reflective of Arab-Muslim socio-political and emotional situation. Finally, the same period groans under colonial domination which then ends with imperialism receding from the lands. Consequently, Arab-Muslims regain independence but also start in a slapdash manner and without intellectual discipline to bob up and down like shipwrecked people. At this juncture, Djait comes along and daringly suggest that Arab-Muslims bracket not only orientalism whose term has ended, but also the ideology of modern thought itself, including the entire imperialist age. In short, he appeals to all Arab-Muslims to let this abominable history go, to forget it so as to make room for a new horizon to come, to let a new vision to come of the East and the West as they would like to see it.

You see, Djait takes off from the point where al-'Urwī and al-Jābiri pin their hope on a two-fold undertaking: by the East to develop a critical understanding of Western rationality, and by both East and West to exert all-out effort to engage in on-going debates, to invent mechanisms whereby they come to be themselves and see eye to eye about things of mutual concern. On the other hand, al-'Urwī, as you also recall, is very depressed about the state of underdevelopment of Arab-Muslim world both materially and intellectually; after all, he's writing in the 70s. It weighs quite heavily on his mind, though such underdevelopment isn't the lot of Arab-Muslims alone, but that of Russia, China, Germany, Japan as well. And yet while these nations have embarked on a modernizing trend, Arab-Muslims are simply marking time. As if waiting for manna to drop from heaven.

Arab-Muslims, unfortunately, are still marking time. I mean currently they hardly appear any different than at al-'Urwī's time. Already al-'Urwī feels this is a crucial matter: it's inevitable, he argues, that they join the march to modernity which, though born in the West, has become an international practice. And such membership won't detract from their theological and philosophical heritage at all; on the contrary, it would be used as a platform, a stimulus toward becoming themselves—becoming here understood not as their true nature concealed deep within them but as their true nature being high above them, or at least above that which they usually take themselves to be. Al-'Urwī's point of departure is, clearly, highly sensitive, though strong as a bulwark against hegemony, that is, domination, while his point of arrival is transcendence of heteronomy. Once again, he and al-Jābiri agree totally on these points.

For example, al-Jābiri agrees that the state of Arab-Muslim backwardness is real. However, to him that doesn't means incapacity, deficiency, or inability to catch up with the modern world. Not at all. Rather, it means something altogether different. It's a matter of a race: there's a race, if I may put it metaphorically, in which West is racing every other region, people, or continent in the world. One day the former, the West, runs ahead of the groups, perhaps exhausting itself and them at the same time. The race, however, is anything but a sports-like race with rules to be observed by all parties. It's an unconscionable race, to be sure, in which the one who jumps ahead stifles its adversaries, and those who fall behind are crushed. Their backwardness is the dark side of the breathless race run by the West, which has chosen the pace, the terrain, and the goal. Backwardness, as the metaphor suggests, turns out to be a perspective, an interpretation or, if you will, a matter of energy to be sustained at every point— not, therefore, a truth or reality.

Because this backwardness exists as such, that is, as perspective or as lack of energy; also because modernity includes important benefits, despite its alienating force, it's still necessary to go on trying to catch up, to stay in the race. But because this gap can't possibly or simply be made up, it's crucial—and here he reiterates what al-'Urwī has consistently argued—to preserve other forms of value: an identity, a culture, a heritage. Though Arab-Muslims may not be able to match the West's technological capacity, its science, or its power, it's not to say that they should drop out of the race, but rather they shouldn't get intimidated or lost in the confusion. In a word, they should safeguard, cultivate, and refine their share, which is relatively great, in human ethics and enterprise.

213

In this context, Djait's final thoughts, dovetailing into those of al-'Urwī and al-Jābiri, acquire weight, if I may so put it, without counterweight: Arab-Muslims must do everything in their power to stay in the race. This sense of urgency signifies something very specific—education. To know what Arab-Muslims don't know, to comprehend the nature and magnitude of the political problem they face, and to acknowledge the inadequacy of their present modes of thinking in relation to it, may be no solution; but they will never find a solution if they don't understand the situation, if they don't impel themselves to seek some way of doing something about it.

To put it otherwise, Djait urges Arab-Muslims to come to terms with the West's modes of life and thought without having to succumb to its other aspects of nausea or disgust. So divested, it becomes, he contends, more palatable, more of a stimulus than a leader to follow, or a paradigm to live by or imitate. The West may be a kind of exemplar, yet it's anything but an instructor, from whom information is received or rules and procedures are learned. The most important things to be learned, however, have to do with admirable traits to be emulated and standards to be aspired to than specific ideas and values to be accepted. In a word, by means of such discriminating tactics Arab-Muslims can now conquer the West—not by adopting it, but by adapting it to things Arab-Muslim.

In urging Arab-Muslims to stay in the race and to re-educate themselves about the West, he doesn't forget the vital role of the West itself in re-educating itself as well. A long story, in fact, too long to sum up here. Let me just say time and again he exposes the West's egregious ignorance of Islam, in particular that of the entire orientalist supreme apparatus of reductionism, of prejudiced and recriminatory judgments of Islam and Arab-Muslims—an apparatus now both futile and emetic, though, like a mockery, it resurges at present. Again, having said that, he hardly exempts Islam and Arab-Muslims, making them out to be innocent or pure; they, too, actually partake of the same reductionism, ignorance and prejudice against the West. Now, given these two forces of prejudice, also this reciprocal finger-pointing, is there anything really more interesting, more amenable to a dialogue between East and West, and precisely on that topic of blind prejudice?

214

It can begin, Djait thinks, when both East and West admit to failure in being reciprocally proactive, that is, in responding actively to one another, in looking each other in the eye, and seeing their reflections therein.[487] Naturally, such failure or inability to respond (which is their next point in dialogue), breeds and has bred hate, and hate, in turn, breeds and has bred distance which otherwise fills and has filled the fantasy with all sorts of fabulations—for example, the fabulation of a concept that legitimates and justifies this inability or failure: the concept we (the West) are good, you (Islam) are bad; and conversely, we (Islam) are good, you (the West) are infidel. So each side incriminates the other, thereby driven to seek its identity within its own space—Islam in *Dar al-Islam*, the West in Christianity. But it doesn't occur and hasn't occurred to either side that

---

[487] Ibid., pp. 131-33.

identity can no longer be defined, experienced, or found in such a narrow space. For it's now lived as a position in history; and as Islamic and Christian faiths (not fundamentalisms) lose ground in societies, their practices become more like belonging to one spiritual family among others in a pluralistic context. That's why Djait exhorts both sides to recognize that they have no meaning apart from each other.[488]

This, then, is how Djait would have East and West broach the subject of impasse in their cultural relations. No politics involved, of course. Only the acknowledgement, and to begin with, that they've lived not just occulted from each other, but they're also still occulting each other—and not even playing hide-and-seek. Djait, you see, wants them to practice what may be called perspectivism: perspective willing, perspective thinking, perspective doing. He thus does something no other Arab-Muslim cultural theorist has done: he advances no system of doctrines, philosophical, psychological, or both, for the instruction of both parties, nor even a set of arguments with the aim of compelling their agreement. Rather, he proffers a variety of intellectual and pragmatic insights with a view to fostering the emergence of the sort of Westerners and Easterners who realize their self-image as free human beings—free from internal hang-ups which, it's said, bloat the stomach.

Education, seeking knowledge and truth is the name of the game. Which, it turns out, he himself has to practice. And he does so in the form of writing the book. It's the kind of book that epitomizes perspectivism, pure and simple. What's more, it makes him feel the discipline of his head, his rationality, to be his pride, his obligation, his virtue; it also makes him feel embarrassed or ashamed by all fantasizing and debauchery of thought, being the friend of healthy common sense. Is there anything else, he wonders, that would better preserve humanity?

215

This pride and this realization and the experience of writing sustaining them involve, I submit, a vision. Or better, a transformation of the way in which

---

[488] Ibid., p. 11.

Westerners and Easterners must learn to understand, to relate to life and the world, along lines that Djait clearly comes to regard as desirable, if not necessary. An indication of his underlying invitation is provided in the last section of the book in which the idea of modernity is set forth with this observation: East and West is not a stand-off between civilizations but a confrontation of each with modernity. That's the major and, I think, the only difference. For he goes on: if there's any sort of solidarity that can provide a basis for a truly universal aspiration, "it is surely the solidarity of cultures, including that of the West, against the enemy that denies them all—uncontrolled modernity. Within this framework Islam can send home its sublime message."[489] An education capable of bringing that about, without sacrificing the intellect, would be an education indeed.

Note that this statement (the pivotal point of the whole book) is devoid of the traditional modes of philosophical and religious thought but also of the available alternatives (theological scholarship, natural sciences). If I read Djait's mind here, I'd say it isn't a matter of education for education's sake, but rather a matter of educating Westerners' and Easterners' aspirations and valuations in a manner conducive of human flourishing in this complex world in which all gods have died. It seems to me, judging from a later remark made in the nineties, Djait has come to see it not only as all-too-human and inadequate but as positively detrimental to that flourishing, having effects that bode ill for the future, and requiring something serving as both an antidote and an alternative.[490] And this antidote and alternative is precisely the book he has written. What Djait has wrought in this book is the means of a remarkable possible educational experience and transformation that may reach into and affect the fundamental character of our humanity—a kind of spiritual work of art.

216

---

[489] Ibid., p. 173.

[490] See Fatema Mernissi, pp. 46-7, p. 54.

This present work will end with Roshdi Rāshed's publication of his article "Science in Islam and Classical Modernity." The article gets translated into both English and French only to mark, if anything, the significant research embedded therein. Which is three-fold, actually: to show up Western overriding claim to rationality; to clinch the bridge-building efforts of our Arab-Muslim cultural theorists; and to encourage other Arab-Muslims to emulate its conciliatory spirit. With that in mind, you should, I presume, come to realize why the West, at least in part, must ultimately apologize to the East for having pre-emptied or occulted the latter's contribution to human advancement. But first there's a brief history I should present to you in order to put things in perspective, as Djait would say; it takes me back precisely to Djait once more and to his comments on the work of the Indian Muslim scholar Muhammad Iqbāl.

On several occasions Djait expresses admiration for Muhammad Iqbāl's work, particularly his capacious, free spirit.[491] He admires the scholar, deeply influenced as he is by Nietzsche, for his unbounded courage during the peak of colonization in posing probing questions that put in question Western philosophy of reason itself. Djait equally admires Iqbāl's solid confidence incarnate in the intellectual tools he possesses, which, of course, include Qur'anic rationality. Such is the capaciousness of a free spirit embracing East and West alike. However—and this is the point I'm trying to bring out—Djait, given his conciliatory spirit, neither casts aspersions on Western rationality, doubts Western reason nor even agrees with Spengler's thesis on the decline of the West.[492] He may put the West in its place, but he certainly doesn't hold it like a whip-lash of ideals either. Besides, the West, the East, or any continent or country is subject to the stern law of life: old age and one day, perhaps, death. Which brings him to the more important problem of future history: he wonders "whether there might not be a new dialectic of the life of civilizations, incommensurable with the

---

[491] For further information on Muhammd Iqbal, see references in Akbar S. Ahmed, *Islam Today: A Short Introduction to the Muslim World* (New York: I.B. Publishers, 1999).

[492] Hichem Djait, pp. 84-96.

dialectic of the past."[493]   You see, as An Arab-Muslim, Djait is a cyclical—but also an exemplary thinker-historian.

217

The age of criticism is on and gaining momentum.   A syncretistic, conciliatory age, to be sure, with galvanizing forces unprecedented in their will to end once and for all the centuries-old dichotomy of Islam versus West.   Such savants as Djait and colleagues are those very forces.   And they have one aim: to shrink this dichotomy by the synthesis of their feeling.   Which, I hasten to add, they achieve through painstaking scholarship—and never through belittling Western rationality.   What, indeed, have they to do with belittling!   The opposite is the case.   For they sing its praises—yet also remind it not to turn up its nose at those who already have it, though of a different caliber, or those who struggle to attain its halcyon heights.   In a word, for them, East and West not only complement each other; they give rise to each other almost simultaneously.   The eighth century proves that.   But so do Science and philosophy: I mean they embrace East and West, as it were, in a geographical-spiritual circle: from west (Greece) they travel to east (Byzantium) and back to west again.   That's why advancement of humanity lies upon their shoulders.

One more step and we come to Roshdi Rāshed.   Muhammad Abd al-Salām of Pakistan, winner of Nobel Prize for physics, must have been profoundly influenced by Muhammad Iqbāl.   In the 30s, Iqbāl suggests new ways to see problems common to both religion and philosophy.   He finishes by asserting, daringly, that it is necessary to examine "without any preconceptions European ideas and the degree to which the conclusions Europe has arrived at can help us to rethink and, if necessary, reconstruct the theological concepts of Islam."[494] Likewise, in the 80s, 'Abd al-Salām shows science to be a domain where diverse peoples nurture each other like family members.   In former times a European

---

[493] Ibid., p. 96.

[494] Muhammad Iqbāl, *Reconstruire la pensée réligieuse de l'Islam* (Paris: Editions Adrien-Maisonneuve, 1955), p. 14.

travels to Tlaytla to acquire knowledge of Greek science and philosophy, and the sources that medieval Latin scientists use are those of Muslim and Arab-Muslim penmanship—for example, al-Rāzi and Ibn Sīna (Avicenna), among others. If knowledge is truly mankind's common heritage, then will it really harm Europe or shake its superior foundation to admit having learned from Arab-Muslims? While, according to the philosopher al-Kindi, Arab-Muslims themselves acknowledge seeking the truth everywhere and anywhere they can lay hands on it? After all, Arab-Muslims creativity in the field of science isn't to be underestimated.[495]

But Arab-Muslims, despite occasional intellectual glow, lose the race. Why, Abd al-Salām asks? He thinks it's alienation from religion, though not in the narrow sense in which *Salafiyya* makes it out to be. In fact, he agrees with Iqbāl that Islam urges its adherents to seek knowledge wherever they can find it. Besides, one eighth of Qur'anic surahs exhort the study of nature, not to speak of Islam according wide protection for scientists and researchers, particularly the association for scientific research which has entire Muslim world in its purview. Despite all that, isolation still sets in, and Muslims and Arab-Muslims fail to keep abreast of what transpires in the West—for example, in the domain of technology. True, during Sultan Selim III's reign, all kinds of modern studies in algebra, mathematics, and mechanics find their way into the Muslim world; the aim is to compete with Westerners in the manufacture of guns. But, again, he fails or neglects to place emphasis on primary scientific research. The same may be said of Abduh in Egypt: it never occurs to him to train Egyptians long enough to match Europeans in the domain, for instance, of the science of geology.[496]

218

In recalling an important Muslim and Arab-Muslim experience, Abd Salām describes its failure in linking the arts and technology with diligent

---

[495] Muhammad Abd al-Salām, "Kayfa Yumkin lil'Ulūm an Tanhad fi-l Bilād al-'Arabiyya wa-l Islāmiyya?" *Jaridat al-Safīr* (Beirut, 1982), p. 11.

[496] Ibid., pp. 12-14.

scientific research. The very cause, he feels, underlying the experience of scientific progress in the West. However, the only drawback in this assessment lies in the double register to which he assigns the two types of experience. When he speaks of the rise or awakening of Arab-Muslim sciences or learning, he emphasizes immaterial causes; and when he speaks of Western scientific advancement, he emphasizes material causes. Granted, there may be a real diversity in motivation between East and West. But is enthusiasm; or better, is the mere awareness of the importance of working out a modern renaissance in the Arab-Msulim world sufficient? Abd al-Salām is aware, though indirectly, how survival of nations depends on their contribution to the funds of human knowledge. My self-respect, he says in effect, suffers terribly from acute wounds when I enter a hospital today and find every treatment used to save a patient's life, starting with penicillin upwards, has been invented—without participation from the Third World, at least from Arab-Muslim world.[497]

Now what's this knowledge that Arab-Muslims ought to participate in developing? In the 80s, Roshdi Rashed first attempts to submit the concept of Western knowledge to a thorough critical review. The upshot of which is this: he calls into question the assertion that classical knowledge is European in origin. After all—and here he looks at it from a European perspective—haven't Western historians and philosophers come to a consensus that classical knowledge in its modern or historical course appears ultimately as if confined to European man alone? Now, it's possible, and has been acknowledged as such, that there are practical types of knowledge invented by other cultures. Yet these cultures remain outside the main stream of history (as presented by said historians), or don't enter history, except in so far as they contribute to the advancement of learning that's European in origin. And so science has been admitted as

---

[497] Ibid., p. 15.

complementary to the concept of modernity which itself has entered into debate with tradition in the eighteenth century.[498]

219

Such is the concept of European science as reported in the works of seventeenth- and eighteenth-century European historians and philosophers: Fontenelle, Condorcet, D'Alembert, Bossuet, among others. This last author says that the progress achieved by the nations of Western Europe in the domain of sciences from the sixteenth century on out-measures that of all other nations put together.[499] But this concept of European science hasn't been truly confirmed until in the nineteenth century and, of all things, until the advent of orientalism no less—that pseudo-science known as the subjective projection of the desires of the scientist onto the world. Besides, the science of language has contributed, in turn, to the molding or shaping of this concept. So, you see, orientalist studies assume the lion's share in establishing the sharp distinction between East and West, not as two geographical entities but rather as two historical attitudes or mentalities, the one being littler than the other.[500]

With respect to the science of languages, it certainly affirms the theory that of the two linguistic groups, the one Indo-European and Semitic, the former stands irrevocably supreme—in which case the history of languages becomes a history through languages. This suprematist thinking reaches its apogee with Renan who makes the great deduction that the Semites, unlike the Indo-Europeans, are incapable of philosophy or science; and, as if to mitigate his sharp remark, he transposes blame onto the language itself, not the people. And Rashed here quotes Renan's well-known statement about how the Semitic people have developed no mythology, no epic, no science, no philosophy, the art of narrative,

---

[498] Roshdi Rāshed, "al-'Ilm Kadhāhira Gharbiyya wa-l 'Arab": *Majalat al-Mustaqbal al'Arabi*, vol 48 (Beirut, 1983), p. 5.

[499] Ibid., p. 6.

[500] Incidentally, that's precisely what has made such a book as *The Measure of reality* possible. Alfred Crossby, without batting an eyelash, or perhaps so cavalierly, being so co-opted by orientalism, places the borrowed French word 'mentalité' as the cornerstone of his book.

etc. As to Arab-Muslim science, Renan thinks it's merely a reflection of Greek sciences with Persian and Indian influences mixed in; in short, Arab-Muslim science is a copycat reflection of the Arian.[501] Even today's historians, though they discounting such anthropological premises, still preserve all inferences born of them. Arab-Muslim science, they say in effect, add nothing to classical Greek science, though it fundamentally depends on the latter. Where, on the one hand, Western science depends on principles and theories as well as determinate measures, Arab-Muslim science, it's claimed, leaves itself to chance and experiment. And yet, it seems Western science has forgotten that the empiricist principle characteristic of modern science—the importance of sense experience to the generation of all genuine knowledge—is one of the meritorious work unique to it and to no other.[502]

220

And so, you see, a whole stage of human history gets occulted for quite a long time simply at a whim and without the slightest worry in the world. In point of fact, orientalism firmly believes, for instance, that algebra is of Italian extraction and later developed further by Descartes and Fiettes, and so on. But Rāshed, quick to parry, refutes and disarms such untenable ideology that's penetrated Western historiography since the second half of nineteenth century. There are certain historical facts and hypotheses to be considered. On the one hand, he cites two scholars, al-Beirūni and al-Khayām, who adduce such facts and hypotheses that the Alexandrian school never deals with. On the other hand, the exposition of other facts pertaining to the relationship of technology to science, to mathematics, and to physics may suffice to indicate that the belief that science is primarily of Western provenance hardly ever takes into account the objective course of history.[503] Consequently, Rāshed feels a careful study of history and

---

[501] Roshdi Rāshed, pp. 9-10.

[502] Ibid., pp. 11-12.

[503] Ibid., p. 15.

through expounding the efforts of scholars such as al-Rāzi and Ibn al-Haytham, one could show how the truncation of the course of history is effected by an ideological will to power, pure and simple.[504]

In the final analysis, Rāshed's critical procedure, like Djait's, is far from being a disparagement of the West. Rather, it's a debunking tool of certain European racist ideology, a.k.a. orientalism, in relation to the concept of science—classical science or early modern science.[505] For example, he recognizes the importance of censuring orientalism's anthropological bias for Greek thought as the sole cradle of European science and progress. As if such science would be terribly embarrassed to wake up to discover it's rooted not only in addition to Greek culture, but also in African and Semitic as well as in medieval Arab-Muslim cultures. Of course, censure hardly satisfies intellectual curiosity in such serious matters. The overarching need for painstaking analysis of historical data must take precedence. That's precisely what occurs in the next publication in 2002, in which Rāshed launches a special probe into Arab-Muslim contribution to the fund of human progress. It's also what all Arab-Muslims, he hopes, ought to do to become interlocutors who carry weight in their future dialogues with the West.

221

Allow me to repeat here a quote I set down at the beginning.[506] (After all, in the beginning is the end.) Rāshed starts off the work with a statement by none other than the German philosopher Husserl: "It's well known that during the renaissance, European humanity underwent a revolutionary turnaround: against the prevailing Middle Ages modes of existence which it now no longer valued,

---

[504] Ibid., p. 16.

[505] It's interesting to note here that Rāshed's debunking method parallels, at a different level of course, Martin Bernal's cultural critique presented in his three-volume work. See Martin Bernal, *Black Athena: Introduction*, vol. 1 (New Jersey: Rutgers University Press, 1987), pp. 1-73. At still a third level Thierry Hentsch's book *Imagining the Middle East* should be studied in tandem with Rāshed's and Bernard's works.

[506] See above, note 10.

preferring instead a new kind of freedom."[507] Rāshed right away sees through it. By "Renaissance" Husserl doesn't mean Italian literary humanism, but rather classical science. That's to say, early modern science. With that Husserl, perhaps unwittingly and without the sense for history, unveils a double-edged sword formerly wielded by others: "a weapon of war and a means of explanation." The former is used by seventeenth century scientists and philosophers in order to mark a safe distance, real or imaginary, from the ancients, and in order to promote their own contribution. One only has to think of Bacon, Descartes, Galileo. As a means of explanation, "renaissance", as Husserl makes it clear, doesn't explain a completely conventional period, but just one moment in the intellectual liberation of Europe as it tears itself away from ignorance and superstition.

This underhanded orientalist ideology, though everywhere its luster seems to dim daily, still surprisingly finds advocates among philosophers and historians even in twentieth century. And if such advocacy signifies anything at all, it surely is nothing less than downright disparagement not so much of historical continuity as of historical data themselves. But there's something already lodged in this ideology, something that forces it to burst at the seams, as it were, with a central question: what are the origins and development of classical modernity, which is closely related to science and its philosophy?

Here Rāshed's painstaking research reveals the fourteenth century to be the date of classical modernity. But then he finds that even this thesis has been contested, so that the debate finally makes it clear that such concepts as 'Renaissance', 'Reform', and 'Scientific Revolution' can't account for the accumulated facts, and that in the evolution of classical science, the fourteenth century has been somewhat eclipsed by the twelve and thirteenth centuries, when the Latins start to make Hellenistic science and Arab-Muslim science their own— and this is in fact three centuries before the 'Renaissance' of which Husserl speaks. Traditional methods of dividing political or cultural periods, therefore,

---

[507] Roshdi Rāshed, "Science in Islam and Classical Modernity." *al-Furqān Islamic Heritage Foundation*, al-Furqan Publications, no. 71 (London, 202), p. 3. The booklet contains the Arabic original and French as well as English translations. I use the English translation.

prove inadequate when it is a matter of understanding and analyzing classical modernity. Original Arab-Muslim works of science are themselves not included here, but they are referred to in their Latin translation, and in this way, maintain a presence in the debate.[508]

222

Rāshed's next step is to demonstrate (which he does thoroughly and thoughtfully) what he calls the progression of science in Islam. There's no need to reiterate the minutiae of technical and mathematical terminologies pertaining to this demonstration; it must be read carefully in the original. In any event, I can offer only a few highlights to maintain the link to my narrative here. Since the ninth century, Rāshed says in effect, Arab-Muslim mathematical landscape gradually becomes the landscape of the Mediterranean.[509] This means that classical scientific modernity has its roots in the ninth century and that it continues to develop until late seventeenth century. You also see that this modernity is written about in Arabic in the early stages, that it's then transmitted through Latin, Hebrew and Italian, before going on to become part of significant new research. This is established by means of a line running from al-Khawārizmi through Ibn al-Haytham down to Kepler and other seventeenth century scientists. And so "knowledge of Arabic science is crucial for our understanding of classical modernity," which Rāshed has just demonstrated.

With this unveiling of historical fact, he now returns once more to Husserl. The new rationality called algebraic and experimental characterizes classical modernity, and is founded between ninth and twelfth centuries by scholars as far apart as Muslim Spain and China, all of whom are writing in Arabic. Appropriation of it by Western scholars begins in the sixteenth century, and a new improved version appears from the sixteenth century onwards. It would therefore seem that whoever wishes to understand classical modernity shouldn't subscribe

---

[508] Ibid., p. 5.

[509] This, incidentally, is the thesis of T. Hentsch: historically, the Mediterranean is the meeting point of diverse cultures.

to the historian's idea of periods or eras, since these are founded on causal links between events of political, religious and literary Renaissance history and events in science: "rather he should go in search of true paths, and leave aside the myths and legends which lead such great minds as Husser's astray."[510]

223

Allow me to sum up by reviewing briefly the facts given so far, so that we can look ahead toward better relations between East and West. First, according Abd al-Salām (whom you met earlier), if knowledge is common heritage to all humanity without national distinction, then to corroborate that truth requires, logically enough, a critique of the concept of Western epistemology. Roshdi Rāshed does precisely that, as you just saw. What's more, it's necessary, as an integral part of this corroboration, to distinguish modernity from what may be called Western particularism. This, too, Rāshed demonstrates both here and elsewhere.[511] Secondly, Abd al-Salām also calls our attention to an important model: the experience of Sultan Selim III of Turkey and his attempt to assimilate European science and technology, both of which parallel those of Muhammad Ali Pasha of Egypt. I referred to these facts in my third chapter. The outcome is failure which, of course, can be explained.

This failure, if you recall, underlines objective factors both external and internal. And yet Sultan Selim's comportment in particular, you discern a tacit acknowledgement of the human dimension of European science, even at a time when the concept of Western science hasn't been firmly or conclusively established. On the other hand, some of the enlightened minds of the time do distinguish between modernity and European particularism—for example, al-Tahtāwi and Ali Mubārak of Egypt as well Sultan Selim's supporters who courageously confront strident pressure by Istanbul's sternest conservatives. All these learned, enlightened men, among others, welcome European modernity to

---

[510] Roshdi Rashed, p. 26.

[511] Roshdi Rāshed, *The Development of Arabic Mathematics: Between Arithmatic and Algebra* (Kluwer: Boston Studies in Philosophy of Science, 1994).

290

whose cause they contribute indirectly precisely by accepting its ideological cause. Certainly, there are, as you saw, interior reasons for such behavior which have to do with a acerbic struggle in both words and deeds between two currents: traditional and contemporary. The rules in Egypt, however, happen to be a bit less stringent than those in Turkey.

224

I review these matter here only to point out that the need for a critique of Western ideology, also of its particularist concept of science and philosophy, hardly rests upon theorems only; it can find support in Arab-Muslim experience prior to the ideological East-West dichotomy or that of Islam-Europe.

True, the return to the works of al-Tahtāwi, Ali Mubārak, and Khayr al-Dīn al-Tūnisi, including some of the most enlightened Turks, may not carry much weight; true, too, the information these works contain may be naïve and simplistic. Still, they embody invaluable and significant history, that which sheds light or clarifies Arab-Muslim view of the West and its progress at the time. More than that, Arab-Muslims ought to probe into the works of those luminous intellects who take no umbrage at or find no hindrance in accepting Europe and the good, beneficial things it offers Arab-Muslims by way of science and arts. Albert Hourani concludes a long chapter by affirming this period in history, though a transitional one, a happy period during which tension between Christianity and Islam is at a minimum.[512]

225

I'd like to leave you with some final, hopeful thoughts. East-West or Islam-Europe dichotomy seems to be receding as much from sight as from mind. According to Djait, there's a good reason for that: "Islam-versus-Europe is now especially outdated because neither Islam nor Europe is a unified entity."[513] That means fragmentation names their lot, at the same time secures their common present and future destinies: it makes of them siblings more alike today than at

---

[512] Alber Hourani, pp. 67-102.

[513] Hichem Djait, p. 168.

any other period in their history. But it also means a fresh clearing for rapprochement between them appears at hand, now more than ever. And of all the tactics in the world that can set forth this rapprochement there's only one— apology. Apology for all previous prejudices and atrocities perpetrated by the West against the East. The East, in turn, forgives the West while cultivating in itself the will to forget. Unless these acts of grace are declared or performed, the practice of the art of criticism marking twentieth century, especially the second half of the century, will come to naught. I discussed this matter in my "Instead of an Introduction."

This art of criticism is far from being one of a recriminating or incriminating manifesto. Such manifesto's outdated, as Djait would say. Rather, it's the art of replacing knowledge that has been formerly erected on a granite foundation of ignorance (orientalism, fear of the West) with knowledge based on the truths of science and history of science. It's the kind of knowledge totally devoid of prejudice, metaphysics, and untruth.

You see, through apology, forgiveness, forgetting, and criticism runs a continuous line that gets stronger as the ensemble works harder to block ideology of the past from governing or controlling the present and the future in both East and West. I say so because I fear danger of such control still lurks around, particularly on the part of Arab-Muslims. After all, they're just beginning to discover the potentialities of criticism, sniff its halcyon airs. Which means the old traditional view of the West still exerts and has exerted deep influence in the last two decades of twentieth century. For all these reasons, it's been necessary for me to reconstitute the past, to describe the evolution of Arab-Muslim view of the West. The idea is to place before the self (which I call the creative force in human psyche) both past and present events and, consequently, to enable Arab-Muslims to see how important, given those events, to cultivate further their art of criticism in order to modify that view.

What Arab-Muslims ought to know—and only education based in truths of science can drive home this knowledge—is that whatever virtues they possess, arise in them, as in all humans, neither by nature nor against nature. It sounds cryptic, I know. Nevertheless, the point I'm trying to make is this: these virtues (forgetting, forgiveness, constructive criticism) don't develop spontaneously, without education and upbringing. Religious education alone is insufficient: true, it evinces a kind of disciplined self-overcoming in its own way, but there's a paradox at the center of such education. Although religion promises great creativity in producing highly sophisticated human artifacts, its resulting products embody core values that culminate and attempt to stamp out the human capacity to create. If Arab-Muslims, then, embody this double way of life (religious and empirical) openly and honestly—who create a table of values informed by a realistic grasp of the workings of the universe and who refuse to fudge or run away from hard truths—they come to see science under the lens of the art of criticism, but also such art under the lens of life.

And speaking of life, what, you may ask, is the difference between mere life and the good life? Well, it means Arab-Muslims shouldn't cultivate their virtues in order to live long and in ease as well as in pursuit of the ideal of mere self-preservation, physical, health, and comfort. Rather, they should want to develop the capacity and desire for greatness. And not only that. They should cultivate self-sufficiency, ability to understand and promote themselves in an autonomous, comparative way. Only then can they contemplate themselves in the Other's soul and thereby recognize their divine element. So, to return once more to how virtues arise in humanity, religious education combined with secular education, that is to say, culture and nature, is what's required. It's what the good life requires.[514] Put otherwise, virtuous action that's part of the creative art of culture is also natural in that it represents the final stage of the correct development of the human being.

---

[514] At least, this is what the Nobel Prize laureate Muhammad Abd al-Salām epitomisez in his very person. That is, he syncretizes science with faith. See UNESCO *Newsletter* August/September issue, 1981.

Must I repeat that Arab-Muslims have already proved their ability to coexist with the other both at the level of dogma and of history? Haven't they lived together with Jews, Christians, Hanafis, Pagans, polytheists in the middle ages and in what's been called *Dar al-Islam*? But is that enough? Not at all. Part of the cultivation of virtue, I should say part of their education is to move beyond the stage of coexistence and evince the courage to effect solidarity and practice exchange. But this may not come to pass unless a special effort—which is empirical education and cultivation of virtue—is exerted in a simultaneous knowledge of self and Other. Once again, must I say this double exertion is still at a minimum today?

This isn't to say that some Arab-Muslims haven't truly engaged in the practice of self-knowledge. However, the fruits of such engagement haven't ripened yet. This is understandable, since a long period of history has had to elapse during which diverse pressures have mounted and finally begun to weigh heavily on their view of self and other. Today more than ever, the opportunity for more and more Arab-Muslims to probe into this view is at hand, if only for no other purpose than to attempt to define their cultural identity. What worries me, though, is that some of these attempts in force center on the inability to perform what I'd call the operation of apperception. That is, is the mind capable of perceiving itself? Perhaps. At any rate, since the question hinges on knowledge of self and definition of identity, this equally demands knowledge of the other in a manner that keeps itself clear of any occultation by fabulated portraits or ideas corresponding to nothing concrete in the real world. The West, after all, succeeds and has succeeded in paving the way for all kinds of mutual misunderstanding. Something demanding immediate collaborative, penetrative efforts to prevent the appearance of new portraits of the West—portraits fostered west of the West.

Bibliography

Abd al-Razzāq, 'Ali. *Al-Islām wa Usūl al-Hukm.* Beirut, 1972.

Abd al-Salām, Muhammad. UNESCO *Newsletter,* August/September (1981).

Abdel-Mālek, Kamal. *America in an Arab Mirror: Images of America in Arabic Travel Literature: An Anthology, 1895-1995.* New York, 2000.

Abul-al Fidā'. Taqwīm al-Buldān. Paris, 1840.

'Abduh, Muhammad. *Risālat al-Tawhīd.* Cairo, 1971.

Achebe, Chinua. *Things Fall Apart.* London, 1958.

Adams, Charles. *Islām and Modernism in Egypt.* New York, 1968.

Al-Antāki, 'Abd al-Masīh. *Nayl al-Amānī fi-al Dastūr al-'uthmānī.* Cairo, 1908.

Al-Afghānī, Jamāl al-Dīn. *Al-A'māl al-Kāmila.* Cairo, 1968.

Al-Ansārī, Muhammad Jabir. *Tahawulāt al-Fikr wa al-Siyāsa fi al-Sharq al-'Arabī.*
Kuwait, 1980.

Al-Bahī, Muhammad. *Al-Fikr al-Islāmī al-Hadīth wa Silātuhu bi al-Isti'mār al-Gharbī.* Beirut, 1973.

Al-Bakrī. *Jughrāfiyat al-Andalus wa al-'Urūba.* Beirut, 1968.

Al-Jābirī, Muhammad 'Ābid. *Al-Khitāb al-'Arabī al-Mu'āsir: Dirāsa Tahlīliyya Naqdiyya.* Beirut, 1982.

Al-Jisr, Husayn. *Riyad, Trablus, al-Shām.* Trablus, no date.

-----------. *Al-Risāla al-Hamīdiyya fi Haqīqat al-Sharī'a al-Muhammadiyya.*
Beirut, 1889.

Al-Istakhrī, Abū Qāsim Ibrāhīm. *Masālik al-Mamālik.* Leiden, 1873.

Al-Maqdisī. *Ahsan al-Taqāsīm fi-Ma'rifat al-Aqālīm.* Leiden, 1877.

Al-Marsifi, Husayn. *Risālat al-Kalām al-Thamān.* Beirut, 1982.

Al-Masri, Husayn Mujīb. *Fi al-Adab al-Turki.* Cairo, 1965.

Al-Mas'ūdī. *Al-Tanbīh wa al-Ishrāf.* Beirut, 1981.

Al-Mawdūdī, Abu 'Ali. *Nahnu wa al-Hadāra al-Gharbiyya.* Beirut, no date.

Al-Nadawī, Abu al-Hasan 'Ali al-Hasanī. *Mādha Khasira al-'Ālam bi-Inhitāt al-Muslimīn.* Beirut, 1965.

Al-Nimr, Abd al-Mu'min. *al-Islām wa al-Gharb Wajhan Liwajh.* Beirut, 1982.

Al-Qalqashandī, Abū 'Abbās Ahmad. *Subh al-'A'sha fi Sinā'at al-Inshā.* Cairo, 1913.

Al-Suyūtī. *Tārīkh al-Khulafā'.* Cairo, 1970.

Al-Tabarī, Muhammad Ibn Jarīr. *Tarīkh al-Tabarī,* vol.8. Cairo, 1966-69.

Al-Tahtāwī, Rifa'at Rafi'al. *Al-Mu'alafāt al-Kāmila* (2 vols). Beirut, 1973.

Al-Tūnisī, Khayr al-Dīn. *Aqwām al-Masālik fi Ma'rifat Ahwāl al-Mamālik.*
Beirut, 1979.

'Amara, Muhammd. *Al-'Arab wa al-Tahāddi.* Kuwait, 1980.

296

Arkoun, Mohammad. *Rethinking Islam*, trans. Robert D. Lee. Boulder, 1994
-----------. *Traite d'Ethique*. Damascus, 1969.
Armstrong, Karen. *Islam: A Short History*. London, 2000.
Arslān, Shakīb. *Limādha Ta'khar al-Muslimūn wa Limādha Taqadam Ghayruhum*. Beirut, no Date.
-----------. *Hādir al-'Ālam al-Islāmī*. Beirut, 1973.
Aslan, Reza. *No God But God: The Origins, Evolution, and Future of Islam*. New York, 2005.
Auerbach, Eric. *Literary Language and its Public in Late Antiquity and in the Middle Ages*, trans. Ralph Manheim. New York, 1965.
Badawi, Abdul Rahman. *Al-Turāth al-Yūnānī fi al-Hadāra al-Islāmiyya*. Beirut, 1980.
Barthes, Roland. "Myth Today." *A Barthes Reader*, ed. Susan Sontag. New York, 1982.
-----------. *Image, Music, Text*, trans. Stephen Heath. New York, 1977.
Bernal, Martin. *Black Athena: Introduction*. New Jersey, 1987.
Berkes, Niyazi. *The Development of Secularism in Turkey*. Montreal, 1964.
Boulares, Habib. *The Fear and the Hope*, trans. Lewis Ware. London, 1990.
Bowker, John. *What Muslims Believe*. Oxford, 1998.
Choeiri, Yussef. *Islamic Fundamentalism*. London, 1990.
Cohn-Sherbok, Dan, ed. *Islam in a World of Diverse Faiths*. New York, 1997.
Crossby, Alfred W. *The Meaure of Reality: Quantification and Western Society, 1250-1600*. Cambridge, 1997.
Dawood, N.J, ed. *The Koran*. New York, 1993.
Derrida, Jacques. *Ethics, Institutions, and the Right to Philosophy*, trans. Peter Perecles Trifonas. New York, 2002.
-----------. *On Cosmopolitanism and Forgiveness: Thinking in Action*, trans. Mark Dooley and Michael Hughes. New York, 2001.
-----------. *Acts of Literature*, ed. Derek Attridge. New York, 1992.
-----------. *Margins of Philosophy*, trans. Alan Bass. Chicago, 1982.
Djait, Hichem. *Europe and Islam*, trans. Peter Heinegg. Berkely, 1985.
Donaldson, Dwight M. *Studies in Muslim Ethics*. London, 1953.
El-Khazen, William. *Al-Hadāra al-'Abbāsiyya*. Beirut, 1984.
Eagleton, Terry. "Death, Evil, and Non-Being." *After Theory*. London, 2003.
Farroukh, 'Omar. *Tārīkh Sadr al-Islām wa al-Dawla al-Amawiyya*. Beirut, 1983.
Fiske, John. *Reading the Popular*. New York, 1991.
Flynn, Stephen. *America the Vulnerable: How Our Government is Failing to Protect Us from Terrorism*. New York, 2004.
Foucault, Michel. "28 January 1976." *Society Must be Defended*, trans. David Macey. New York, 2003).
-----------. *Disciline and Punish: The Birth of the Prison*. New York, 1079.
-----------. "21 January." *Society Must be Defended,* trans. David Macey. New York, 2003.
-----------."Truth and Power." *Foucault Reader*, ed. Paul Rabinow. New York, 1984.

trans. Robert Hurley. New York, 1998.

----------. "The Ethics of the Concern of the Self as a Practice of Freedom." *Ethics,* vol. 1. New York, 1998.

----------. "On the Genealogy of Ethics: An Interview of Work in Progress." *Foucault Reader.* New York, 1984.

----------. *Power: Essential Works of Michel Foucault: 1954-84,* vol. 3. ed. James D. Faubian. New York, 1994.

Gibb, H.A.R. *Mohammadanism.* New York, 1962.

Grunebaum, Gustav Von. *Medieval Islam.* Chicago, 1954.

Hadas, Moses. *A History of Greek Literature.* New York, 1965.

Hapwood, Derek. *The Russian Presence in Syria and Palestine, 1843-1943*: *Church and Politics in Near East.* Oxford, 1969.

Harik, Judith Palmer. *Hezbollah: The Changing Face of Terrorism.* New York, 2004.

Hasan, 'Ali Ibrāhīm. *Al-Tārīkh al-Islāmī al-'Ām.* Cairo, 1965.

Hecht, Jennifer Michael. *Doubt.* New York, 2004.

Hentsch, Thierry. *Imagining the Middle East,* trans. Fred A. Reed. New York, 1992).

Heyd, Unis. "The Ottoman Ulama and Westernization." *Scripta Hierosolymitana* IX (1961).

Hillenbrand, Carole. *The Crusades: Islamic Perspectives.* New York, 2000.

Hofmann, Murad Wifried. "Muslims As Co-Citizens of the West: Rights, Duties, and Prospects." *Online Document,* 2002.

Horani, Albert. *Arabic Thought in the Liberal Age 1789-1939.* New York, 1962.

Husayn, Tāhā. "Mustaqbal al-Thaqāfa fi Misr." *Al-Majmū'a al-Kāmila.* vol. 9. Beirut, 1973.

Husayn, Muhammad Muhammad. *Al-Islām wa-l Hadāra al-Gharbiyya.* Beirut, 1979.

Ibn Fadlān. *Risālat Ibn Fadlān fi- Wasf al-Rihla ila Bilād al-Turk wa al-Khazar Wa al-Saqālibah wa al-Rūs.* Damascus, 1977.

Ibn Hawqal. *Kitāb Sūrat al-Ard.* Leiden, 1938.

Ibn Khaldūn. *The Muqaddimah,* trans. Franz Rosenthal. Princeton, 1969.

Ibn Khuradadhbeh. *Kitāb al-Masālik wal-Mamālik.* Leiden, 1883.

Ibn Nabī, Malek. *Ta'mulāt.* Damascus, 1979.

----------. *Wujhāt al-'Ālam al-Islāmī.* Damascus, 1981.

----------. *Shurūt al-Nahda.* Damascus, 1981.

Ibn Rusteh. *Kitāb al-A'lāq al-Nafīsa.* Leiden, 1892.

Iqbāl, Muhammd. *Reconstruire la Pensée réligieuse de l'Islam.* Paris, 1955.

Al-Jabarti, Abdul Rahman. *Tārīkh 'Ajā'ib al-Athār fi- al-Tarājim wal-Akhbār* (3 vols.). Birut, 1978

Jad'ān, Fahmī. *Usus al-Taqadum 'Ind Mufakkirī al-Islām fi-al-'Ālam al-'Arabī al-Hadīth.* Beirut, 1987.

Jan Mohammad, Abdul R. "The Economy of Manichean Allegory." *Post-Colonial Studies Reader.* New York, 1995.

Kaylānī, Najīb. *A'dā' al-Islamiyya.* Beirut, 1981.

298

Keddie, Nikki R., ed. *An Islamic Response to Imperialism: Political and Religious Writings of Sayyid Jamāl al-Dīn al-Afghāni*. Berkeley, 1983.

Keegan, John. *The Iraq War*. New York, 2004.

Khālidi, Walid. *Islam and the West, and Jerusalem*. Washington, D.C., 1996.

Khalil, Ahmad. "Dār al-Islām and Dār al-Harb: Definition and Significance." *Online Document*, 2003.

Kratchovskii, Ignatius. *Tārīkh al-Adab al-Jughrāfī al-'Arabī* (3 vols.). Cairo, 1963.

Lakoff, George. *Don't Think of an Elephant*. New York, 2004.

Lewis, Bernard. *The Muslim Discovery of Europe*. New York, 2001.

----------. *What Went Wrong? A Clash between Islam and Modernity in the Middle East*. New York, 2002.

----------. *The Emergence of Modern Turkey*. London, 1961.

----------. "The Impact of the French Revolution on Turkey." *Journal of World History* 1 (1953) 105-125.

Maalouf, Amin. *The Crusades Through Arab Eyes*. New York, 1985.

Madelung, Wilfred. *The Succession to Muhammad: A Study of the Early Caliphate*. Cambridge, 1997.

Mazhar, Ismā'īl. *Malqā al-Sabīl fi- Madhhab al-Nushū' wa al-Irtiqā'*. Cairo, 1926.

Manji, Irshad. *The Trouble with Islam*. New York, 2003.

Marcus, Gary. *The Birth of the Mind*. New York, 2004.

Mernissi, Fatema. *Islam and Democracy*, trans. Mary Jo Lakeland. Cambridge, 2002.

Mirsepassi, Ali. *Intellectual Discourses and Politics of Modernization*. New York, 2000.

----------. *Islam and Democracy: Two Centuries After the Persian Letters*. New York, 2003.

Mubārak, 'Alī. *The Complete Works* (2vols.). Beirut, 1979.

Nasr, Vali. "Iraq's Real Holy War." *New York Times* (March 6, 2004).

Nietzsche, Friedrich. *Beyond Good and Evil*, trans. Walter Kaufmann. New York, 1989).

----------. *Will to Power*, trans. Walter Kaufmann, New York, Vintage Books, 1968).

----------. *Zarathustra*, trans. Walter Kaufmann. New York, 1982.

----------. "On the Genius of the Species." *The Gay Science*, trans. Walter Kaufmann. New York, 1974.

----------. *Genealogy of Morals*, trans. Carole Dieth, Cambridge, 2000.

----------. *Daybreak: Thoughts on the Prejudices of Morality*, trans. Hollingdale, R.J. New York, 1999.

Nouryeh, Christopher. *Translation and Critical Study of Ten Pre-Islamic Odes: Traces in the Sand*. New York, 1993.

Nussbaum, Martha. "Tragedy and Self-Sufficiency: Plato and Aristotle on Fear and Pity." *Essays on Aristotle's Poetics*, ed. Amelie Oksenbery Rorty. Priceton: Princeton University Press, 1992.

Priceton: Princeton University Press, 1992.

Parkinson, Northcote. *East and West*. Toronto, 1963.

Peters. F.E. *Judaism, Christianity, and Islam: the Classical Tests and their Interpretation*. Princeton, 1990.

----------. *Aristotle and the Arabs*. New York, 1968.

Peters, Rudolph. *Jihad in Calssical and Modern Islam*. Princeton, 1996.

Piven, Frces Fox. *The War at Home*. New York, 2004.

Plato. *Alcibiades, The Dialogues of Plato*, trans. B. Jowett, vol. 2. London, 1891).

Qurdāwī, Yusif. *Al-Hulūl al-Mustawrada wa Kayfa Janat 'ala Ummatina*. Beirut, 1980.

Qutb, Muhammad. *Al-Insān bayna al-Mādiyya wa al-Islām*. Bierut, *1978*.

Qutb, Sayyid. *Ma'ālim fi- al-Tarīq*. Damascus, 1965.

Rahman, Fazlur. *Islām*. New York, 1968.

Rāshed, Roshdi. *Science in Islam and Classical Modernity*. Al-Furqān Publications: No. 71. London: 2002.

----------."Al-'Ilm Kazāhira Gharbiyya wa al-'Arab." *Majallat al-Mustaqbal al -'Arabī* 48(1983).

----------. *Science in Islam and Classical Modernity*. London 2002.

----------. *The Development of Arabic mathematics: Between Arithmatic and Algebra*. Boston, 1994.

Rau, Santha Rama. "By Any Other Name." *Gifts of Passage*. New York, 1951.

Rida, Rashīd. *Rahlāt*. Beirut, 1971.

Rodinson, Maxine. "The Western Image and Western Studies of Islam." *The Legacy Of Islam*, eds. C. Bosworth and J. Schacht. Oxford, 1974.

Rushdie, Salman. *Fury*. London, 2001

Rousseau, Jean Jacques. *Julie, ou la nouvelle Heloise*. New York, 1956.

Said, Edward. *From Oslo to Iraq*. New York: Pantheon Books, 2004.

----------. "What People in the USA Know About Islam is a Cliché." *Power, Politics, and Culture: Interviews with Edward Said*. New York, 2002.

----------. *Covering Islam*. New York, 1997.

----------. "Gods that Always Fail." *Representations of the Intellectual*. New York, 1996.

----------. *Orientalism*. New York, 1979.

Saigh, Faiz. *Arab-Unity*. Beirut, 1958.

Salāhī, 'Ādil. *Muhammad: Man and Prophet*. Boston, 1998.

Sayyid, Lutfi. *Mabādi' fi al- Siyāsa wa al- Adab wa al-Ijmā'*. Cairo, 1963.

Shakespeare, William. *Othello*, ed. Edward Pecher. New York, 2004.

Shanks, Niall. *God, the Devil, and Darwin*. New York, 2004.

Shaw, S.J. *Between Old and New: The Ottoman Empire under Sultan Selim III*. Harvard, 1971.

----------. *History of Ottoman Empire* (2vols.). Harvard, 1970.

Shīrāzī, Hasan. *Kalimāt al-Islām*. Beirut, 1964.

Tibāwī, Abdul Latīf. *British Interests in Palestine*, 1800-1901. London, 1961.

----------. *Al-Mustashriqūn al-Nātiqūn bi al-Inglīziyya*, ed. Muhammad Bahī.

Beirut, 1963.

al-'Urwī, Abdullah. *Al-Idolojiyya al-'Arabiyya al-Mu'āsira*. Beirut, 1980.

----------. Al-'Arab wa al-Fikr al-Tārīkhī. Beirut, 1980.

----------. "'uropa wa Ghayr 'uropa." *Majallat Qadāyā 'Arabiyya* 4 (1979).

Wajdi, Muhammad Farid. *Al-Islam fi 'Asr al-'Ilm*. Beirut, no date.

Yakun, Walī al-Dīn. *Al-Sahā'if al-Sūd*. Beirut, 1970.

Yusuf, al-Yusuf. *Maqālāt fi al-Shi'r al-Jāhilī*. Al-Jazā'ir, 1980.

Zai'our, Ali. *Al-Tahlil al-Nafsi lil-Dhāt al-'Arabiyya*. Beirut, 1982.

Zaki, Mahmūd Najīb. *Tajdīd al-Fikr al-'Arabī*. Beirut, 1982.

Ziyada, Khalid. *Iktishāf al-Taqaddum al-'urupī: Dirāsa fi al- Mu'thirāt al-'uropiyya 'ala al-'uthmaniyīn fi al-Qarn al-Thāmin 'Ashar*. Beirut, 1981.

Zin, Howard. *A People's History of the United states*. New York, 1980.

Zurayk, C., ed. *Tahdhīb al-Akhlāq*. Beirut, 1960.

Index